THE ETHICAL PROBLEM

THE ETHICAL PROBLEM

THREE LECTURES ON ETHICS AS A SCIENCE

PAUL CARUS

GYAN

Published by

Gyan Publishing House
5, Ansari Road
Daryaganj, New Delhi-110002
Phone: 011-47034999, 9811692060
E-mail: books@gyanbooks.com

Distribution Network
gyanbooks.com
India, USA, Canada, UK, Australia

ISBN: 978-93-7169-712-5 (PB)

First Published, 1899

2nd Impression 2025

Printed at: Gyan Press, Delhi.

THE ETHICAL PROBLEM
Author: PAUL CARUS

THE ETHICAL PROBLEM

THREE LECTURES

ON ETHICS AS A SCIENCE

BY

DR. PAUL CARUS

SECOND EDITION

ENLARGED BY A DISCUSSION OF THE SUBJECT BY

WILLIAM M. SALTER, JOHN MADDOCK, F. M. HOLLAND,
PROF. FRIEDRICH JODL, DR. R. LEWINS, PROF.
H. HOEFFDING, PROF. L. M. BILLIA

WITH REPLIES BY THE AUTHOR

CHICAGO
THE OPEN COURT PUBLISHING COMPANY
LONDON AGENTS:
KEGAN PAUL, TRENCH, TRÜBNER & CO.
1899

PREFACE TO THE SECOND EDITION.

THIS second edition of *The Ethical Problem* contains besides the original three lectures the entire controversy that was thereby elicited, and also the author's replies to some prominent thinkers holding different views on the subject. The history of the lectures, the occasion of their delivery, and the incidents through which the controversy originated, are sufficiently explained in the preface of the first edition, which with a few unimportant alterations is here republished in its original form. While the circumstances under which the three lectures and the ensuing controversies originated are indifferent, they served to ventilate some of the most important questions of ethics, such as the nature of conscience, the distinction between moral law and moral rules, the ultimate basis of morality, the relation of pleasure and pain to moral motives and kindred topics.

P. C.

PREFACE TO THE FIRST EDITION.

The ethical problem has come into great prominence in these days. The importance of ethics has been brought home to us more than ever. An ethical movement is taking place, affecting all the interests of humanity. Chairs of ethics have been created in our universities, and the churches are more and more urged to set aside for awhile their useless disputes about dogmas and to devote themselves to ethical work. Yet it has been found that it is impossible for the churches to set aside their dogmatic creeds for the sake of ethics, because these creeds form the very basis of their ethics; that which religious people conceive to be ethical depends upon their religion; they cannot ignore the dogmas, for the dogmas are the very instruments of their morality; they are the guides that teach and advise them as to their conduct in life. If the dogmas of the churches have for some reason become unsuitable as a basis of ethics, and I believe that at least in their traditional interpretathey have indeed become so, the churches cannot simply ignore them; they will have to revise them, and the revision will have to be made with special reference to their ethical importance.

An important sign of the times, proving the great prominence of the ethical movement, is the foundation of the Societies for Ethical Culture. These societies are devoted to the advancement of the ethical movement, and many earnest friends of progress have watched their development with the keenest interest. *The Open Court* having been founded to afford a place for the discussion of phliosophical and ethical subjects with the purpose in view of establishing ethics and religion upon a scientific basis, has devoted considerable space to the publication and examination of the views brought forward by leaders of the Societies for Ethical Culture. Yet in spite of all the agreement that obtained between the tendency of *The Open Court* and the aims of the Societies for Ethical Culture a mutual understanding on the most important point, viz., that concerning the basis of ethics, could not be arrived at. *The Ethical Record*, of Philadelphia, maintained that the Societies for Ethical Culture had taken special care not to commit themselves to any religious or philosophical view, while *The Open Court* declared that some religious or philosophical view was indispensable. Ethics must have a basis to rest upon. Without a philosophical or religious view that gives character to the different conceptions of what is to be considered as good or bad, ethics would be an impossibility.

The standpoint taken by *The Open Court* was embodied in a short article which is here reproduced :

THE BASIS OF ETHICS AND THE ETHICAL MOVEMENT.

"We are strongly in sympathy with the Societies for Ethical Culture, because among all the liberal movements of ethical aspirations they show the greatest sincerity and earnestness with regard to moral ideals. Yet there is a point of fundamental importance in which we have not as yet been able to ascertain whether we agree or disagree with them. It is the problem as to what is the basis of ethics. The solution of this problem is for every one of greatest importance; it must become the corner-stone of the ethical movement, and it is concerning the problem and its solution that we are anxious to come to a mutual understanding.

'*The Ethical Record* says: 'We think there is some lack of clearness as to what a basis of ethics means.'

"The basis of ethics is the 'reason why' man must regulate his actions in a certain way, and thus it is the philosophical foundation upon which ethics rests. The moral 'ought,' which involves that which we call good, depends upon the basis of ethics. Our definition of 'good' will be different according to the different answers given to the question, Why must I feel bound by any 'ought' or 'moral law'?

"It might be maintained that a philosophical foundation of ethics is of secondary importance: the first demand is to obey the moral 'ought.' And certainly we admit that action is more than knowledge. But let us not forget that ethics, if it means anything, is the regulation of action conformably to some principle or maxim. The ethical man is first of all a thinking man. He acts in a certain way because he considers this kind of action as good and another as bad. What would ethical action be without the ethical principle by which we have to regulate it?

"Man '*considers*' something as good, we say. But the question is not what a man *considers* as good. The question is, What *are* good, and what bad, actions? Professor Adler says: 'Concerning them (the facts of moral obligation) there is a general agreement among good men and women everywhere.' This is an ethics of mere conventionalism. Moreover, that general agreement is an error; for while the Spartan thought stealing without being caught was a virtue, the Athenian considered it a shame. Yet Professor Adler limits the agreement concerning these facts as obtaining 'among *good* men and women' This would stamp everybody who disagrees with Professor Adler, as bad; and that can scarcely be his meaning.

"The answer given by *The Ethical Record* to the question, Why should we act morally? is: 'We conceive that the obligation of justice and love is self-evident to rational beings.' This conception of ethics would be intuitionalism, a theory which we thought belonged to the dead past.

"Justice and love are admirable words, but they are too general to give a clear idea regarding what they mean. We all agree that justice and love must be the impulses of our actions. In the name of justice and love the anarchists demand the abolition of all law, the nationalists demand the removal of 'wolfish' competition, the single-taxer asks for the confiscation of land, and for justice and love charitable people feed paupers. How widely different must their conceptions of justice and love be!

"Schopenhauer says: 'Moral predigen ist leicht, Moral begründen schwer' (to preach morals is easy, but to place it upon a philosophical foundation is difficult).

"*The Ethical Record* says; 'The ethical movement has taken special pains not to commit itself to the philosophical views of its lecturers.' The ethical lecturers represent the ethical movement, and if the ethical movement has taken particular pains not to commit itself to their views, this is equivalent to saying that it has no views whatsoever. The ethical movement, we are informed, 'made a statement of its aim (in the constitution of the "Union") after mature consideration, and expressly welcomes to its fellowship those who sympathize with its aim (the elevation of the moral life) *whatever their theological or philosophical opinions.*' How can we have a common aim in the 'elevation of moral life,' if we are not agreed upon what a moral life is, if our philosophical opinions about good and bad differ? If the ethical movement welcomes people of any creed and of no creed, they cannot expect that its members will have the same or even a similar and harmonious ethical ideal.

"Peoples of various opinions may very well band themselves together for the purpose of searching for the truth and discussing it; but the ethical societies are apparently not debating clubs.

"To have an opinion and to dare to be of one's opinion; to stand up for it bravely; and in case we have not as yet an opinion of our own, to search for it and have no rest until we have found it,—this is the very first step in ethics, the most indispensable condition of ethics. The man who has a wrong opinion and holds it in good faith is more ethical than he who waives the question. How can we, when building a good house adapted to our needs, invite all our neighbors to assist us, whatever be their opinions with regard to the plan of the house, with regard to what must be understood by a good house?

"Before we commence building let us have a plan. Philosophical views and also theologies are by no means mere theories having no practical value. They are, or rather they become, if they are accepted as true, the maxims and regulative principles of our actions; and any ethics without a philosophical view back of it is no ethics, but ethical sentimentality. It is like a wanderer in search of a goal, who has lost his way and does not care to be informed about the right direction.

"We maintain that dogmatic religion can no longer serve as a basis for ethics. We no longer believe in the possibility of a supernatural revelation, and search for another and a natural reason why we should live morally. If the ethical teacher preaches the moral ought, everybody in his audience has the right to ask the question: 'By what authority do you sustain this command?' If the moral ought of the ethical teacher is merely an expression of his individual opinion, he has no right to preach it to others. If he no longer believes in the supernatural God, he must give account of that God who gave him the authority to preach.

"The Ethical Society, as I understand it, has been founded because, in the opinion of its members, dogmatic religion no longer suffices as a basis of ethics. But if the leaders of the Ethical Society refuse to lay a new basis this undertaking has no meaning. We deem it their duty that they should speak out boldly and with no uncertain voice. A non-committal policy in the face of other views, religious as well as philosophical, is just as good as giving up the attempt altogether.

"Many clergymen and many rabbis are very clear-sighted on this matter; they seem to know the needs of the time; they earnestly and judiciously work for a purification of religion. And we wish that those who profess to carry out the ideal of the present age, namely, the foundation of a purely ethical religion, should not remain behind; they should know, and if they do not know, they should search for, the ground upon which we are to stand. The question, 'What is the basis of ethics? is of paramount importance to all of us, to the religious dogmatist, to the freethinker, and above all to the members of the Societies for Ethical Culture. The success of the ethical movement will in the end depend upon how their leaders solve this question."

THE THREE LECTURES ON ETHICS.

Soon after the publication of this article, which appeared in No, 140 of *The Open Court*, the board of trustees of the Society for Ethical culture of Chicago invited the editor of *The Open Court* to present his views of ethics in a series of lectures. These lectures were delivered in Emerson Hall on the first, second, and third Sundays of June, 1890, at 11 a. m.

These three lectures on the Ethical Problem delineate a system of ethics which is based upon a unitary conception of the world. This system takes exception to the vagueness of *The Ethical Record*, whose ethics as a matter of principle has no foundation; and it attempts to settle the dispute between Intuitionalists and Utilitarians. Objection is made to Intuitionalists because of their supernaturalism, to Utilitarians because of a mistaken interpretation of the facts of nature.

Perhaps the best defence of Intuitionalism is made by Professor H. Sidgwick of Cambridge, who in his personal attitude is neither a Utilitarian nor an Intuitionalist. But since he considers the moral ought as an "ultimate and unanalysable fact" (see *Mind*, October, 1889) he is to be classed among Intuitionalists.

Mr. John Stuart Mill defines Utilitarianism as follows: "The "creed which accepts as the foundation of morals Utility, or the

"Greatest Happiness Principle, holds that actions are right in pro-"portion as they tend to promote happiness, wrong as they tend to "produce the reverse of happiness. By happiness is intended "pleasure, and the absence of pain; by unhappiness, pain, and "the privation of pleasure."

The most prominent Utilitarians of the living generation against whose doctrines the ethics here defended are set forth are Mr. Spencer of England, Madame Clémence Royer of France, Professor Georg von Gizycki of Berlin, and Professor Harald Höffding of Copenhagen.*

The data of Mr. Spencer's system of ethics are well known to all English readers.

Madame Royer, in her latest book on ethics, advance sheets of which were kindly sent me by the author, pursues the same direction as Mr. Spencer. In the Conclusion she defines "the good as the sum of pleasurable feelings (*jouissances senties*) in all con-

*The great English historian of European morals, W. E. H. Lecky, leads us to infer that ethical systems must be either intuitional or utilitarian. He does not take into consideration that there might arise a theory of ethics in opposition to these "two rival theories of morals." And yet there is a great English thinker who is not an Intuitionalist and at the same time stands in strong opposition to the favorite doctrines of our most prominent utilitarians. W. K. Clifford says in his essay "The Scientific Basis of Morals":

"The end of Ethic is not the greatest happiness of the greatest number. Your happiness is of no use to the community, except in so far as it tends to make you a more efficient citizen—that is to say, happiness is not to be desired for its own sake but for the sake of something else. If any end is pointed to, it is the end of increased efficiency in each man's special work, as well as in the social functions which are common to all. A man must strive to be a better citizen, a better workman, a better son, husband, or father.

"Again, Piety is not Altruism. It is not the doing good to others as others, but the service of the community by a member of it, who loses in that service the consciousness that he is anything different from the community."

Professor Wilhelm Wundt expresses similar ideas, rejecting both, utilitarianism and intuitionalism, in his *Ethik: Eine Untersuchung der Thatsachen und Gesetze des sittlichen Lebens* (Stuttgart, 1886).

If the generation of pleasurable feelings is not the aim of ethics it follows as a matter of logical consequence that altruism is just as wrong as egotism. The aim of ethics is neither the welfare of self nor that of other individuals but of those interests that are super-individual.

Such men as Professor Clifford and Professor Wundt are certainly not benighted by theological prejudices or vague *a priori* speculations. They stand upon the solid ground of mathematical and empirical methods, and I value an agreement with these thinkers highly.

scious beings; the bad as the sum of their sufferings." The moral good is the remedy of the bad, it tends to decrease the sum of the bad and to increase the sum of the good.

Madame Royer's book is clear and to the point; the style is lucid, and not the least interesting part of her work is her attempt to define the absolutely good of the Universe in terms of pleasurable feelings by the help of algebraic formulas—a method, that from her standpoint must be considered as the only correct way of making ethics a science. I have anticipated this error, in *Fundamental Problems*, p. 217, where it is said that "ethics is not an arithmetical example by which to calculate how we can purchase, at the least sacrifice, the greatest amount of happiness."

In her Preface Madame Royer says in an italicised passage: "That which increases in the world the quantity of conscious existence is good, that which diminishes it is bad." I consider it as a proved fact, that consciousness is caused by pain.* An unsatisfied want intensifies our dim feelings, and renders them conscious; and a perfect adaptation makes consciousness sink again into the dream-like state of unconscious soul-life. Human life is so intensely conscious because man has constantly to adapt himself to new conditions. If there were no progress, if we lived in that state of perfect adaptation which is Mr. Spencer's ideal, men's lives would elapse in idyllic harmony and with the mechanical rhythm of a machine. It would be the state of a happy dream; consciousness would disappear as it has disappeared in those movements of our body which we execute as pure reflex motions, without further thought, because they are perfectly adapted to their ends. Therefore "the good" or that which produces consciousness, is want, disturbance, pain.

Accordingly the definition of good in the preface of Madame Royer's book does not agree with the definition proposed in the conclusion.

Professor Gizycki's work on ethics has the merit of being very popular—a virtue which is rare in the books of German professors.† He has to some extent abandoned the principle of utility

*See the editorial article on "Pleasure and Pain," *The Open Court*, No. 120, Vol. III., p. 1987.

†The chapters on Determinism and Indeterminism in Professor Gizycki's *Moralphilosophie* appeared first in an English translation in *The Open Court*, Nos. 25 and 26. Other passages, remarkable for their beauty and strength, appeared shortly after the publication of the book in *The Open Court* under

and formulates the maxim of ethics in the sentence: "Strive for peace of soul by devoting thyself to the welfare of humanity."

Professor Gizycki maintains that "feelings are the ultimate basis of morals." He says "the moral feelings—reverence and contempt, esteem and indignation, peace of soul and remorse—are not activities of reason, but simply feelings." This is an error. So long as we possess feelings only, we can have none of what Professor Gizycki calls "moral feelings." Every one of the so-called "moral feelings," for instance, esteem or indignation, is a judgment; and how can we pass a judgment of esteem or indignation unless we compare and reason concerning certain feelings? It is true that if man were not a sentient creature he could have no ethics. But the properly ethical element in ethics does not consist in feelings, but in the judgment concerning feelings.

Brutes possess feelings just as much as man, but man alone is in possession of reason, and the regulation of his feelings by reason makes him ethical. The conduct of brutes exhibits, with rare exceptions, a lack of morality; and in the measure that a creature begins to judge, it becomes ethical.

Professor Harald Höffding of Copenhagen, is perhaps the most advanced of the Utilitarians. He goes so far in the statement of his principle of ethical estimation as to object to the very words "happiness or utility" (*Nutzen oder Glück*, German translation of his "Data of Ethics," p. 37). In their stead he proposes to put the term "welfare" (*Wohlfahrt*) in order to embrace also the higher wants of man's nature. Professor Höffding defines welfare (p. 98) "as a continuous state of pleasurable feeling" (*Wohlfahrt ist ein dauernder Zustand des Lustgefühls*). The present edition contains an exposition of his views in his own words which, in criticism of the author's positions, he kindly consented to write as a contribution to *The Monist* (Vol. I., No. 4, pp. 520–551). His statement is perhaps the best and most scientific formulation of Hedonism, the ethics based upon man's pursuit of happiness.

We may say that the pursuit of happiness is a natural right of man, but we cannot derive the moral ought from the pursuit of happiness. And the mere pursuit of happiness is not sufficient to make a complete and worthy human life. On the contrary, the

the titles; "Death and Life" (No. 70) and "Nature and Eternal Youth" (No. 72).

mere pursuit of happiness wherever it prevails unchecked in the soul of man is a most dangerous tendency, which unfits man for business as well as for family life, and above all for ideal aspirations. What is the reason that trustworthy persons, competent workers, dutiful men and women, are so rare? It is simply because most people are too eager in their pursuit of happiness.

The pursuit of happiness is not wrong. Enjoyment is not a sin and recreation is not improper. Yet it is wrong to make happiness the sole aim of existence. We cannot live without enjoyment; enjoyment keeps our minds healthy and buoyant. Yet enjoyment is not the purpose of life. Recreation is the rest we take after our work is done. We do not work in order to have recreation; but we seek recreation in order to do more work.

If the pursuit of happiness is not sufficient to make man's life complete and worthy, what then is needed to make it so? We all know what is needed: it is ethics. Then let us have ethics—not theories about procuring pleasurable sensations, but true ethics—ethics that are nobler than the mere pursuit of happiness.

* * *

Criticisms are solicited from all who dissent from the views set forth in the following lectures. I shall be glad to learn from my critics, and wherever any one will convince me of an error he will find me ready to change my opinion and to accept the truth whatever it be.

P. C.

TABLE OF CONTENTS.

INTRODUCTION.

In endeavoring to establish ethics as a science, the author's aim has been on the one hand to point out the intimate and inalienable connexion of morality with religion; and on the other hand to show that ethics can by no means be derived from mere sentiment. Both the intuitionist and the hedonist are wrong, the former in seeking the ultimate foundation of ethics in the sentiment of moral impulses called conscience and the latter in determining moral worth by a consideration of pleasure and pain.

In order to find the objective element that constitutes the nature of morality, we must discover the objective element of man's soul. Man's soul is not merely subjectivity. The fact that he feels is an indispensable condition of his existence as a living and thinking being, but it is not the essential feature of his humanity. He does not consist of feelings pure and simple, but of feelings of a definite kind and nature. The most important part of man's existence is his character, and character is quality; a man's character is not the feeling element of his feelings, but is determined by the forms of his feelings, by his thoughts, and his intentions. And forms are, if our philosophy be right,* not mere subjective semblances (as Kant would have it), but objective realities.

*See the author's *Primer of Philosophy* and *Fundamental Problems*.

The problem of ethics presupposes the solution of the psychological question as to the nature of the soul, which has been treated elsewhere, and can here only briefly be dealt with.

In reply to the question, What am I myself? we say, the self of every man is his character. I am not my body, but that which determines the actions of the body. I am the longings, the impulses, the ideals which inspire me, and, above all, the actions which I do. In brief, the soul consists of thoughts and volitions. Accordingly, I am a certain form of life,—a form formed and forming. I am formed by formative factors that existed before I was combined into this peculiar idiosyncrasy, and I in my turn am forming the idiosyncrasies of future generations with whom I come directly or indirectly into contact. In this sense, I (that is, the forms of life which make up my personality) existed to a great extent before I was born, and shall exist in the reproductions of my most personal features after the dissolution of my body. The indestructibility of every event that ever happened is especially true of the form of life, the soul, which at every moment of its existence is simply the summed up result of its entire previous history, beginning with the first appearance of life on earth. And as the past is immortalised in us so we shall be immortalised in the future; and this immortality of the soul is a fact in spite of the transiency of every successive moment of our life as well as the final dissolution of the body.

Morality is a formation of character; it is the acquisition and preservation of those forms of life which, in our best judgment, must be deemed worthy of existence. We have been built up by the soul-life of the past, and we are building up the soul-life of the future. Our self extends into both directions, into the ages that have been and into the ages to come. The present temporary incarnation of this soul-life is transient, while its forming factors are enduring.

Self is a word of doubtful significance; if we understand by self our body in its material concreteness, life teaches us the transiency of self, and ethics would practically consist in the eradication of all selfishness. We must cease clinging to the self of this transient incarnation of our form of life, which is most easily done by overcoming the delusion that this bodily self is neither a reality of permanence nor does it possess any absolute dignity. If, however, we understand by self the form of our soul-life, our character, the ideals that inspire us, and the aims which we pursue, ethics would be simply the science of self-culture and self-preservation. In this sense morality is the highest, the best, and most consistent selfishness.

Taking this attitude, the contrast between egotism and altruism breaks down: ethics is as little egotistic as it is altruistic. Ethics is antagonistic to self in its narrow and bodily sense, but if we understand by self that which constitutes the character of our life, viz., the form of our being, the essential feature of that which constitutes our personality, ethics is simply the enhancement of our self. It will in the long run, and if methodically considered, teach us the selfishness that does not cling to the heap of atoms called body, but to its more important formal and formative features, our ideals, which will continue to exist after the breakdown of our material existence.

If by individual we mean the concrete and material embodiment of our soul, and by personality the characteristic features of our aspirations, the form of our life, our spiritual being: we would say that ethics as a science finding an objective foundation in the realities of life must transcend the realm of the individual, and establish solidly and forever our personality. Our personality and our conception of personality must be lifted into the domain of the super-individual; we must learn to regard the fleeting as fleeting, and appreciate the value of permanence. The individual is not only subject to a constant change, but it is finally doomed to die. The individual should therefore be the instrument of personality; it is the occasion through which our personality can make its influence felt in the development of the entire life of mankind; and ethics is simply a method of improving this opportunity.

Ethics is not altruism, although it sometimes prompts us to altruistic deeds, because the enhancement of our self-interest in the higher sense of the word naturally leads to the enhancement of our own self as incorporated in our fellow-beings. Helping others is not moral on the principal that they are others, but rather because they are or may become like unto us: they represent our own life-form which is in need of assistance. Hence charity extended to people who are unworthy is no virtue; and goodnaturedness without circumspection is either weakness, or negligence, or foolishness, but never meritorious.

The idea is very prevalent that ethics is goody-goodyism, that it is anti-selfishness, that it is a suppression of our own personality in favor of other personalities. If a man from sheer good nature yields to the unreasonable demands of another, or if he confides in him without a sufficient guarantee, he may be unselfish, but he is therefore not moral. Many people who lack the strength of saying "no" at the right time, when the results of their false altruism become apparent, console themselves with the thought that they were too good; but they are mistaken; their conduct is not moral, but weak, and weakness is immoral. The acquisition of strength which may often appear as sternness is one of the most urgent duties of life, and goodnaturedness as a rule is merely a euphemism for a lack of character, implying a deficiency in the power of resistance.

An example of these wrong ethics is the sheep, for the sheep in its meekness and weakness is supposed to be moral, while its enemy the wolf is represented as the incarnation of immorality. We would say that neither the sheep nor the wolf is moral; but if the simile is understood as a parable, we might just as well take the wolf as the representative of morality; for while the sheep sets an example of cowardice and indifference, the wolf at least exhibits courage; he stands up for his own self, and fights the struggle of life energetically and boldly.

Courage is not a vice, but one of the cardinal virtues, although its significance as a virtue has been underrated in the centuries during which through a literal acceptation of the lamb as the symbol of innocence an ovine morality was preached and the theory of an absolute non-resistance to evil had become the highest moral ideal.

There is a certain sense in the religious injunction, "Resist not evil," but as it is commonly formulated the statement is wrong, and ought to read, "Resist not evil with evil." The principle of retaliation is wrong, but the principle of fighting error, vice, and falsity, is not only not immoral, but it is the main duty of morality.

Evil is exactly the thing to be resisted, only we should not overcome evil homeopathically by increasing the evils of the world. Lao-Tze expresses the right sentiment in the *Tao-Teh-King* when he says:

> "Requite hatred with goodness."—Chap. 63.
>
> "The good I meet with goodness; the bad I also meet with goodness; for virtue is good (throughout). The faithful I meet with faith; the faithless I also meet with faith; for virtue is faithful (throughout)."—Chap. 49.

The old Buddhist Scriptures say of a saintly man:

> "Anger he conquers by calmness,
> And by goodness the wicked;
> The stingy he conquers by generosity,
> And by truth the speaker of lies."

A prevalent error is the idea set forth by many men of great prominence that ethics has nothing to do with religion. For instance, Professor Petrie says:*

> "That the idea of personal morality is not an integral part of most religions, is obvious to any one who has had a practical view of them. Right and wrong do not enter into the circle of religious ideas to most races. The piety of the Carthaginian before Moloch, of the Roman as he sent his captives from the capitol to be slaughtered in the Colosseum, of Louis XI. as he confided his duplicities to the Virgins in his hat-band, or of Louis XV. as he prayed in the *Parc-aux-Cerfs*, show what the brigand who pays for his masses, or the Arab who swindles in the intervals of his prayers, prove in the present day—that the firmest religious beliefs have no necessary connection with the idea of moral action."

The error of this view consists in the fact that our own views of morality are imputed to people of either a different religion or a different religious conception. The savage who worships his deity by slaughtering

** Religion and Conscience in Ancient Egypt*, pp. 14–15.

the captives is subjectively (viz., before the tribunal of his conscience) as moral as the Christian general who would be intent on saving their lives. Saul was rejected by Samuel simply because he did not slaughter all the captives, and did not destroy the property of a conquered race, and he was deemed irreligious; his act was considered by Samuel as decidedly immoral. The immoral actions of savages are the best evidence of the close connection between religion and morality. A savage religion produces savage views of morality. The Carthaginians who sacrificed to Moloch, and I might say, by way of parenthesis, the Israelite king, Manasseh, too, who made his sons and daughters pass through the fires of Baal, were subjectively considered moral; they did not perform these acts on account of a perversity of their moral fiber, but on account of a perversity of their religion. They believed in a savage religion. Undoubtedly, they performed these horrible rites with fear and trembling, and against their better instincts, simply because they deemed them right, and the proper thing to do. They thought that God, or the gods, demanded such sacrifices. Their religion is at fault, not their morality.

The same is true of the ethics of the promotors of the Inquisition, and of the popes who introduced and sanctioned this inhuman system of making propaganda for the religion of love. Torquemada, the Grand Inquisitor of Spain, is reported even by his enemies to have been a pure-minded man, of best intentions, and he was at the same time so tender-hearted that he left the room as soon as the suspected heretic was put on the rack. Subjectively considered, he certainly was moral, and acted under the impulse of high motives against the better instincts of his humanity. His fault is not one of wickedness, but of belief; and his errors are not due to the viciousness of his heart, but to the errors of his religion.

We insist, therefore, on the truth that religion is closely connected with morality. And how could it be otherwise? For religion is the conviction we have of the truth,—the conviction which comprises our conception of the universe, and becomes as such the determining factor of all our actions.

Religion need not be a belief, but it is always a faith. Belief is opinion; it is a taking for granted, without having evidence; but faith is a synonym for conviction. Faith is the determination to be true to one's ideal. It is true that many deem belief to be an essential element of religion, but this is only an emergency for those who are lacking in comprehension. The belief that justice extended to enemies is the proper thing to do, does not become less religious when through a deeper insight into the interrelations of human life it is changed into positive knowledge. We would here call attention to the fact that the Hebrew word for belief, אֱמוּנָה (amuna), means firmness, or character (connected with the word אָמֵן (amen), which means "it is established"); and the Greek word for belief, *πίστις*, means fidelity, and ought to be translated by the English word "faith," and not "belief."

It goes without saying that religion originates with mere opinion, but it progresses more and more to a clear comprehension. First we know in part and we prophesy in part; but when that which is perfect is come, then that which is part shall be done away.

THE ETHICAL PROBLEM

ETHICS A SCIENCE.

THE ethical problem is the burning question of to-day. It is a fact that the majority of civilized people demand obedience to certain ethical rules of conduct. To some extent they enforce them by law, yet it is generally agreed upon that the statutes would not be sufficient to ensure the observance of those rules unless the members of society possessed the spirit of which those laws are merely an expression; and the laws of a country can only prescribe in roughest outlines the most general demands of the community. The laws rest upon the ethical spirit that animates a nation. The motive to do right must be a living power in every citizen, and if we speak of the ethical problem we demand an answer to the question, How can we plant that motive in the souls of men?

The ethical problem accordingly is a practical problem. It is no mere speculation for theorizers. It is the living question of to-day which is at the bottom of all questions, and we may justly say that it has been the burning question of all the ages past, and will remain the chief interest of human life in all the centuries to come.

Yet because the ethical problem is practical, we cannot dispense with theoretical enquiries. Theories and their practical applications are inseparable. Theorizing without practical use is a Vanity Fair of mental exertions. Theories, if they are correct theories, if they are properly derived from, and if they agree with, facts, are the most practical inventions made. The savage may build his hut without a knowledge of mathematics, but the study of mathematics is no mere and useless theorizing for the architect who builds a dome or who bridges an arm of the sea. A correct theory makes a man more efficient in his work; and indeed right theories are the indispensable conditions of all progress in practical life.

It will be impossible to implant in the souls of men the motive of doing right without telling them what is meant by "right." We cannot inculcate ethics without laying down a principle or standard by which a man may decide for himself what is right and what is wrong. If we demand that he refrain from doing wrong and be guided by what is right, we are bound to give him a reason why. If right-doing were always advantageous to him, he might, as a matter of course, obey the moral behest and we should need no ethics. But if it sometimes conflicts with his personal interest, we must give him a reason that will be stronger than his egotism, we must implant the ethical motive in his soul. How can we do that without enquiring into the principles of ethics, the factors of moral life, without understanding the origin and evolution of ethics, without digging down to the roots from which the ethical spirit grows?

I.

The ethical problem is as old as the human race. Humanity has always been in search of certain rules to regulate the conduct of society. These rules must have had a very slow growth at first; they developed unconsciously in the era when man was still an animal living in herds. Civilized society evolved from savage life in the degree that certain rules of conduct were more and more clearly recognized. It is natural that those tribes prospered best in whom the ethical spirit was comparatively well developed, and in the process of natural selection the growing nations of the world were sifted with ruthless cruelty "like as corn is sifted in a sieve." Thus humanity was educated in the hard school of experience, to find out the basic principles from which to derive the rules of conduct.

The ethics of a people at a given time, being the result of their experience, is naturally the practical application of their conception of the world. There is no action, i. e., purposive motion, without knowledge. Knowledge transforms motion into action. Action depends upon knowledge, and the sole purpose of knowledge is its application to action. Knowledge and ethics are correlatives, they are brothers, yet knowledge is the elder, he is always a little in advance of his younger brother, ethics. The evolution of knowledge will necessarily promote the evolution of ethics.

Ethics, in the widest sense of the term, means regulation of action. And in this sense every knowledge must have its ethical application. If the savage knows that friction produces fire, this knowledge finds its practical application in the ethical rule: In case you want fire, produce it by friction. There is no scientific discovery, be it ever so small or ever so great, that cannot be formulated in the shape of an ethical injunction. For instance, in order to build a house, observe the laws of gravitation. Sometimes a very crude knowledge suffices to perform a certain work; sometimes man, unconsciously, without a clear knowledge of what he is doing, succeeds in doing something that is right, but it cannot be doubted that the more knowledge he has, and the clearer he understands the science of a thing, the better will he perform a special work, and the more properly will he be enabled to attend to it.

All science has its ethical application—ethical in the widest sense of the term. And we may, in this way, consider all practical instruction, and the application of all human activity as ethical. Yet there is a special usage of the term ethics, the science of which is more difficult to understand, and this special ethics is meant if we speak of ethics in general.

Ethics, in the more definite sense, represents those duties which must be performed in the interest of society. Very often these can be performed only by a certain self-sacrifice; and yet they must be done. They have to be performed not only under the compulsion of law from the motive of fear, but of free will from the motive of love. Penal laws can serve for extremities only; they are mere safety-valves for protecting society in desperate cases. They are not the factors that make the community grow. The members of a society must be willing to sacrifice some of their individual interests, and if they are not animated with this spirit, our legislative apparatus can be of no avail.

The ethical stimulus has been implanted into man by religion. All the religions of the world are justly considered ethical movements. Confucius inaugurated an ethical movement, the decalogue of Mount Sinai is an ethical movement, Buddha is the founder of an ethical movement, and Christ's Sermon on the Mount is intended to replace a slavish obedience to the letter of the law by the ethical spirit of religious aspiration.

What is religion? Religion is a conception of the world applied to practical life. It is a theory of the universe in its ethical importance. It is a philosophy employed as a regulative principle for action.

If there is a difference between philosophy and religion it is this: The word philosophy is mostly employed when we speak of the world-conception of single thinkers; the word Religion signifies a philosophy endorsed by a whole society. In addition to this distinction we notice that religion always includes the ethical application of a conception of the world, while a philosophy may imply, but need not necessarily contain its ethical corollaries. In a philosophy the theoretical part, in a religion the practical application, is predominant, yet there is no difference in principle; every philosophy is a religion and every religion a philosophy.

The history of all the sciences begins with the belief in magic. The inventor who has made himself useful in this or that way has accomplished something extraordinary, something wonderful, something impossible; it appears impossible to the natural abilities of man. Accordingly, it is argued, he can have done it only by the aid of supernatural forces. And the man who made the invention is under the same impression. He did not make his own ideas, but the ideas grew in him as the flowers grow in spring. They came to him like a revelation from above. He felt himself inspired.

And there is a great truth in this conception of inspiration—a truth which is at present little heeded. All growth comes to us like a gift from on high. It is true that we have created by our own efforts the higher life of a civilized humanity; yet on the other hand, it is true also that all our efforts would have been in vain, did nature not contain the conditions for evolving that higher life. Man is a conscious being and he can learn to understand his wants, he can represent in his consciousness the growth of his body as well as his mind and the conditions that favor this growth. He can also scan the future so as to provide for emergencies and to protect himself against dangers. Thus consciousness becomes a factor having great influence upon man's life for properly directing his future evolution and for preserving the health of his life. Yet it was not his consciousness that made man grow. Humanity is of a natural growth not otherwise than is the unconscious growth of plants.

There is no science and no application of science which at first was not considered as magical. How could it be otherwise with the science that forms the basis of ethics? Almost all the old religions are still in the state of infancy; they represent the phase of astrology before it developed into astronomy, the phase of alchemy before it developed into chemistry. Yet like the sciences, religion also will develop into a state of scientific maturity.

Religion was supposed to have come to man by inspiration. And it did come to him by inspiration in a certain sense, as an idea comes to a poet, as a discovery comes to a scientist. The inspiration of religious prophets was not different from that of scientists, poets, or social reformers. Yet it was considered different, and up to this time the magical phase of religious views has with the majority of mankind not yet developed into that scientific state reached by the other branches of human experience. This step however must be made, and the signs of the time indicate that it will be made in the near future of humanity. Indeed the ethical problem at present is nothing but our desire to make this step.

The vanguard of those thinkers who are the leaders of human progress feel the necessity to place religion upon a scientific basis. The religion of magic, of supernaturalism, of superstition, must develop into a religion of science, it must become the scientific basis of ethics. Religion will remain a conception of the world that serves as a regulative principle for action. Yet this conception will cease to be the product of an instinctive imagination, it will become a scientific system of certain truths that have to be examined and proved by the usual methods of scientific enquiry.

The religion of science will have no dogmas, the truth of which is asserted on grounds of assumed authority; yet it will have truths, the authority of which depends upon on their capability of proof. The religion of science accordingly is not a religion of sentimental toleration which endures any and every opinion with equal indifference. The religion of science will be the most exclusive and orthodox religion that ever existed—orthodox in the proper sense of the word: having the right conviction, or being in possession of provable truth. And if the term is not misunderstood, we may add, that the religion of science will also be the most intolerant religion, for it will destroy all the views that are incompatible with it.

It will no longer suffer them to exist. However it will not destroy antagonistic views by putting opponents to death or persecuting them, but by convincing them of their errors.

II.

The ethical problem of to-day can be formulated in the question: "Is ethics a science; or if it is not at present, can ethics be founded upon a scientific basis?" This question is substantially the same as the effort to conciliate Religion with Science, or to evolve Religion from its state of infancy into its state of manhood; from dualism, into monism, from the mysticism of vague supernaturalistic speculations to the clearness of positive certainty, from authoritative belief and credulity into that of knowledge.

We want new ethics but no new morality. The morality of the old religions is not wrong. Their injunctions upon the whole are right. The commandments: "Honor thy father and mother," "thou shalt not steal," "thou shalt not kill," "thou shalt not bear false witness," are to-day as valid as they ever were. They have rather gained in meaning, for the consciences are more sensitive to resent any injury done to a neighbor since Christ taught us to consider even sinful desire to be culpable as though the sin itself were committed. It is not the morality of the old religions we object to, but it is the argument upon which the old religious morality is based.

You may say it matters not why a man leads a moral life, so that his life be moral. And to some extent it is of little consequence indeed, namely, in so far as morality has become a habit of his character which he could not change even though the motive that impelled him to do right should disappear. However it is by no means indifferent if we consider the necessity of educating the growing generation whose characters are plastic like clay in a potter's hand. Man wants motives for his actions, and above all he wants motives for those actions that appear to run counter to his personal interests. Man wants strong motives for those actions which he would not perform, if his egotism had the sole decision. And man has a right to demand motives for he is a thinking being and it is his prerogative to be guided by reason.

The old reasons of religious ethics have become untenable, and it is therefore, solely therefore, that the ethical problem has become a burning question. If the belief in a supernatural and personal God, as taught by the churches were as strong to-day, as it was centuries ago, if the authority of church doctrines were as firm and undisputed as it was formerly, we would have no ethical problem. There would be no meaning in the very phrase "the ethical problem." It is this need to supply a new and tenable basis for ethics which lies back of all ethical aspirations to-day.

There is no ethical problem to the dogmatic believer, for he imagines that God in person has spoken through the mouths of his prophets and his only beloved son, and whosoever believes and obeys God's commands will, after death, receive the crown of life. And yet such is the imperative demand of progress that even to the thoughtful dogmatist the ethical problem is brought home. He may conceive the increase of unbelief among the thinkers of mankind as a sign of depravity in the human race; nevertheless this state of things demands his attention likewise. If he has an interest in the welfare of society, he must see the need of teaching ethics to unbelievers. The dogmatist is an ethical teacher, an ethical missionary also. He knows that a teacher must go down to the level of his disciples, and from their stand-point raise them to his own. Every missionary must speak in the language of those whom he wishes to convert. Thus even a dogmatist, from his stand-point, can appreciate that an appeal to the accounts of revelation would be useless with regard to those who have ceased to believe them. He himself will be obliged to appeal more to natural and demonstrable arguments than to his creed, and thus it will happen that the churches themselves, even though they retain their denominational names, will, under the pressure of facts, by the gentle influence of the times, change into societies for ethical culture.

There is one point you ought to understand well. The ethical movement will work for the progress of mankind whatever you do; for it will, under all circumstances, help to ethicalize our churches. But if you intend to give permanence to your work in the ethical movement, if you wish that the Societies for Ethical Culture shall continue, you must not rest satisfied with negations, you must do the positive work of affirmation. It is not sufficient to drop the antiquated creeds of supernaturalism, which furnished in former centuries the motives for moral action, you must replace them by new motives that can stand scientific criticism. It is not sufficient to propound the ethical problem and to push it to the front of human interests, so as to call to it all the attention that it deserves; you must also solve it.

The work done by the leaders of the ethical movement is undoubtedly a great achievement, and the mere selection of the name is most appropriate. The mere formulation of a problem, said David Hume, is almost half of its solution. You have elicited sympathies all over the world among the learned professors of ethics as much as among the liberal clergy who are willing to follow the spirit of scientific progress. Will you now leave the task undone? Will you shrink from completing the work lest you commit yourselves to a real solution of the ethical problem? I hope, and indeed I believe, that you will not. Does not Christ's word apply to you as well as it did of yore to the multitude that listened to his words in Galilee: "Ye are the salt of the earth, but if the salt have lost its savor wherewith shall it be salted. It is thenceforth good for nothing, but to be cast out and to be trodden under foot of men." If you leave the work undone, if you positively refuse to do it, it is certain that your societies will pass away, for, in that case, they would have no reason to exist, they would be meaningless, like the salt that has lost its savor.

Your failure to solve the ethical problem would be a serious loss to the cause of progress; yet if the ethical societies would pass out of existence, the ethical movement would remain. Though you misunderstood your own ideals, your ideals would live in spite of you. They will take root in the hearts of others who possess the strength and the courage to realize them.

After all, it is not impossible that the churches may be roused, for there is still much power for good in them. The churches have not lost the capability of regeneration; the demands of the time press them very hard; they feel no less than you the urgency of the ethical problem, and why should not a spirit of reform seize them as happened in the era of Luther? The leaders of the churches will become aware of the fact that they are losing contact with their times. If they continue in the old rut, their numbers will diminish and their influence decrease. But, in that case, is it not most probable that in the last moment of necessity the clergy will understand the dilemma: Either the churches have to adapt themselves to the needs of the time, or they will cease to exist? If they understand this, an ethical revival will undoubtedly animate church life and with all the advantages of their organization, with their historical inheritance and traditions, they will evolve into that higher phase of religion which is free from the superstition of magic. They will purify their faith so as to shake off the illusions of supernaturalism, and unequivocally take their stand on the solid ground of scientific truth.

There can be no doubt, if there is any truth in the law of evolution, that the ethical movement will be victorious in the end. Its enemies cannot suppress it, neither can its friends nor its founders. It must have its way. We can hinder its growth, we can retard its progress by miscomprehending it, but we cannot undo it. Yet we can also promote its progress, we can enhance its growth, we can mature its harvest: and in doing so we shall work for the cause of humanity.

III.

The question now arises: How can we have a scientific basis of ethics? How is the transition from the old state to the new to be effected? And which philosophy shall give us the theoretical assistance of method for our operation?

Which philosophy? There are so many! And one philosopher contradicts the other. There is materialism and spiritualism, realism and idealism, monism and agnosticism. Which shall we select as a basis for ethics? I believe the bewildering number of so many different systems hindered the leaders of the societies for ethical culture from endorsing any one of them. We have so many little systems of world-theories as to what the essence of the world might be like, that an outsider can only reserve his judgment. I can only approve of Professor Adler's proposition that an ethical movement must not commit itself to any one of these thought-constructions of theorizing philosophers.

Yet if there is no philosophy of permanent value, the ethical movement must contribute as much as possible to create a philosophy that will be sufficient for our needs. And at present it is not so much a philosophical system that is needed, as clearness about the principle by which to guage the depth and the importance of world-conceptions.

Schiller said in one of his xenions:

> "Which will survive of the many philosophies?—Surely I know not!
> Yet Philosophy will, truly, forever remain."

There was a time when we had several astronomies. Which of them survived? Only one, that of Copernicus. We name it after the man who first discovered it; yet we might have named it the astronomy of facts. All the ingenious theories and fantastic speculations had to be abandoned, when this most simple theory was propounded, which rightly considered was in need of no hypothesis and although it did credit to the imaginative power of its inventor, it was merely a consistent and simple explanation of facts. So it will be with all the philosophies. All the thought-constructions of absolute being must go, and only the philosophy of facts will remain. And the new ethics in order to become a science must be established on facts.

Here is the line of demarcation between the new ethics and the old. The old ethics is based upon revelation, upon absolute ideas, upon anything, but not upon facts. The new ethics is based upon facts and is applied to facts.

There are perhaps many among you who would say: "Facts are a poor capital to start with. What are facts? Are they not the realities of life, the sensory impressions we have, the happenings and events of history and of our individual experience, the natural processes that take place around us?" Certainly all these things are facts, and facts are the realities of life.

Laplace searched the skies and he could not find God. In the same way, you may search the facts of reality and you will not find ethics. Ethics is not ready made; it is not the one or the other fact among all the realities of the universe. Ethics is our attitude toward the facts of reality.

The objection that can be made to the proposition of basing ethics upon facts can be stated as follows: "The realities of life are often very sad; and they are especially insufficient in the properly moral element. Ethics therefore wants something greater and grander than facts. Science may explain the things that are;

science may be satisfied with facts, but ethics deals with things that ought to be; ethics is not satisfied with facts but it brings us ideals. The basis of ethics and of ethical ideals must be sought in something superior to facts, in something absolute."

It is true that ethics is not satisfied with the present state of things; ethics attempts to improve the state of facts as they are. Ethics deals with ideals. Yet these ideals whence do they come? Are they really derived from the absolute? Do ideals come to us from fairy land? Are they really of a mysterious and a superterrestrial origin? If so, supernaturalism would be right after all!

What are ideals? Ideals have a very humble origin; they are not of celestial or transcendental parentage. Ideals are the children of our needs. If an inventor is engaged in inventing a machine for filling some need in human life, he has an ideal, for an ideal is an idea to be realized.

Ideals do not come down to us from the skies, nor are they mere dreams, mere poetical visions of our prophets. Not at all! Man wants something, so he conceives the idea how good it would be if he had it. If a man is a mere dreamer, he is pleased with his imagination, and complains about the hard facts of reality. However, if he is a thinker, that is, a dreamer who, in addition to his imaginative faculty, possesses self-discipline, will, and the ability to prune his imagination, and to criticize his dreams, he will study facts.

And only by studying facts will he be enabled to realize his ideal. Those apparent ideals which, for some reason, are not adaptable to facts are no ideals, but dreams.

The ethical ideal rises as all other ideals, from the wants of man. Humanity is in need of a better state of things, of more benevolence in our mutual intercourse, of more justice in our dealings, more enthusiasm for the common good. This produces conceptions of a higher conduct than humanity at present possesses, of better laws and institutions, and we are constantly investigating the different plans to decide whether or not they would be an improvement if realized. If ethical ideals do not agree with the laws that science, after a careful examination, has derived from facts, they are mere dreams, and are just as worthless, perhaps also just as misleading, as is the mirage of a *fata morgana* in the desert, or an *ignis fatuus* in a marshy region.

The religions of supernaturalism teach that the source of all goodness and morality is a great personal being residing beyond the skies; and he, by means of magic, implants into man's bosom the ethical ideal. No wonder that Laplace could not find God! A medicine-man, who works miracles, has no room in nature even though he were omnipotent enough to let the stars spin around his fingers. Yet there is a great truth in the idea of God. The religion of science recognizes that there is a power, an all-pervading law in the universe, which is not personal, but superpersonal. And this superpersonal power not only obtains in the motions of the stars and in the laws of cosmic life, but also in the destinies of nations, in the growth of society, and in the fates of individuals. It wrecks those who do not conform to its injunctions. If Laplace had sought for this God, for the God of science, who is a reality of life no less than the law of gravitation, he would not have failed to discover him. We need not search the skies in order to find this God. We need but look into our own hearts, for there he lives in our ethical aspirations and ideals. He is not far from every one of us, for in him we live, and move, and have our being.

The old religion of magic teaches that God works by magic, and can in turn be worked upon by magic. Hence the institutions of prayer and adoration in spite of Christ's command that God is spirit, and those who worship him must worship him in spirit and in truth. The new worship is no adoration, but obedience to the ethical laws, as Christ says: "Not every one that saith unto me, Lord, Lord, shall enter into the kingdom of heaven, but he that doeth the will of my Father which is in heaven." The God of science demands no creed, but deed. What is creed but the belief in the letter of parables? And is it not expressly and repeatedly stated that Christ's words are truths symbolically expressed? "All these things spake Jesus unto the multitude in parables; and without a parable spake he not unto them." (MATT. XIII, 34).

What would Christ say, if he saw the modern paganism of Christianity which has retained a modified idolatry, instead of realizing the purely ethical religion of a worship in spirit and in truth? His word that "God is spirit" is wrongly translated by the phrase "God is a Spirit." This insertion of the article alters the entire sense of the passage. It changes God into a Ghost, into a bodiless person, and gives new occasion for the continuation of pagan rites and customs.

There is a tendency now along the whole line of scientific enquiry to prove that every one of our sciences ultimately stands on facts. Mathematics and logic were formerly supposed to hang in mid-air, their fundamental truths were said to be axioms that need no proof because they are self-evident. Modern mathematics has succeeded in proving that mathematics is ultimately based on facts no less than any other science, and the same has been proved of logic. Modern Mathematics has not superseded Euclid, and modern logic has not superseded Aristotle. Yet the modern conception of these sciences has made an amendment which will guard against the error that the formal sciences are anything like an unexplainable miraculous revelation.

We are so much accustomed to respect those things only, the origin of which we do not comprehend, that it seems to us like a disappointment if we are told we should be able to understand the foundation of ethics and to search for its basis among facts. Indeed those who yet believe in absolute ideas, those who have not as yet succeeded in coming down to facts, still stand beyond the line of demarcation that separates the old view from the modern or scientific view. The idea to base ethics on absolute conceptions, on mystic emotions, on vague methods of intuition, or on incomprehensible ideals, is in principle not very different from the old method of a supernatural revelation of ethics. The line of distinction is sharper than any color line can be, and those who have not as yet felt the need of basing ethics upon facts cannot be said to be imbued with the spirit of modern ethics.

Here is an ideal worthy of the noblest efforts of our enthusiasm. Ideals may have, as I said before, a lowly origin. This detracts not in the least from their divine grandeur. On the contrary this adds to their greatness. This world of ours is not a world suited to the taste of the pleasure-seeker, yet it affords an ample field to the man who finds his satisfaction in realizing ideals.

Ideals are born of want, and the birth of ideals is often accompanied by painful throes, by suffering, anguish, and anxiety. Yet all the affliction man has to undergo is fully compensated in the noble satisfaction he enjoys in the work of realizing his ideals.

Be not afraid lest in this world the Ideal
  Should disappear, or like a flower fade;
  For she is not mere fancy's fickle shade.
She is a glowing presence, true and real.

Still firmly an alliance hymeneal
  Joins her to Human Progress, as a maid
  Is wedded to a hero, whom his blade
Protects; thus faithfully he shields the Ideal.

Wondrously from this bridal union springs
  The life which, breathing through the human race
  In ardent youth shines forth from every face;
It lends to the inventor fancy's wings,
And stirs the poet's heart, who gaily sings
  The Ideal's beauty and the Ideal's grace.

THE DATA OF ETHICS.

ALL knowledge is a representation of facts in sentient beings. Those facts which form the subject-matter of a special branch of knowledge are called its data. For instance the data of astronomy are the motions of the celestial bodies, the data of botany are the phenomena of plant-life.

What are the data of ethics?

The data of ethics are the motives for human action.

In order to understand the laws that regulate the motives for human action, we must study the soul of man, the origin and mechanism of its ideas, their relations to the surrounding world and above all the interconnections that obtain between man and man.

It devolves upon us to explain how man happens to be a moral being. Having motives, man must have aims, and he can have aims only by being able to forecast future events and calculate the consequences of his intended actions. We must further understand how man can have motives of duty stronger than his personal interests. The motives of duty are called conscience. This will lead us to the ultimate purpose of ethics: How can we make man responsible for his actions and how can we educate him to obey the behests of his conscience, the motives of duty, in preference to all egotistic desires?

I.

Man is the only creature on earth that is an ethical being, because he alone is able to think. The beginning of all ethics is thought. Before I act, I think, I can forecast the probable result of my action; yea, even more than the probable result. If I know all the conditions and control them, I can with certainty foretell the consequence. It appears wonderful that man can know something before it happens, and yet it is a fact; and if it were no fact, how could we have ethics?

This is the old problem of Kant's *a priori*, which has caused much dispute among philosophers. Mr. John Stuart Mill has tried to do away with it, he put it down and denounced it; but the *a priori* is like a stand-up, that queer wooden toy-man standing upon a rounded leaden base. You may knock down the stand-up as often as you please, it will spring to its feet again. So the *a priori* has been declared to be an impossibility, but here it is again.

Says Kant*: "We say of a man who undermined his house, he might have known *a priori* that it would fall; that is, he need not have waited for the experience that it did actually fall."

The *a priori* is the foundation of all our ethical action in the widest sense of the term ethics; it is the

* "Critique of Pure Reason," 2d Edition, Introduction.

basis of all practical application of knowledge. If we were not able to forecast the result of our actions, there would be no ethology.

Is it not marvelous that man can know something before gaining the actual experience of it? Is this not an inexplainable mystery, the influence of some supernatural power?—No. The mystery of the *a priori* is easily explained as soon as we understand the nature of formal laws.

If I construct a number of triangles all different in shape, rectangular, obtuse, and equilateral, I shall find that the sum of the angles of each of them measures one hundred and eighty degrees. This is wonderful indeed; but it is not miraculous. It is a necessary consequence; in all these cases like conditions produce like results. And mathematics as a science is engaged in showing how the conditions are the same, although they may at first sight appear different.

It is true that we cannot determine beforehand how some substance which we have never seen before, will be affected by this or that treatment; but we do know beforehand the laws that underlie *one* quality in all the things which in our experience we can possibly meet. We do know beforehand the laws of form, and everything that exists, everything that can become an object of our experience, is equally subject to the laws of form. If I put twice two apples into a basket, I have put four apples into it. "Twice two are four" is perhaps the simplest statement of a formal law, and we know beforehand that wherever the same action of two being doubled takes place, the result will always be the same; it will be the product of twice two, which we call four. When we know that a result will *always* be the same, we call it necessary.

Thus we can formulate all the formal laws and we can know beforehand that no experience ever will refute them. The formal laws of numbers we call arithmetic; those of spacial relations "mathematics," those of thinking "logic," and the formal laws of natural sciences are sometimes called "metaphysics."*

The formal laws being universal are, objectively considered, the conditions of the regularity that prevails in nature; subjectively considered, being conceived as necessary, they afford us the means of comprehending the phenomena of nature. Comprehension is nothing but the recognition of the regularity that prevails in the facts of experience, and comprehension enables us to suit our actions to special purposes, and thus to determine the course of events.

Ethics, accordingly, is ultimately based upon the same universal order of things that makes mathematics, arithmetic, logic, and human reason, possible. Reason is that quality of man that makes him an ethical being.

*The word metaphysics has often been defined as the science of the mystical essence which underlies the existence of reality. Metaphysical was (according to a wrong etymology of the word) supposed to be that which lies behind the physical. This kind of metaphysics has long since been superseded by positivism. The most important law of true metaphysics, i. e., purely formal natural science, is that of the conservation of matter and energy.

Reason has been supposed to be of supernatural origin; yet reason is no more supernatural than is the ability to understand that twice two will always be the product of twice two, that is four. This very ability *is* reason, for all the complicated activities of our mind in logical argumentation and ratiocination, all methods of induction and deduction are the same thing over again, they are formal thought or applications of formal thought.*

The laws of form being the key to our understanding the regularity of the course of nature, reason, as it were, reveals to us the unity of All-existence. This revelation is no revelation in the old theological sense, it is a natural revelation, the origin of which we can trace in the formal laws of existence. This revelation is not the inexplicable act of an extra-mundane deity; it is no mysticism, no supernaturalism. It is simply the recognition of the universal order of things. Knowledge being the representation of facts, this revelation is nothing but the recognition of the regularity that prevails among these facts, and this recognition pours

* Kant distinguishes between "transcendental," i. e., formal, and "transcendent," i. e., that which transcends all comprehension. Everything supernatural is transcendent; but those truths which Kant calls "transcendental" are by no means "transcendent"; they are the clearest thoughts possible, the laws of logic, arithmetic, mathematics. If there is anything transcendent, our knowledge of it is necessarily mysticism.

Kant made a grave mistake when he called formal thought "transcendental." For Kant's disciples confounded both words and considered transcendental truths as transcendent. Thus the radical Kant became, in their minds, a supporter of supernaturalism, and those thoughts of his which destroyed all mysticism, became a new basis of it.

a flood of light over this world of ours, for while the many various facts of experience at first appeared to us as a bewildering chaos without rhyme or reason, we now learn to consider it as a cosmos in which the minutest detail is ordained by an immanent and intrinsic law.

* * *

Kant has written an excellent little book in which he lays the foundation for a metaphysics of ethics. It is entitled *Grundlegung zur Metaphysik der Sitten.* In this book he enquires into the purpose of reason. Is happiness the end of reason? Kant says, no! He argues:

"In the physical constitution of an organized being we take it for granted that no organ will be found in it for any purpose but such as is also the fittest and best adapted for that purpose. If in a being possessing reason and will, the preservation, the prosperity, in a word, the happiness of that being constituted the actual purpose of nature, nature had certainly adopted an extremely unwise expedient to this end, had it made the reason of that being the executive agent of its purposes in this matter. For all actions that it had to perform with this end in view, and the whole rule of its conduct, would have been far more exactly prescribed by *instinct*, and this end would have been far more safely attained by this means than can ever take place through the instrumentality of *reason*.

"As a matter of fact we find, that the more a cultivated reason occupies itself with the purpose of enjoying life and happiness, the farther does the person possessing it recede from the state of true contentment; and hence there arises in the case of many, and pre-eminently in the case of those most experienced in the exercise of reason, if they are only frank enough to confess it, a certain degree of "misology" or hate of reason; for after weighing every advantage that they derive, I will not say from the invention of all arts facilitating ordinary luxury, but even from the sciences, (which after all are in their eyes a luxury of the intellect,) they still discover that virtually they have burdened themselves more with toil and trouble than they have gained in point of happiness, and thus, in the end, they are more apt to envy than contemn the commoner type of men who are more immediately subject to the guidance of natural instinct alone, and who do not suffer their reason to influence in any great degree their acts and omissions."

What then is the use of reason, if its purpose cannot be found in producing happiness? Reason enables us to comprehend the regularity of the order of nature and the unity of cosmic existence. Everything that exists conforms to it. And if some combination of things ceases to conform to the laws of cosmic existence, it will ultimately meet with destruction.

We have learned in our previous lecture that all knowledge can be formulated as an ethical prescript. Thus we express the same truth ethologically as follows: If you wish to exist, obey reason. Reason teaches us how to regulate our actions in conformity with the order of natural laws. If we do regulate them in conformity with the order of natural laws, they will stand; otherwise not. In the former case they will be good, they will agree with the cosmical conditions of existence; in the latter case they are bad, they will not agree with the cosmical conditions of existence;

therefore they will necessarily produce disorder and evil.

Kant calls this attitude of man, produced under the influence of reason and prompting him to conform to universal laws, "the good will." This attitude of the will, Kant says, "is not the sole and whole good, but it must still be considered as the highest good and the condition necessary to everything else, even to all desire of happiness."

The conclusion derived from these premises Kant formulates in the following statement:

> "To know what I have to do in order that my volition be good, requires on my part no far-reaching sagacity. Unexperienced in respect to the course of nature, unable to be prepared for all the occurrences transpiring therein, I simply ask myself: Canst thou so will, that the maxim of thy conduct may become a universal law? Where it can not become a universal law, there the maxim of thy conduct is reprehensible, and that, too, not by reason of any disadvantage consequent thereupon to thee or even others, but because it is not fit to enter as a principle into a possible enactment of universal laws."

II.

Kant's ethics has been criticized of late as "mere formalism;" yet could we not on the same ground reject all the sciences because they are based upon the laws of formal thought? It proves the superiority of Kant's reasoning that he so clearly shows the formal side of ethics. We cannot treat of grammar without understanding logic! Or if we do, our discussions will be idle talk. Any investigation into ethics accordingly must be based upon clear notions of the metaphysics of morals, or as we would prefer to call it of "purely formal ethics."

The criticism of Kant's ethics would be justified, if formal ethics were the whole of ethics. However formal ethics is as little the whole of ethics as logic is the whole of grammar. The principle of modern ethics is to base ethics upon facts, and the formal laws that regulate the interconnection of facts is one part only of all the facts. Purely formal ethics, like all the purely formal sciences, is empty. The contents of formal ethics must be derived from the actual facts of our experiences.

The application of the precept "so to will that the maxim of thy conduct can become a universal law," depends entirely upon the society of which an individual is a member. The same formal law might be applicable to the code of a band of robbers no less than to the customs of peaceful citizens. How can we determine whether the maxim of a certain action is "fit to enter as a principle into a possible enactment of universal laws," otherwise than by experience? Man being a rational animal, he naturally will employ his reason; but reason can be employed to advantage only if it uses the material of facts, as we find it in experience. Ratiocinations of pure formalism may be good mental exercises, they may be indispensable for training the mind, yet if they had no practical purposes, if they were not applied, and never to be applied to actual facts, they would be as sounding brass or a tinkling cymbal.

* * *

The facts to be considered in ethics are the many and various relations in which man stands to his surroundings. These relations produce the many different motives that prompt man's actions. The most important relations of all for ethical consideration are those which connect the life of a single individual to the fates of all his fellow beings. The relation between man and man constitutes that super-individual soul-life which we call society.

Relations are not material things, and it is difficult therefore to understand that they are actual and most important realities. Relations are facts of experience also. Let us for the sake of illustration imagine that all the relations of a man to his surroundings are so many invisible silken threads, fastened to those spots of his body where the objects affect him. Every contact with the outer world sets some of these threads in vibration, thus causing a commotion among the innumerable plugs or hooks to which they are fastened. This commotion is the pulsation of man's physical and mental activity. The contact of his breathing organs with the oxygen of the air keeps the flame of his life aglow, and the constant consumption of the energy with which the structures of his organism are freighted, causes the need of renewing them for a continuation of the process of life.

Among all the threads that connect man's body with the outer world and the different parts of the body among themselves, there are some that pass through the sensory organs to his brain; the end stations to which they are hooked, are the different places where a commotion produces a state of consciousness representing that object with which it stands in relation. The hooks in man's brain are not only connected with threads that pass through the sensory organs into the brain, but also with others that connect the hooks among themselves and connect some hooks with the muscles of the body. Thus a commotion caused among the cerebral hooks will set the muscles in motion.

Now suppose that a consumption of energy has taken place through the contact with the outer world, there will result a strong pull of certain threads to the brain and a state of consciousness will be produced which we call hunger and thirst.

This state of consciousness acts as an irritation upon man. It prompts him to action, and in so far as it is the cause of some motion, we call it "motive." Motive is that which moves, and the distinction we make between cause and motive, is that a motive is a cause which in its action is accompanied with consciousness. The motion of an organism that is accompanied with consciousness is called "action," or an "act," and the attitude of passing into action is called "will."

The hooks on which the innumerable threads are fastened, represent man's soul. What are these hooks and how did they originate?

The world-substance cannot be dead matter; it must contain, in its simplest and most elementary forms, the germs of life, so that in special combinations, as we find them in organized animal substance, the motion of atoms is accompanied with feeling.*

In consideration of the fact that the whole world in all its dimensions is a most complicated network of causes and effects, it will be natural that an animal organism, which has been formed somewhere, will be affected by innumerable impressions that show an unfailing regularity. The different impressions will produce different forms of structure in the organism, and the motions vibrating through the different structures will be accompanied with different feelings. The preservation of these forms is called "the memory of living substance," and modern investigations of physiology teach us that all the various functions of the different organs and nerve-cells are due to the unconscious memory of the living substance inherited from countless ancestors. Accordingly, these hooks of our soul of which we spoke, are nothing but the

* Compare the article "Is Nature Alive?" in *Fundamental Problems*, pp. 110–133.

effects which the threads of causal relations have produced by constant contact.

Innumerable sensory impressions have produced in the feeling substance representations of their causes in the surrounding world; and many of these representations act as stimuli, they are motives for action.

* * *

Ethics is an estimation of the motives for action, whether we shall yield to them or suppress them, and in case we have to choose among several motives of which one only can be selected, ethics has to instruct us as to which motive is to be preferred. But ethics can be of service only if it gives us a principle according to which we can form our judgment. Ethics without a principle or maxim, without a standard for discrimination, is no ethics. It may be enthusiasm, it may be sentimentality, it may be zeal for some unknown good; it may be mysticism or romanticism, but it is not ethics, for judgment as to right and wrong, according to a definite conviction, is the very nature of ethics. Take away that conviction, deprive ethics of the principle of estimation, and ethics will cease to be ethics.

Ethics by passing judgment upon man's motives will under ordinary circumstances always strengthen some of them and weaken others. Yet, an ethical man is he whose aspiration it is to live in perfect harmony with the moral law. To him it will be impossible to let any motive pass into act upon which the verdict of "wrong" has been pronounced by the jury of his ethical consideration.

* * *

The most important relations of a man are the relations that obtain between him and his fellow-beings. They form the soul-life of a super-individual organism which is called society. The importance of these connections is enormous, and their overwhelming influence upon the emotions of every individual cannot be overrated. Every individual is, by the thousands of threads that connect him with wife and children, with friends and fellow-citizens, tied to society. Consider the immense power of the inherited memory of sociological functions in past generations, and we shall easily comprehend the strength of social motives.

Some philosophers are prone to consider egotistic motives as the natural springs of action, while they look upon purely altruistic motives as something extraordinary and inexplainable. They are wrong; egotistic motives are no more and no less natural than altruistic and social motives. Both have developed at the same time, both have differentiated from morally indifferent and simple reflex actions. Morally indifferent are those actions concerning the motives of which no ethical estimation is required. The lowest stages of animal development know neither egotism nor altruism. The differentiation of both appears simultaneously at a later period. It is remarkable that in the mental development of a child, the ability of speaking in the first person with the pronoun "I" signifies a comparatively mature state of mind.

When some egotistic motive impels man to do an act that is injurious to one or several of his fellow beings, he experiences a pull of the social threads which is sometimes very strong even in the thoughtless. It often acts like a thunderstorm with the irresistible force of elementary powers. And the behests of conscience overruling with imperative command man's individual interests appear to him, and indeed they are, invested with that superindividual authority which conscience represents. The behests of conscience confront us as an "ought" and we call them our duty, obedience to which is as a rule tacitly admitted.

Conscience is nothing supernatural, it is of a natural growth. Man being a social animal, it is all but impossible that the social instinct and the motives for actions in behalf of society should not have been strongly developed. There are people in whom egotistic desires possess greater strength than moral impulses, but it is all but impossible that a man should be void of all conscience.

The animal allows itself to be guided by instinct, but it is the prerogative of man to regulate his actions by reason. Conscience as a mere moral instinct is certainly, as experience teaches in many most perplexing situations, often the safest and best guide. Nevertheless conscience as a mere instinct can by no means be considered as infallible; nor must we lose sight of the fact that the different behests of conscience very often come in conflict among themselves. But even if it were not so, the dignity of man as a rational being demands that he should examine all his motives and also the behests of conscience.

III.

The purpose of ethics is to determine the moral import of the different motives, and we ask now what is the principle that should guide us in our estimation concerning the worth of motives.

When we try to explain the growth and origin of man's soul, we must go back to the first appearance of living substance. Human soul-life would be an inexplainable mystery if we did not consider the continuity of soul-life through all the generations of man's ancestors from the very beginning. The facts that scientists have brought to light in studying the phases of evolution require us to regard humanity as one great and immortal organism. The soul-life of our ancestors continues in us and at the same time must we know the most important fibres of our emotional and intellectual soul-life originate in the relations that bind us to our fellow-beings. These considerations remove the barriers that seem to obtain between the individual and humanity—aye, and the whole creation of cosmic existence.

We are apt to think that our soul-life is something quite distinct from the outside world. The subjective world of representations is so different from the objective world of things. Nevertheless they are one. Every sensation is a subjective state, but it is such only through the objective state that causes it. It is no mere internal act but it is a relation between object and subject—a relation in which neither subject nor object is a redundant element. In the course of evolution and in the development of human soul-life, the representations of the surrounding world and of man's relations become increasingly distinct. The regularity that obtains in nature around him and within him is more clearly recognized; and man's power over nature grows in the same measure as the human soul expands in the comprehension of facts. In this sense we speak of a higher evolution of the human soul. The facts carefully gathered by all the sciences, by comparative physiology, history, psychology, prove that the tendency of growth of a higher evolution is intrinsic. As a child grows whether he will or not, so humanity develops, and it has often developed differently from what the philosophers expected; and there are many in whom the spirit of progress was active who "builded better than they knew." Yet while the growth and progress of humanity, of the soul-life of society as well as of the individual soul, is of a spontaneous nature, man can, to a great extent, make or mar his own fate and that of his race. Man certainly cannot make the details of his physical growth, yet he can easily mar it by negligence. And his mental development depends entirely upon a wise choice and direction which is of his own making.

We can thus promote or retard the development of human soul-life: all the efforts that tend to preserve and to promote it, are "good," while all the efforts that tend to dwarf it, are "bad."

* * *

The task of ethics is to expand the interests of each individual so that they embrace the weal and woe of the whole human race in all its future generations. It is not enough to take into consideration the narrow span of our present life, we must regulate our motives according to an ethics of eternity. We must not think and feel and act as individuals who care nothing for future generations; we must think, and feel, and act, as the immortal human soul, which is the soul of mankind. It began with the beginning of all life upon earth, it lives now in us, it glows in our thoughts and hopes, and it will continue to live in future humanity.

There will be a time when this generation will have passed away, when we shall be no more—and yet we shall continue to live; our work done in the interest of humanity, our soul-life will continue beyond the grave.

The efforts we have made in childhood and in youth to expand our soul, say, for instance, in studying at school, continue to live in us even now. The material particles that did the work at that time, have long since passed away in the flux of matter, but the structures in our brain (representing the physiological basis of our memories), as they were shaped through our former activity, remain, because the renewal of our brain tissues, indeed the renewal of all living structures, preserves the forms once produced, thus constituting a continuity of soul-life.

The continuity of soul-life and the preservation of the forms of brain tissue which are the physiological basis of thoughts and the memories of thoughts, are patent to every one of us. But the continuity of soul-life is a law also in the development of our whole race. The souls of our ancestors and their thoughts are as little lost as is the work of our school days. They continue to live in us, for our souls have grown from theirs, they are a reproduction, a re-formation, a continuation of their soul-life.

The continuity of the soul-life of humanity is as strong and demonstrable as that of the individual. The ethical duty for the single moments of man's life and the individual atoms of his body is based on the very same principle as the ethical duty of individuals toward humanity. A single motive in our soul that presses upon our will to pass into act, has no right to be considered for itself alone; all the other motives have at least the same right. Thus we ought to compare them and decide which will contribute most to enhance human soul-life. Every motive must be weighed against all other motives of the present and the future; and those which tend to lower the standard of human soul-life in ourselves or in the race should never be permitted to pass into action.

If all the motives of man were so many single and isolated or sovereign feelings, there would be no ethics. The data of ethics are not motives that are equivalent, i. e., of equal value, but unequal motives; unequal in their worth, and those which either promise or actually afford the greatest pleasure are by no means those which deserve the highest ethical approval.

What a poor creature man would be if we could deprive his soul of all those thoughts that represent his connections with mankind! The strength of a tiger chiefly lies in his muscles and his teeth; yet the greatness and the strength of man lies in his relation to the human race. The human soul is powerful because of its connections with mankind, which form the superindividual element of the soul. The data of ethics therefore cannot be found in the individual alone as a separated being, but in the super-individual relations of the individual; and the social motives like so many invisible threads pull in his mind powerfully so that for the peace of his soul and for his own satisfaction he must obey; or he will ruin himself.

IV.

Having sketched as briefly as possible the conditions of ethics that make ethics possible, that condition its growth and its importance, I will not conclude without touching an important point concerning which there is little agreement and still less clearness. It is the problem of man's freedom of will. Is there free will, or is free will an illusion?

It is generally conceded that a free man only can be held responsible for his action; a slave who does not act from free will, who is compelled to do this and to leave that alone, cannot be held responsible.

Epictetus said: "No one can deprive us of our free will," and Schiller said: "Man is free e'en were he born in chains."

All the sages of mankind, all the great moral teachers of the world have inculcated the truth that a man can be free if he wants to be, and that freedom of will is possible only by observing the moral law. The man who yields to his passions enslaves himself, he commits actions which later on will bring consequences upon him that he will have to regret; or they will entangle him in a net of circumstances that will be like iron fetters upon his will. But he who controls his passions by self-discipline, will preserve his freedom of will.

This doctrine of free will has on the one hand by

theologians been declared to be an inscrutable mystery, and on the other hand it has been denounced by so-called freethinkers as an illusion. The idea of freedom of will has been represented as if it were an exception in the course of natural processes. All phenomena are determined by causes, yet the actions of a free will were supposed not to be determined by cause.

The cause that sets the will into motion, we call motive. If free will meant a will not determined by motives, it would indicate a state of disease; for an unmotived action is, properly considered, no action, but a mere reflex motion, caused through pathological conditions. The action of a free will of this type must appear to us as the arbitrary whim of an alienated person; and people whose actions are not determined by motives cannot be considered responsible, and ought to be confined in an asylum.

The old theological conception of the freedom of will is not only untenable, it is self-contradictory, and will not stand a close examination. It is erroneously defined, not as "the freedom to act as one wills," but as "the freedom to will as one wills,"—as if there were any sense in the conception that a man can will differently from what he wills!

In opposition to this false statement of a free will, the adversaries of religious ethics rose and declared that there is no such a thing as freedom of will. Every act of ours is determined; and therefore they declared we are compelled to act as we do. The criminal acts as he does of necessity and a moral man also acts morally, of necessity; both are, so they say, slaves of their motives. Both obey the compulsion of a natural law.

Strange these very same men who object so strongly to the idea of free will, are the very same men who clamor for freedom of thought, and generally call themselves "freethinkers." If there is no freedom of will, there is certainly no freedom of thought, for the laws of thought are very rigid and admit of no freedom.

The mistake made by both, the old school of theologians as well as their antagonists, is a lack of distinction between necessity and compulsion. Necessity is that which is determined by law; compulsion, however, is an act of violence to force a man to do something against his will. A slave that is compelled to work for his master, is not free; he would not work if he were not forced to do it. A free man, let us say an artist full of an idea, executes his work without any compulsion, he works of his own free will. His actions are determined by a motive of his own, not by a foreign pressure. Therefore we call him free.

A freethinker tells me that a man's motive compels him to act as he does; accordingly, man is a slave of his motive. I would have no objection to the usage of the word compulsion in that sense, if it were properly understood. In that case the free man would be he who himself compels himself to whatever actions he undertakes while the slave is compelled by other things, for instance, by his master's whip. But this usage of the word compulsion is contrary to custom, and we would, if we changed our language in this way, produce the impression in our mind as if the act which is determined by a motive that resides within a man's soul and is a part and a characteristic feature of himself, is exactly the same as that act which is the result of compulsion. It would produce the impression as if a free man were as irresponsible for his action as is a slave. A free man, in that case, ought to be called a slave, and a freethinker an enslaved thinker.

Freedom of thought can mean only the absence of all compulsion, that prevents thought of thinking in accordance with the laws of thought. Yet in the absence of all compulsion thought, in order to be correct, has rigorously to obey the laws of thought. There is no freedom of thought in the sense that we may reach this or that conclusion just as we please.

There is no doubt that the actions of a man are strictly determined by his motives. A will not determined by a motive is as nonsensical as an effect not produced through a cause. And if actions could be willed by a will not determined through motives, ethics would have no sense. What would be the use of implanting moral motives into the minds of men, of teaching them the laws of nature and the laws of society, to which they have to conform, if their actions after all would not be determined by these or any other motives?

Responsibility is the consciousness of a free man, that he is the author of his actions and of their consequences. He, himself, and also others have to bear the consequences of his actions, be it for good or for evil. A man who knows the laws of nature and especially also the moral law that pervades and builds up society, and who has at the same time the good will to conform to it, is a law unto himself. He will act morally, not from compulsion but from free will; and this attitude of being a law unto himself, we call the autonomy of will, derived from *αὐτός*, *self*, and *νόμος*, *law*. The autonomous man alone is a free man; he alone is an ethical man; and the autonomy of man constitutes the dignity, the majesty, the divinity of man.

Ethics alone can make a state of society possible which consists of free men. Ethics instructs men about the moral law, and by implanting the moral law in their souls so as to rule the habits of their lives, it makes them autonomous. If there is a millennium possible upon earth, it can be realized through ethics only. We shall not be able to abolish all pain, and struggle, and anxiety, for life is strife, and there is no growth, no progress, without disturbances, pains, and anxieties. Yet we can abolish the worst evils of existence, which are those produced by our own ignorance and narrowness. Let every man be a law unto himself and society will be better than it is now; it will be the realization of the highest ideals of mankind, of justice, of order, and of freedom.

Man's freedom means not licence:
  Nor action without cause:
Man's freedom is obeisance
  Unto the soul's own laws.

For Anarchy unruly
  Must leave, a slave, you still.
Mark! Liberty is, truly,
  Autonomy of will.

A weakling seeks for pleasures.—
  Results learn to foresee;
Heed Nature's laws and measures
  Truth only makes you free.

THE THEORIES OF ETHICS.

Ethics as a science began with doubt. It was doubted whether or not there is any true ethics, whether or not non-egotistical motives can exist; and if they exist, whether their origin might not be of a natural growth.

Prescientific ethics was mythological, as it had to be. How could uneducated people understand the application of abstract principles otherwise than in parables. If ethics were not of such paramount importance, it would scarcely have arisen before the discovery of mathematics or logic. Being indispensable to the welfare and progress of the human race, ethics was first taught in myths and legends, which were accepted not in their allegorical but in their literal meaning. Belief in their literal meaning was very soon considered indispensable for all who sought participation in the sacred rewards promised in ethical myths. It was feared, that if the letter should go, the spirit would have to go also.

All myths in their literal meaning involve the mind in absurdities, and so all mythological dogmas, unless allegorically interpreted and understood according to the purpose for which they were invented, are contrary to human reason. They convey truths which in their mythological garb must appear paradoxical. The unbeliever objected to dogmas incompatible with reason and he objected also to any ethics based upon mythological ideas.

The development of ethics as a science has been a continuous battle between the infidel doubter and the pious believer; the former generally aggressive, the latter defensive; the former negative, bold, hasty, radical in convictions, prone to make sweeping assertions, and ready to welcome any new discovery that would seem to overthrow the old established views; the latter conservative, more scholarly than scientific, rather slow to understand new truths but greatly appreciating the valuable gold contained in the old truths. We find—how could it be otherwise?—misunderstandings on both sides.

The path of science in its victorious progress is strewn with errors of heroes who fought for truth. The mistakes of the searchers for truth have often been decried or at least ridiculed not only by their respective adversaries, but also by the following generations who knew better than their predecessors because they had reaped the fruits of their labors. Let us therefore bear in mind that every scientific truth has become a possession of the human mind only through an examination from many different points of view. The defenders of those conceptions which had to be rejected did no less valuable and indispensable work than those who were on the right track. For in the search for truth every path has to be followed and every possible solution must be considered. Most of the errors in the development of the sciences are necessary errors; they are attempts to find the truth and often contain germs of the truth or represent one phase of it which is distorted only by a one-sided conception.

I.

The old dogmatic teachers of ethics, anxious to establish their mythology as indispensable, used to argue in this way: "All the sciences may be able to prove that within each sphere of their investigations natural laws rule supreme. Yet the conduct of man differs from natural phenomena; if a man is guided by moral motives, we must assume that a supernatural influence is at work in his heart. If man were merely a child of nature, he could follow the natural motives of egotism only. Since he possesses motives that are altruistic and non-egotistic, this is an indubitable sign that he carries within his soul a spark of the supernatural, the divine. Conscience is the voice of God; conscience teaches man his duty; and the presence of conscience proves that man is created in the image of something supernatural—of God, and that this supernatural being must exist."

From the standpoint of supernaturalism, the presence of conscience in man's soul remains unexplained and is considered as inexplicable. The sense of duty is declared to be a miracle; the idea of what is right and the meaning of the ought are treated as facts not capable of analysis, which stand in contradiction to natural laws and which come to us by an act of divine revelation. The idea of right, we are told, is within us, and all we can do is to discover it there by an introspection into the secrets of soul-life. From the method recommended by this class of ethical enquirers, their conception of ethics is called intuitionalism.

In opposition to the intuitionalist, some infidel philosophers denounced the idea that man could be in possession of any other than natural motives; they declared it irrational, and in their zeal to defeat their adversary they maintained that man followed only egotistic motives. They denied the existence of purely altruistic motives altogether; and examples from real life, where no egotistic motive could have influenced a man, were so explained that altruistic motives appeared as a special and refined kind of egotism. A man loves *himself* in his wife, in his children, in his friends, in his countrymen; sacrifices brought for their welfare, spring from mere egotism; nothing more. It not only gives him satisfaction to bring such sacrifices, but he is also supposed to have brought them in order to get fair returns for them. He is said to be like a man who gives away money in the expectation of receiving it back with interest.

The religious teacher of ethics had always insisted

upon the sovereignty of the moral command; it must reign supreme over pleasures and pains. The unbeliever attempting to undermine an important argument of the believer, maintained that ethics did nothing of the kind. Ethics, if it tried, could not suppress the natural desire to seek pleasure and to avoid pain. The whole purpose of ethics, he declared, is to avoid those pleasures which in the end will necessarily cause pain, and to endure with patience those pains which are unavoidable conditions for future pleasures. The good, it was maintained, is the very same thing as the useful; every thing that is useful is good, and useful is that which affords more pleasure than pain. From their definition of good, this class of ethical enquirers adopted for their view the name "Utilitarianism."

Bentham is generally looked upon as the most consistent and classical representative of Utilitarianism, and his works are a model of psychological insight and keen judgment. Nevertheless, we must regard his views as one phase in the history of ethics only which is now recognized as one-sided. The failure of Bentham's ethics is conceded even by those who are his followers and disciples.* Bentham's utilitarianism was an attempt to base ethics upon purely egotistic mo-

* Höffding criticizes Bentham in his "*Grundlage der humanen Ethik.*" Bentham's error, he says, is the supposition that there is a perfect harmony among the egotistic interests of all individuals, if they are but clear concerning their own interests.

tives; modern Utilitarianism recognizes the necessity of admitting non-egotistic motives. Not the happiness of the individual is maintained to be the aim of ethics, but the greatest happiness of the greatest number. This step, however, is inconsistent with Bentham's principle and overthrows the whole system. It is a surrender of the cardinal point of egotistic ethics.

The weakness of intuitionalists is their despair of ever explaining the natural origin and meaning of moral motives. They are so overawed by a reverent admiration of the presence of super-individual motives, that they bow down in the dust and worship the unknown power which they suppose to be the originator of these motives. The weakness of the Utilitarians is their denial of the possible existence of super-individual motives; they argued that all our motives, being parts of our own personality, must be egotistic. And yet the non-egotistic, the super-individual motives, the impulses that urge us to obey a higher law than self-interest, are indubitable facts of soul-life. However, though they are super-individual, they are not supernatural, as is claimed by intuitionalists. The relations of man with his surroundings and with his fellowmen establish so many connections which, like invisible threads, powerfully pull on man's mind and set the springs of his action free, in which he recognizes the representation of a higher interest and a greater concern than his pleasures and individual welfare.

Now we may consider as correct the view of the intuitionalists, if their theory is interpreted to mean that ethics must be based upon the study of the human soul; there we find a moral instinct that teaches man to be guided by higher motives than those of egotism. At the same time we may side with their adversaries, when we construe their ethics in the sense that the moral motives can in so far be called egotistic, as they are actual parts of our soul. Moral motives are of a natural growth, and their origin can by scientific investigation satisfactorily be accounted for. However, we must emphatically object on the one hand to the mystic element that attaches to intuitionalism, and on the other to the identification of pleasure with the idea of moral goodness that is unwarrantably introduced by Utilitarianism.

It is true that the good is always useful, but we cannot invert the sentence and say the useful is always good. Blue is always a color, but not every color is blue. Utilitarians are right in saying that every act which is morally good, must be useful. Moral acts are not always useful to him who does them, but they are always useful either to society, to our country, or to humanity in general, in promoting the welfare, the power, the nobility, the ideal of human soul-life. But Utilitarians are mistaken if they make utility the standard of measurement for that which must be called good.

There are acts which under certain circumstances

may be productive of good, if good means pleasurable to individuals. Take for instance the well-known Broadway street-railway case. It is undeniable that the enterprise of running horse-cars on Broadway in New York is useful not only to the company who undertook the work, but also to society. Franchises, according to a law of New York, which has been altered since then, must be given by twenty-four aldermen. Now there were some doubts, not concerning the usefulness of the enterprise, but whether another proposal by some other company to lay the tracks of the railway through another street might not be preferable, and there may have been still more points of deliberation. Let us suppose that the Broadway scheme was preferable. But the manager was pained by the loss of time caused through protracted deliberation. He was a practical man, he wanted to push matters and keep the majority of the aldermen in good humor. He succeeded by sending envelopes containing eighteen thousand dollars to thirteen aldermen, and the franchise was speedily given.

Every act was useful to somebody, and the whole scheme was useful to society also. It is true that offering money was a degradation of the moral character of the aldermen. But after all, they did not mind, and their characters were not so pure as to suffer greatly. In that direction no harm could be done. The only thing that could bring harm was publicity. Now if the useful were the standard of morality, the act of the manager ought to be condemned on account of his carelessness, that he neglected the necessary precautions to secure secrecy.

The first jury did not agree on the case and had to be dismissed. This roused a storm of indignation and the second jury was selected with great care. The second jury brought in a verdict of guilty.

The conscience of the people at large condemned the act; and yet there were many opinions in favor of the manager on the ground that though he had acted from private interest, his enterprise had been for the public benefit. The bribery was committed as a means to a good end and it was rather unfortunate that it had become known.

We do not decide here whether bribery is excusable in a state where honorable enterprises can prosper only by means of bribing. We only inquire whether the utility of consequences constitutes the morality of an act. And we answer this question in the negative.

Similar acts may happen which do not become public. Who dares to defend them on the ground of Utilitarianism. Indeed no one does. Not even Utilitarians! Utilitarians would, if they had to give their opinion on such examples, explain that by useful, they do not mean that only which benefits the material interests of men, but also that which promotes their intellectual welfare and ennobles their characters. They would fit the facts to their principle instead of trying to find a principle that should be suited to all facts.

In order to suit the facts to the principle of utility, they would limit the idea of usefulness to that which we call moral goodness.

We have no objection to Utilitarians who use the word "useful" in this narrow meaning. Yet we would advise them to be careful lest the meaning of their words be misunderstood. The average man is not accustomed to use the word "useful" in the purified and transfigured meaning which it has received at the hands of some noble-hearted Utilitarians. The average man calls useful that which affords him tangible advantages of some kind; and common parlance distinguishes very well from useful acts those which are good. Our language and the meaning of words are only an expression of the instincts of our soul. Common parlance mirrors in this distinction between good and useful, the voice of man's conscience which very often impels him to acts that are not useful to him and prevent him from doing what he naturally considers as extremely useful.

II.

Bentham goes very far in the defense of the Utilitarian principle; he maintains that the most abominable pleasure of a criminal act could be justifiable if it remained alone. It is to be condemned solely because of the evil consequences of the pain incurred, the chances of which are so great that in comparison to them the pleasure of a crime is reduced to zero.

It is very valuable for ethical teachers to know that men of such extreme views as Bentham recognize the overwhelming evils consequent upon immoral acts. Bentham in his search after truth could not discover the sacred feelings of purely altruistic motives that are often too deeply concealed in the human heart, and therefore he denied their existence. The truth is, that should the moral motives be lacking in their moral purity, man would nevertheless be forced to act morally from the mere egotistic interest of self-preservation. But this is no reason for maintaining that moral acts are always done from a conscious or unconscious self-interest.

If Bentham's views were correct, our moral teachers ought to be faithful to truth, and ought to appeal to the egotism of mankind only and not to the higher motives of super-individual duties. These higher motives would be at best a self-delusion, and it would be immoral to elicit artificial and unnatural feelings. Yet it cannot be denied that an appeal to the higher duties of man is always more successful than to the lower desires of selfishness. The higher motives accordingly are live presences in the soul of man which, for the reason that they are not always patent, cannot be disregarded.

An ethical teacher ought to appeal to the highest motives man is capable of. But information concerning the futility of selfishness should at the same time not be neglected. It is an important truth; so it ought not to be omitted. Every one of us should know that pure egotism always defeats its own ends. The natural institutions of society are such as to make the life of a man who seeks his own exclusive advantage, unbearable and full of bitterness. And if the life of an egotistic pleasure-seeker could be full of unmixed joy, the approach of death would teach us to look out for something higher than the gratification of our fleeting propensities. The effects of our life, of all our actions whether good or evil, remain, long after we have passed out of existence. The examples we set, the thoughts we have uttered live on in the souls of our friends and our children. We contribute in forming the souls of the following generations, and to the extent that we have done this our soul-life will be preserved in theirs. A thoughtless man is biased by the impressions of the fleeting moment; the ethical man however bears in mind the importance of his soul-life after death.

There are sometimes dark moments in our lives when we do not know how to decide, and the decision as to what is right and proper may be very difficult. In such moments, we should soar above the narrowness of the present life and look down upon our own fate from the higher standpoint of eternity. Let us in such moments imagine that we had died; that we are no more, and that our lives have long been ended. While our bodies rest in the grave, our deeds, our thoughts, our words continue to influence humanity. The idea of eternal rest will calm our passions and

soothe our anxieties. When such peace comes over our soul, then let us confess unto ourselves what we wish we had done while alive. From this standpoint we shall best be able to silence the tumultuous desires of the moment and let our nobler self come to the front.

* * *

Ethics is a practical science, and we must never lose sight of its aim, which is to give man motives for doing right. Should we now tell people that the old ideas of "right and wrong" are merely vague notions of what is "useful and obnoxious"? Should we tell them that they must be guided by what they would, according to their very best knowledge, consider as most useful? I believe that ethical teachers will not be inclined to throw so lightly overboard the most valuable ideal of mankind, or to barter moral goodness for material goodness; for what is "the useful" but material goodness?

The Utilitarian makes moral goodness a subdivision of general goodness. By goodness he understands the quality of being adapted to some end. A good apple is adapted for serving as food, a good knife is adapted for cutting; so the actions of man are declared to be good if they are adapted to increase the happiness of the greatest number.

A moral teacher will not take so easily to Utilitarianism, because it slurs over the difference between moral goodness and material usefulness. He will

rather point out that there may be conflicts between moral goodness and usefulness; and if such conflicts happen to take place in our soul, if a lie, according to our best knowledge, promises to be more useful than the truth, he will help us and advise us not to do what appears as useful to our, and perhaps also to other people's, material comfort and well-being, but to prefer that which is useful for increasing the health and nobility of our soul.

If ethics is based on facts, and applied to facts, it will recognize as a basic principle the search for truth and the adaptation to truth. Facts are the data of reality with which we have to deal in our experience. Truth is a correct representation of facts in our mind. An honest search for truth is the condition of all ethics, and being faithful to truth includes all the various moral commands, which a system of ethics can contain.

So long as we are honest disciples of truth, we have a good guide to lead us. We may go astray, we may make mistakes, yet we shall never be so completely lost, as to be unable to rectify our course of action. With the love of truth as our source of inspiration, and the desire to remain in accord with truth, we may often find occasion to regret not having had more complete knowledge, but we shall never be in the plight of self-condemnation.

The principle of truthfulness is a far more definite and correct basis of ethics than the principle of utility.

III.

Those who did not feel inclined to accept the supernaturalistic theory of ethics, felt that an analysis of the ethical motives ought to be the first step in the foundation of ethics on a natural basis. The intention was good, yet the execution was made on the hypothesis that egotistic motives are natural, altruistic motives unnatural. It was supposed that feelings of pleasure are desirable, they are eagerly sought for by all creatures, and feelings of pain are not desirable, they are avoided by all creatures. It is a fact, however, that some pleasurable acts have very painful consequences; and some painful acts have pleasureable consequences. Accordingly, some philosophers proposed as an explanation of moral actions the theory that men are always guided by motives seeking pleasure and shunning pain. Ethics, they said, is and ought to be based on a calculation of what will in the end be most pleasurable.

This theory is called Hedonism. It explains the sacrifices that one man brings to relieve others of pain on the supposition that the idea of relieving his fellow-beings of pain gives him so much pleasure as to fully overbalance the pains he suffers. This may, occasionally, be true, although it need not be true. The explanation is inadequate, for it is certain that there are cases in which the pleasurable emotion that accompanies such noble ideas is not the motive of

the act. If a feeling of pleasure accompanies a noble act of painful sacrifice, it is an unexpected enjoyment, an incidental effect, *but it was not the purpose for which the act was performed.* Thus the explanation explains nothing.

* * *

It is possible that those who believe in a future life in Heaven where they expect to be rewarded for their virtues exercised here upon earth, may be guided by the motive that the future joy is preferable to the present pain. This motive might account for the firmness of Johannes Huss; although it seems to me, that it does not sufficiently account for it. But how can we explain the martyrdom of unbelievers, who, like Giordano Bruno, suffer a painful death for their convictions without any possible expectation of pleasurable returns. Giordano Bruno could by no means expect that future ages would pay homage to him as a martyr of free thought. His death was by no means a great event in his time; it excited little or no comment, and no one, with the exception of a few isolated savants, had sympathy with him. It is beyond dispute, that no consideration of pleasure or pain entered into his mind, but simply love of truth irrespective of any consequence. Adolf Lasson says in the introduction to Bruno's essay on "The Cause, the Principle and the One":

"Bruno had a profoundly pious heart, full of enthusiasm for every thing holy. He had in all his adventures not freed himself

from his attachment to the faith of his childhood, and from the reverence for the authority he had long respected. So long as his religious sentiment was appealed to, he was ready to yield. Yet his judges, according to the usual method of inquisitors, attempted to persuade him of his errors by scientific arguments, and hoped so to force him to recant. But he did not find himself refuted, and he could not abjure his philosophy without renouncing truth. Thus he deluded himself and his judges for some time with the false hope of being able to recant; he demanded again and again new respites for deliberation.

"What tortures this once so serene and self-confident man must have suffered in this deep and inner struggle, deserted by all the world and alone in the hands of his jailors . . . . ."

"The year in which Bruno was burned (Febr. 9th, 1600), was a jubilee year. Millions of pilgrims visited Rome, but there was no one among them who had sympathy with his lamentable death. The only person from whose venomous and heinous report we know some particulars about the history of Giordano Bruno's death, is that spiteful Scioppius, called *canis grammaticus*, a protestant renegade."

* * *

Hedonist philosophers, in their eagerness to lay a natural basis for ethics, overlook several points of great importance. Above all they overlook the fact that the data of ethics are not isolated feelings, but a complex of feelings, bearing upon the relations in which man stands to the world and to his fellow beings.

Bentham speaks of pleasurable feelings as being always good so long as they remain isolated and unconnected with evil consequences. This betrays a fundamental misunderstanding as to the nature of ethics. Single and isolated feelings are the data of

reflex actions, but they cannot constitute any basis of ethics. The feelings we have, are different in intensity, degree, and kind, and all together in their totality form our life. Because they are different, we must have a criterion by which to judge them. We maintain that there is a criterion which does not depend upon whether they are pleasurable or painful. It is this criterion of ethics which enables us to gauge their moral worth. The data of ethics are motives of action, and the object of ethics is to find a standard by which to estimate these motives.

It is a mistake to make pleasure and pain the standard of moral estimation. And indeed ethics have been invented in order to counterbalance the power of the many motives that allure man to immoral acts. If there were no principle above the feelings of pleasure and pain according to which we must regulate our actions, we ought to say that the ideal of ethics is an impossibility. For ethics introduces a criterion for judging about the worth of motives irrespective of the feelings of pleasure and pain that may accompany the intended actions of these motives.

The answer of Hedonists to these objections as a rule consists in complaints of being misunderstood. They maintain, that not the intensity and quantity of pleasure has to be considered, but the the kind and nature of the pleasure only. The nobler and higher kinds of pleasure are preferable to the lower kinds. Very well! If the quality of the pleasure is that which

makes its value, we must consider the standard with which this "quality" is to be determined as the criterion of ethics, but not the pleasure itself. The pleasure might be exceedingly great or small, if its quality be such as to range high according to the ethical standard it would outweigh the greatest quantities and intensities of lower pleasures. And if the accompanying pleasure were absent altogether, would that not leave the action just as moral?

The duty of ethics accordingly would be to determine the nature of that higher quality of human motives and make it so strong that it will overrule in our hearts all fear of pain and desire for pleasure.

An anecdote is told about a little village urchin who was dressed in black for attending a funeral. The boy wanted to wear his red jacket and weepingly said: "If I can't wear my red jacket, the whole funeral will give me no pleasure." How childish is this expression, and it would be barbarously rude if a man who knows the seriousness of the occasion could think in this way. Will Hedonists be ridiculous enough to maintain that the boy ought to wear black, because that color being more appropriate ought to give him a higher kind of pleasure?

Any normal man would be shocked at himself, if under solemn and grave circumstances, he should discover himself regulating his actions according to the principle of gaining more or less pleasure. Nay, even the consideration of a higher kind of pleasure in cases where no pleasure at all is involved, would be incompatible with true morality.

Hedonism, accordingly, would be correct only if we understand by pleasure that attitude of independence and self control which raises man above pleasures and pains.

In addition to all these objections, we have to remark that pleasure and pain are by no means simple and definite feelings so that they could be employed as a standard for an objective estimate of action. That which gives happiness being different according to age, temperament, hereditary character, and habits, the plan to make happiness the aim of life has no meaning. A pleasure to one person is very often an abomination to another. One man finds his happiness in natural, and another in unnatural enjoyments. One man is pleased with a rational use of his energies, while another delights in follies or even in vices. We can educate men to find pleasure in war or in peaceful pursuits, in intoxication or in sobriety, in smoking or chewing, in fishing or swimming, in playing mischievous tricks or in performing noble deeds.

* * *

Pleasure has erroneously been identified with growth, and pain with decay. If that were so, childbearing ought to be the greatest pleasure; and death the greatest pain. But it is a fact that all growth produces disturbances, and thus in most cases it causes pain. Teething is a growth, but it gives no pleasure to babes. Death in itself, however, is no pain; only the resistance of man's vitality against the decay of death is painful. The struggle of death being over there is no pain, but a peaceful fading away of consciousness. Death in itself is no more painful than sleep.

The fact is, that pleasures consist always in the satisfaction of wants, and wants are either natural or artificial. If our nature has become accustomed to certain wants, the amount of pleasure in satisfying them depends upon the intensity of the wants. Pains are either wants unsatisfied or other disturbances that are perceived by consciousness. Growth as well as decay may produce disturbances, both accordingly can become causes of pain. If then the greatest amount of pleasure were to be considered the purpose of life, we ought to educate ourselves to such wants as are noble and elevating, such as widen the range of our soul-life, and make man greater, kinder, and more powerful. In that case, however, not the sum or the amount of pleasure would have to be considered as ethical, but the kind of pleasure. Before we make happiness the aim of life, we must let ethics so educate us that the most imperative want of our soul will be the performance of our duties.

* * *

Man has a natural desire for activity. This desire is natural because man is a living machine freighted with vital energy; the desire to use this energy is ever present. In case man does not spend his energy in useful work, his natural want for activity will compel him to do something, never mind what. To a man who has or who knows of no duties, the motives which promise to give him pleasure will become the strongest; they will direct his energies, as it were, in the line of least resistance. Hence rises the so-called natural desire for pleasure. But this so-called natural desire for pleasure is the greatest danger for a man. And wherever we investigate the methods of progress we shall find that it is far from taking place in the line of least resistance. On the contrary almost every progress leads in the line of greatest resistance. The development in the line of least resistance leads to inevitable ruin.

Hence it follows that the greatest blessing for a man is to have duties which coerce him to perform some useful work. Rich people who, without becoming exactly criminal, can allow themselves to let their action follow the line of least resistance, are in a most dangerous plight. "How hardly shall they that have riches," attain a normal, not to say a strong, development of their souls! Those that are rich, that can live well, that can live for the sake of enjoying life, should for the sake of their own soul-life impose upon themselves heavy duties, as heavy as they can bear. They should educate their children so that they feel unhappy unless they have great duties to perform. The moral worth of a man does not depend upon the amount of pleasure he provides for himself and others, but upon the amount and scope and weight of duty he is able to carry.

* * *

We have made a brief survey of the most important issues between the old religious and the irreligious conceptions of ethics, between the moral views of the believer and those of the unbeliever. We have seen that the unbeliever was right in the one main point which induced him to criticise and overthrow the old system of ethics. His attempts to base ethics upon a natural basis are justifiable, yet the believer was right upon the whole in all single points of dispute as regards the substance of ethical injunctions.

It is perhaps natural that the dogmatic moralist with all the traditional experience of past ages in his favor should have arrived at the truth so far as the practical execution of ethics is concerned. All the different theories which were invented to deny the properly ethical spirit of super-individual motves in morality are exploded. We have to recognize the fact that there are motives active in the soul of man, higher, greater and nobler than egoistic desires. Yet although the moral motives are to be recognized as super-individual factors of man's soul-life, they are by no means supernatural.

IV.

All religions are systems of ethics; and ethics by the very fact that it teaches man how to regulate his conduct is a religion. Every religion comes, or pretends to come, as a salvation. It throws light upon the world around us in which we live and thus it aids us in our endeavors to escape from the miseries caused by our ignorance and folly.

The religion of science like all other religions comes to the rescue of man. It is true that the truths of science appear at first sight to be destructive. They destroy the illusions of a childish faith which has become dear to us. But truth, be it ever so sad, is the only means that can cure the ills of life. If there is any salvation it must be gained by truth and by boldly facing the truth. If truth cannot help, nothing can, nothing will help. A salvation by illusions is like the joy of intoxication. It is neither lasting nor is it wholesome, and when it is gone it will leave us sadder than before. Instead of helping, it will harm.

Among all the philosophies with which I became acquainted, there is one that at a certain period of my life attracted me most powerfully; it is that of Arthur Schopenhauer, the great pessimist. Schopenhauer describes the misery of life in most vivid colors, and what makes him so impressive, is that he does it without exaggeration. He says:

"Having awakened to life from the night of unconsciousness, the will finds itself as an individual in an endless and boundless world among innumerable individuals, all striving, suffering, erring; and as though passing through an ominous, uneasy dream, it hurries back to the old unconsciousness. Until then, however, its desires are boundless, its claims inexhaustible, and every satisfied wish begets a new one. No satisfaction possible in the world could suffice to still its longings, put a final end to its cravings, and fill the bottomless abyss of its heart. Consider, too, what gratifications of every kind man generally receives: they are usually nothing more than the meagre preservation of this existence itself, daily gained by incessant toil and constant care, in battle against want, with death forever in the van. Everything in life indicates that earthly happiness is destined to be frustrated or to be recognized as an illusion. The conditions of this lie deep in the nature of things. Accordingly, the life of most of us proves sad and short. The comparatively happy are usually only apparently so, or are, like long-lived persons, rare exceptions—left as a bait for the rest.

"Life proves a continued deception, in great as well as small matters. If it makes a promise, it does not keep it, unless to show that the coveted object was little desirable. Thus sometimes hope, sometimes the fulfilment of hope, deludes us. If it gave, it was but to take away. The fascination of distance presents a paradise, vanishing like an optic delusion when we have allowed ourselves to be enticed thither. Happiness accordingly lies always in the future or in the past; and the present is to be compared to a small dark cloud which the wind drives over a sunny plain. Before it and behind it all is bright, it alone casts a shadow. The present therefore is forever unsatisfactory; the future uncertain; the past irrecoverable. Life with its hourly, daily, weekly, and yearly small, greater, and great adversities, with its disappointed hopes and mishaps foiling all calculation, bears so plainly the character of something we should become disgusted with, that it is difficult to comprehend how any one could have mistaken this and been persuaded that life was to be thankfully enjoyed, and man was destined to be happy. On the contrary the everlasting delusion and disappointment as well as the constitution of life throughout, appear as though they were intended and calculated to awaken the conviction that nothing whatever is worthy of our striving, driving, and wrestling,—that all goods are naught, the world bankrupt at all ends, and life a business that does not pay expenses,—so that our will may turn away from it.

"The manner in which this vanity of all objects of the will reveals itself, is, in the first place, time. Time is the form by means of which the vanity of things appears as transitoriness; since through time all our enjoyments and pleasures come to naught; and we afterward ask in astonishment what has become of them. Accordingly our life resembles a payment which we receive in copper pence, and which at last we must receipt. The pence are the days, death the receipt. For at last, time proclaims the sentence of nature's judgment upon the worth of all beings by destroying them.

'And justly so; for all things from the void
Called forth, deserve to be destroyed.
T'were better, then, were naught created.'—*Goethe*.

"Age and death, to which every life necessarily hurries, are the sentence of condemnation upon the will to live, passed by nature herself, which declares that this will is a striving that must frustrate itself. 'What thou hast willed,' it says, 'ends thus; will something better!'

"The lessons which each one learns from his lifeconsist, on the whole, in this, that the objects of his wishes constantly delude, shake, and fall; consequently they bring more torment than pleasure, until at length even the whole ground upon which they all stand gives way, inasmuch as his life itself is annihilated. Thus he receives the last confirmation that all his striving and willing were a blunder and an error.

'Then old age and experience, hand in hand,
Lead him to death, and make him understand,
After a search so painful and so long
That all his life he has been in the wrong.

"Whatever may be said to the contrary, the happiest moment of the happiest mortal is still the moment he falls asleep, as the unhappiest moment of the unhappiest mortal the moment he awakens.

"Lord Byron says:

> 'Count o'er the joys thine hours have seen,
> Count o'er thy days from anguish free,
> And know, whatever thou hast been,
> 'Tis something better not to be.' "*

"It is indeed incredible how stale and empty are the fates of most people, how dull and heedless are all their feelings and thoughts. Their lives consist of flabby longing, and pining of dreamy reeling through the seven ages to death, and this is accompanied with a number of trivial thoughts. They are like clocks wound up to go and do not know why. Each time when a man is born the clock is wound up again to play off the same hackneyed tune, bar for bar, measure for measure, with unimportant variations."†

Yet is there not some hope that in the course of evolution humanity may attain a state of perfect adjustment, so that every man can enjoy undisturbed happiness? Even that hope is a flattering illusion of optimistic thinkers; it can never be fulfilled. Our wants are unlimited, and happiness depends upon the satisfaction of our wants. Happiness, accordingly, is relative, and Schopenhauer justly likens it to a fraction, the denominator of which represents our desires and the numerator their gratifications. Every progress allows the increase of both.

Schopenhauer's pessimism is not exaggerated. His dreary description of life is a faithful portrayal of the facts of reality as they must appear from the standpoint

* Schopenhauer, W. a. W. u. V., Vol. II, Chap. 46.

† Ibid., W. a. W. u. V., Vol. I, p. 379.

of egotism. The man who seeks exclusively his own, will be disappointed wherever he goes. His very pleasures turn either into gall or the disgust of satiety. If the satisfaction of desires is recognized as the supreme and only purpose of life, man will in the most fortunate case, if Mephistopheles gives him the opportunity of unlimited enjoyment, exclaim with Faust:

> "Thus in desire I hasten to enjoy,
> And in enjoyment, pine to feel desire."

A man who, like Faust, can satisfy all his desires, is truly in the hands of Satan, as Goethe in his great philosophical allegory demonstrates. Only a strong character, as is Faust, who yearns for a higher life can overcome all the temptations. He tastes of the pleasures of life and finds them shallow. There is no satisfaction for the longing of his soul in any one of them. Yet as soon as Faust abandons the standpoint of egotism, he finds a satisfaction which he had never expected. He forgets the impetuous desire for pleasures in a great work that he undertakes for humanity. He finds that satisfaction lies not in the aim solely, but in the effort to reach the aim; not in liberty, but in attaining and deserving liberty; not in the harmonious enjoyment of life, but in being the master of one's fate, in building one's own life and making it harmonious:

> "Yes! To this thought I hold with firm persistence;
> The last result of wisdom stamps it true:
> He only earns his freedom and existence,
> Who daily conquers them anew."

Faust has become too old to enjoy the fruits of his labor himself, but he feels eternity breathing through his soul. His work will live after him and be a blessing unto thousands:

> "The traces cannot of mine earthly being
> In æons perish,—they are there!—
> In proud forefeeling of such lofty bliss,
> I now enjoy the highest moment,—this!"

Faust had pledged his life to Mephistopheles as soon as he should enjoy a moment of satisfaction. The moment is come and Faust dies. But that which gave him this satisfaction was none of Satan's gifts. It was none of the pleasures of egotism. It was a higher kind of pleasure which has nothing in common with that which is generally called pleasure. For it is a satisfaction of the powerful super-individual yearnings of the soul. And this is the only happiness that man can attain.

Mr. Herbert Spencer builds his system of ethics upon the supposition that "conduciveness to happiness is the ultimate test of perfection in a man's nature." He quotes Aristotle's view, that the proper work of man "consists in the active exercise of the mental capacities conformably to reason," and that "the supreme good of man will consist in performing this work with excellence or virtue; herein he will obtain happiness." Mr. Spencer blames Aristotle for "seeking to define happiness in terms of virtue instead of defining virtue in terms of happiness," and he seriously attempts to justify the opinion, that if immoral acts caused agreeable sensations, we would not call them crimes.

There is a great difference between pleasures and the peace of soul that a good conscience alone can give. Mr. Spencer classes both as "pleasurable sensations" and makes them the test of ethics. The happiness of which Aristotle speaks consists in the satisfaction of having done one's duty, which has nothing in common with any "pleasurable sensation"; for it is no sensation and has as little to do with sense-activity as for instance has our satisfaction at the correctness of a logical judgment. Mr. Spencer might with the very same arguments he uses for his theory of ethics, declare that the ultimate test of logical truth is its "conduciveness to happiness." Those logical arguments, he might say, which cause pleasurable sensations are correct, those which have pain-giving effects are incorrect; and the same holds good for all the departments of human activity and the truths of scientific inquiry. But who would maintain that the solution of a mathematical problem is right in so far and because it gives pleasure to him who has solved it? I know of circle squarers who derive a greater satisfaction from their most ridiculous blunders than any discoverer or inventor possibly can attain by most important and useful discoveries. Yet a moral act, we are told, is good solely because and in so far as it produces pleasurable sensations.

Gœthe who, like Aristotle, defines happiness in terms of virtue, objects most strongly against any other kind of happiness. In the second part of Faust the young emperor is described not as vicious, but as a man desirous to enjoy himself; and Faust pronounces a very severe judgment about a tendency of finding virtue in happiness instead of happiness in virtue. He says:

> Enjoyment makes us gross,
> *Geniessen macht gemein.*

If pleasurable sensations were the standard according to which we have to gauge the ethical worth of actions, they would form the quintessence of ethics and a saying like that of Gœthe's would be extremely immoral. Yet it is not so! Is there any one who denies that enjoyment and the hankering after enjoyment weaken the character? To measure the ethical worth of actions by pleasurable sensations is not superficial; it is radically erroneous. We might just as well let the judge give his decisions in court according to the principle that his sentence must produce a surplus of pleasurable feelings in all the parties concerned.

Nature has not intended man to live for the mere enjoyment of life. All egotism will in the end defeat itself. Man's life has a meaning only if he lives the higher life of super-individual aspirations. The individual must cease to consider himself as an individual; he must consider himself as a steward of the soul-life of mankind.

Every one of us has at his birth and through his education received a rich and most valuable inheritance from his fathers, and it stands in every one's power to increase the spiritual treasure of human soul-life which he has received. The question, Is life worth living, accordingly, depends exclusively on the purpose to which life is devoted. Life is not worth living if a man seeks his own, if he uses his rich inheritance like the prodigal son and wastes his substance to get as much pleasure as possible out of the treasures that his fathers have gathered. However, life is worth living if but the aim of life is high enough to give value to the work of life.

Pessimism has taught that life from the standpoint of a pleasure-seeker has no value; if we expect a satisfaction of our egotistic desires, life will not be worth its own troubles. Life can acquire value only by the use to which it is put. If our days are empty of any action worthy to be done, then they are indeed spent as a tale that is told, although they may be four-score years or more. Our actions only can and must give value to the days of our life. Yet is their strength labor and sorrow; for a life worth being lived is one that is full of active aspirations for something better and higher.*

* The ethics here presented I have called in former publications of mine, "Meliorism." The word Meliorism has been used by some authors as a modified optimism, as something that is midway between optimism and pessimism. By other authors the same term has been employed in the sense that humanity though at present not in a state of happiness, will nevertheless

The ethical life accordingly affords indeed the only salvation for man, and the old religions have been religions of salvation to the extent that they have helped man to raise himself above his egotism. The old religions are not wrong; they contain all of them this all-important truth. Yet the truth is wrapped in myths; and the time has come that we are no longer satisfied with myths. The apostle says:

"When I was a child I spake as a child, I understood as a child, I thought as a child, but when I became a man, I put away childish things."

Mankind has passed through the phase of childhood in which it could be taught only by myths and parables. As says St. Paul:

"And I, brethren, could not speak unto you as unto spiritual, but as unto carnal, *even* as unto babes in Christ.

"I have fed you with milk, and not with meat: for hitherto ye were not able *to bear it*, neither yet now are ye able."

We do not intend to abolish the truth of the old religions, but to purify them from their mythological character. We do not come to destroy, but to fulfil. Therefore, the solution of the ethical problem in the sense indicated, will not endanger, but will revive church life. It will make all things new.

reach by and by such an existence, in which all miseries will be impossible. The Meliorism here proposed fully accepts the truth of pessimism, that life is not worth its own troubles if we live merely for the enjoyment of life. Meliorism places the value of life in ideals that transcend the narrow limits of individual existence. The greater, the stronger, the more earnest are the ideals that animate the soul of a man, the more valuable will be his life and the more will his life be worth living.

The ethical movement thus cannot help bringing us a new religion. And the new religion of ethics will not be a new creed as are the old dogmatic religions, but a religion of facts, a religion of science.

The creeds of old are crumbling ;
  And were their revelation
The only hope in living,
  Life would be desolation.
But lo ! a new religion
  Bursts from the germs decaying ;
A new faith in our bosoms
  Is growing, light-displaying

Great truths with broader outlook
  New missions have created.
By purified Religion
  Our souls are elevated.
New aims, new hopes, new doctrines,
  Old prophecies fulfilling !
And through our hearts is rapture
  Of progress warmly thrilling.

We do not combat freedom
  Of art, nor that of science.
Nay, both with our religion
  Are joined in firm alliance.
Though high, our aspiration
  Is yet concrete and real.
To render life more noble
  Is our sublime ideal.

Of this denomination
  Are they, in life's confusion,
Who further human progress

And sweep away illusion;
Who have ideals dearer
Than self and self-existence,
And love them, although knowing
Their vast, enormous distance.

Thinkers who muse and ponder,
Instructors theoretic;
And poets whose ideas
Are radiantly prophetic;
The warrior, who for Freedom
Fights and for Freedom dieth;
The great, whose noble fortune
With their souls' greatness vieth;

The hand which with heart's trouble
For wife and children toileth;
The man who doth his duty
E'en if his fate him foileth;
And he who kindly comforts
The sick, who gladly shareth
His bread with his poor neighbor,
Our badge and symbol beareth.

DR. CARUS ON "THE ETHICAL PROBLEM."

BY W. M. SALTER.

THE capital point under discussion in this little volume is the basis of ethics. Dr. Carus is mistaken in saying in the Preface that it was in consequence of an editorial on "The Basis of Ethics and the Ethical Movement" in *The Open Court*, that he was invited to deliver these lectures. It was at my suggestion that the Board of Trustees of the Chicago Society for Ethical Culture extended to him the invitation, and my feeling simply was that so interesting a set of philosophical ideas as Dr. Carus was advancing in *The Open Court* should have a hearing *viva voce*, as well as through the printed page. Dr. Carus accepting, I announced his lectures on my own concluding Sunday, asking our members and friends to give them attention and careful consideration. Inasmuch, however, as Dr. Carus has taken the occasion incidentally to reinforce his earlier criticism upon the Ethical Movement; to emphasize the differences (real or supposed) between himself and those of us who are active in this movement; and indeed to take us somewhat severely to task, it becomes proper and, perhaps, necessary that I should say something by way of reply.

First, let me endeavor to understand as nearly as I can what Dr. Carus means. For our Ethical Societies the case is a grave one, in his judgment. There is something we are to do of a more pressing nature; if we do not heed the call, we shall "pass out of existence." We are not to "rest satisfied with negations"; we should cease a "non-committal policy"; should "speak out boldly and with no uncertain voice." We are reminded of our proper place; for, says Dr. Carus with something of a prophet's impressiveness, "There is one point you ought to understand well: The ethical movement will work for the progress of mankind whatever you do." Indeed he gives us such a sense of our insignificance that we are led to feel that more for our own sake than for the cause of progress we should apply ourselves to the all-important task; since the cause of progress will be served in any case.

This task is to answer the question, What is the basis of ethics? Assuming that the ethical movement was started because dogmatic religion no longer serves as such a basis, he asks, What new basis do we offer? I confess to having had some difficulty in finding out just what the author means by "basis" in this relation. Speaking generally, it is declared to be "the philosophical foundation upon which ethics rests," and so "the reason why man should regulate his actions in a certain way"; it is "a philosophical view back" of ethics. We get light from a concrete illustration, namely, the old religion which once served as a basis, the 'reason why' being found in 'the will of God.' Every religion is really, according to Dr. Carus, "a conception of the world applied to practical life"; it differs from philosophy simply in that such a world-conception is treated practically and is endorsed by a whole society (instead of single thinkers). The basis of ethics thus turns out to be a certain conception of the world or "theory of the universe"; it corresponds to what is called philosophy or theology; indeed, our author makes the broad statement: "The ethical stimulus has been implanted into man by religion,"* and he adds with sufficient vigor, "any ethics without a philosophical view back of it is no ethics, but ethical sentimentality."

What "basis of ethics" does Dr. Carus himself present? For it is not mere criticism that he offers; indeed, the criticism of the Ethical Societies is but incidental, and the author's evident intention is to present a positive solution of "the ethical problem," i. e., to point out the *true* basis of ethics. "Religion," he declares, "will *remain a conception of the world* that serves as a regulative principle of action. Yet this conception will cease to be the product of an instinctive imagination, it will become a scientific system of certain truths that have to be examined and proved by the usual methods of scientific enquiry" (the italics are mine). What then is the scientific world-conception, the true basis of ethics? I confess to having been completely taken aback, when as I read on I discovered that Dr. Carus declined to answer the question, contenting himself with vaguely saying that the true philosophy will be one which is in accordance with facts, which seems equivalent to saying that the scientific system will be a scientific system. The different philosophies are mentioned, viz., "materialism and spiritualism, realism and idealism, monism and agnosticism," and the author actually approves of Professor Adler's proposition that an ethical movement should not commit itself to any of them. Does

* How much foundation such a statement has as matter of history is tolerably well known to students of Sociology and Primitive Culture. I would commend to every interested reader the article on "Ethics and Religion," by the learned Professor C. H. Toy, of Harvard University, in the *Popular Science Monthly* April (or May), 1890.

any reader wonder that I am at a loss to know why Dr. Carus should have taken the attitude to our societies which he has, almost twitting us on our lack of courage, suggesting that our ethics is but "ethical sentimentality," and saying that if the ethical societies do not increase as they ought to, it is because they have no definite opinion, because they lack a foundation, trying to be broad and becoming vague (x. xi)? What I had at least hoped for was an exposition of the way in which the monistic world-conception would serve as a basis of ethics; for to me personally at any rate and, I think, to many more this would have been of considerable interest. But monism is classed along with agnosticism, and materialism as one of the "thought-constructions of theorizing philosophers," (16. 17); so that after all the high notes, the vigorous charging and counter-charging, we are left with the barren dictum, "The new ethics is based upon facts, and is applied to facts." Taking this into account I am not at all sure that I know what Dr. Carus means by a "basis of ethics," and as it is not wise to criticise till one knows what he is criticising, I will forbear criticism. I will not say that the author is not clear as to what he means, but generally speaking the remark of *The Ethical Record* which he quotes seems to have fresh illustration: "We think there is some lack of clearness as to what a basis of ethics means."

There are, however, two distinct questions: What is the true world-conception, upon which every special science may, in a broad and rather loose sense, be said to be based; and secondly, what is the ultimate principle in ethics itself? The second question might be more distinctly stated as follows: Not what is the *basis of* ethics, in the sense of "a philosophical view back" of it (a theology or philosophy), but what is the basic principle *in* ethics? Ethics, in the popular sense, being a system of rules for conduct, it is necessary, if it is to be treated scientifically, that there should be some supreme rule, by their agreement or disagreement* with which all lesser rules should be judged. Now the most charitable construction I can put on Dr. Carus's method of proceedure is that he has confused these two questions; and indeed, in the last two chapters of the book he more or less leaves the realm of world-conceptions and devotes himself to the humbler question of the standard (or what I have called the supreme rule) of right action. Yet in the treatment of this second question, I am sorry to say that I find the author's thought more or less confused and inconsistent. Ethics, it is repeatedly insisted, must be based on facts; yet in one clear-sighted passage he says, "Ethics is *our attitude* toward the facts of reality" (the italics are mine). The latter remark seems to imply that the same facts may be looked at from different attitudes; yet if so, how are the facts themselves to decide which attitude we shall take? It is true, as Dr. Carus happily says, that "all knowledge can be formulated as an ethical prescript." For example, the knowledge that friction produces fire finds its practical application in the ethical rule: In case you want fire, produce it by friction. But the facts in the case do not in the slightest determine whether we shall produce fire; we may contemplate the

* This rule, it is needless to say, would itself be interpreted or "based" in terms of the world-conception or theory of the universe which one holds, just as the first principles of the other sciences would be; the theist would interpret them in one way, the monist in another, etc.; but the first principles of all special sciences *qua* special sciences are peculiar to themselves; otherwise taken, they would be identical, i. e., be the ultimate principles or principle of the universe itself.

facts with purely speculative curiosity and do nothing, or we may have an aversion to fire and so do nothing, or we may wish fire and then we shall produce it by the method indicated. It is evident that not all the knowledge of all the facts of the universe would by itself lead to moral action, or indeed to action of any kind; so that it would be more accurate, and so more clarifying to the mind, to say that ethics should face, regard, or know the facts of the universe rather than to say that it should be based upon them. Evidently the root-question in ethics is, what should we wish? Once knowing what we wish, the knowledge of the facts and the laws of nature is valuable to us; and once knowing what we should wish, acquaintance with such facts and laws becomes ethically valuable and we have a standard for our entire conduct. It is at this point that I find Dr. Carus's views radically insufficient; indeed, his ethics seems a something "in the air." "*If*," he says, "you wish to exist, obey reason," (italics are my own). But the very question is, not what or whether we wish, but what we should wish? To say, "If you wish fire, produce it by friction," does not say whether we shall so produce it; to tell us, "In order to build a house, observe the laws of gravitation," does not call us *to* observe the laws of gravitation; to say, "If you wish to exist, obey reason," puts upon us no obligation to obey reason. It is true most persons do wish to live and in consistency therewith we may well say that they should act in such and such a manner; but if any one says, I do not care to live, moral obligation, according to this view, ceases to have any application to him. If any one says, I do not care about my health, the *laws* of health are meaningless to him; if another says, I do not care about my family, the whole of family-ethics loses its validity for him. It has long been plain to me that resting ethics on our matter-of-fact wishes or instincts is not establishing ethics, but undermining it and leaving it a something "in the air." There must be a rational consideration and rational settlement of the question, What of our desires or wishes or instincts *have a right to rule in us?* before there can be any such thing as a scientific ethics.

Notwithstanding, however, this lack of thoroughness in Dr. Carus's treatment of the question, his discussion of some of the different standards of right and wrong is interesting. He defends the naturalness of altruistic and social motives, against those who hold that only egotistic motives are natural to man. He goes too far, it appears to me, in identifying ethics with the social duties, there being as much rational foundation for an "ought" in relation to one's self as in relation to others. He conducts an excellent polemic against those who would find in pleasure or happiness the end of all action, though he surely does an injustice to Utilitarianism in saying that "it slurs over the difference between moral goodness and material usefulness." The standard of good and bad which he appears to reach (after sundry physiological and psychological observations) is "the development of human soul-life"; whatever tends to preserve and promote this is good, while all efforts to the contrary are bad. By "soul-life" is meant the soul-life of the whole race, including all its future generations. But is not this rather vague? Is not the standard an uncertain one? "Soul-life," we are told, is made up of representations of the surrounding world and of man's relations thereto, and includes an increasing power over nature along with an increasing knowledge. But do we not require to know what type of soul-life we shall seek to further and promote? Persons of large knowledge and ample power over nature may be of one kind or another: they may be modest or vain, friendly or unfriendly, truthful or false, chaste or licentious, public-spirited or selfish. In following the injunction to preserve and promote soul-life, should we not have our minds directed to the sort of soul-life that is truly desirable? Dr. Carus does, indeed, speak vaguely of "the standard of human soul-life," and elsewhere uses the expression "health and nobility of our soul," but without indicating what he means. The point is of importance because, as the author in substance says, the effects of all our actions whether *good or evil* remain, long after we have passed out of existence, because the examples we set and the thoughts we utter, whether good or bad, live on in the souls of our friends and our children, and the motive for living for eternity, of which the author makes impressive use, would seem to appeal as much to the bad man who wishes to perpetuate his badness, as to the good man who wishes to promote soul-life of a different type. I do not say that these difficulties are insuperable, and simply record my impression of the author's failure to deal with them.

In still another sense of the word "basis," Dr. Carus proposes the principle of truthfulness as a basis of ethics. In fact, so much "Zweideutigkeit" in the use of terms, I think I have rarely seen in any other ostensibly scientific treatise. It is difficult for me to understand further how Dr. Carus could proceed so carelessly in treating of ethical "theories." Intuitionalism is identified with supernaturalism, and Paley on the strength of his theology is called an intuitionalist, while he was in fact one of the founders of Utilitarianism. Hedonism is treated separately from Utilitarianism, although every form of Utilitarianism has been hedonistic, modern utilitarianism being simply universalistic hedonism.

I have spoken of two distinct questions, which Dr. Carus seems to confuse; there is a third which he fails to distinguish from the others, and in the treatment of which I am glad for his sake to say that he falls into a happy inconsistency. This relates to *the motive for regulating our conduct* according to the standard which has been supposably discovered. It is one thing to know what is the true world-theory, another to know what is the standard of right, another to know the true motive for regarding that standard. The position which I have always taken (and I think all the other ethical lecturers have taken), is that when we once really know what right is, there is no other course for us but to obey it, simple reverence for the right being the only true, the only moral motive. We have to most carefully study what the right is, but once knowing it our only attitude is (i. e., should be) obedience. To ask *why* we should do the right is meaningless, it is to go out of the moral region altogether. Now when Dr. Carus proposes the question, "Why must I feel bound by any 'right' or moral law," when he says that if we demand of a man "that he refrain from doing wrong and be guided by what is right, we are bound to give him a reason why," he seems to join with those who are not satisfied with the moral motive, and after reading those remarks in the opening pages of his volume, I observed with particular closeness the subsequent course of his argument to see what "reason" or "why" he would give. Yet he had already casually spoken of the "motive to do right"; and what was my surprise and gratification to find him later on speaking distinctly of the "aspiration to live in perfect harmony with the moral law," (p. 37); of the "moral motives in the moral purity," (p. 61); and boldly saying that "an ethical teacher ought to appeal to the highest motives man is capable of," (p. 61.) In fact, Dr. Carus gives no "reason why" in the sense of a motive beyond the moral motive; and is well aware that so to do would be not to explain, but to degrade morality. Yet if so, what necessity was there for him to take such an attitude of antagonism to us? We too are trying, in the measure of our ability, to plant (or better, to develop) the moral motive in the souls of men. Dr. Carus said, addressing the Chicago Ethical Society, "You may say it matters not why a man leads a moral life, so that his life be moral." This is a grotesque description of our position. The motive of right conduct is what makes it moral; if that has been said once, it has been said a hundred times on the Chicago platform.

To conclude then this, I fear, already too long article: It is true that the ethical movement has not committed itself to a particular world-theory; it leaves its members and lecturers free to adopt whatever theory most approves itself to their reason; instead of setting up a standard of philosophical orthodoxy as Dr. Carus seems to propose (though he fails at the critical moment), it believes that philosophical systems should have a free field and no favor and that *that* one should survive whose claims prove the strongest in the struggle for existence—and all within the fold of an ethical fellowship, held together by community of moral aim.

Dr. Carus, I am sorry to see, has not outgrown the sectarian principle of the churches and would apparently give us another sect as "exclusive" and "intolerant" as any in the past, though (Gottlob !) it will slay with the sword of the spirit and not with the arm of flesh. Secondly, it is *not* true that the ethical lecturers have not furnished a "basis of ethics" in the sense of a standard of right and wrong; each of them has done so and estimated all particular duties by their relation thereto; and although on some points of speculative significance all may not be agreed, they are sufficiently so for practical sympathy and co-operation—certain great duties being recognized by all alike. Our highest aim is to make men autonomous in their moral conduct, as indeed Dr. Carus thinks we should, (p. 49,) apparently forgetting his earlier challenge that if we no longer believe in the supernatural God, we should give account of "that God" who gives us authority to preach (xii). What is more, any of us may believe in the "Supernatural God," if so it seems reasonable for him to do; the movement is by no means committed to Anti-Supernaturalism, as he seems to think, whatever were the motives of some of those active in the beginning, and it has quite another reason for being than that which Dr. Carus ascribes to it.* Thirdly, as to the much abused "basis" in still another possible meaning, namely, of a *motive* for the regulation of one's life, we have from the beginning recognized the same "basis" which Dr. Carus suggests, viz., the motive to do right, the aspiration to live in perfect harmony with the moral law.

* That reason is stated in the concluding chapter of my *Ethical Religion*: and still more simply and clearly and convincingly in the first two chapters of Dr. Stanton Coit's just published *Die Ethische Bewegung in der Religion*. (Leipsic: O. R. Reisland).

MR. SALTER ON "THE ETHICAL PROBLEM."

BY DR. PAUL CARUS.

Mr. Salter thinks that I have not properly understood the position of the leaders of the ethical movement. But Mr. Salter's reply is good evidence that I did not misunderstand them. He says: "It is *not* true that the ethical lecturers have not furnished a basis of ethics in the sense of a standard of right and wrong;" and yet he takes pains to explain that by this basis of ethics he understands certain ethical rules, and especially the supreme ethical rule, but not the reason of his ethical rules which finds expression in a philosophical or religious view back of ethics. The latter alone can properly be called a basis of ethics, and all the ethical teachers agree that that which *we* call the basis of ethics is not needed. They look upon it as of mere speculative significance.

Mr. Salter fails to see the indispensability of a philosophical or religious view back of ethics; he fails to see that it alone can give character to ethics, it alone can change the instinctive morality of our conscience into truly rational and self-conscious ethics.

Conscience and the moral law are not so absolute as Mr. Salter in his book declares them to be. Religion and ethics have developed: the facts of an erring conscience as well as of the religious superstitions prove that both have grown from experience. Both religion and ethics have developed together; they are twins.

When saying religion and ethics have grown from experience, I mean that the stern facts of life have taught us what desires should be suppressed and what wishes should rule supreme. The facts of life themselves have taught us our attitude toward our surroundings; they have taught us the moral laws.

It appears that the "moral law" has a different meaning with Mr. Salter than with me. The moral law, whenever I use the word, is simply a formulation of the lessons taught us by experience. Moral laws are—like the laws of hygiene—statements of those conditions which will keep our sentiments and motives in perfect health.

Mr. Salter knows no 'reason why' for his moral law, and he imagines that to give a reason why "would be not to explain but to degrade morality."* In this way ethics is, in Mr. Salter's mind, inseparably intertwined with mysticism.

Our intention is indeed to explain morality, and here arises our conflict with the policy pursued by the ethical lecturers. We consider scientific enquiry into the reason why of ethics, not as a degradation, but as a duty. The ethical lecturers do not acknowledge the

* Mr. Salter writes in a marginal note on the proof of this article:

"You must be aware that I use this language in *another connection*: viz., in speaking of the *motive* for right-doing."

I am accustomed to distinguish between motive and reason. (See Fundamental Problems, p. 80, lines 24—25.) Motive is the cause that effects an action. A cause in the domain of human action is called motive, for it is that which makes the will move. I distinguish between motive and reason, but I cannot think of a motive without a reason. A motive is a cause that consists of an idea, the idea acting as an irritant or stimulus upon a man, thus provoking him to action. The contents of this idea is called reason.

I maintain that the motive to do this or that must have a content. This content is its reason. The rule "do that which is right" (or the intention "I wish to do that which is right") is without practical value, unless I know what is right. In order to know what is right I must ascertain it, and I can do so only by enquiring after the reason why it is right. Thus the 'reason why' is inevitable whatever standpoint we take.

'reason why' presented by orthodox theology. They are therefore bound to give a new reason why. If they refuse to do so, their whole movement is founded on sand.

It is an old experience which perhaps most of us who have sought for light and endeavored to understand our own ideals and aspirations have felt, that every enthusiasm, above all religious enthusiasm, regards science and all close scrutiny with suspicion. The relentless dissections of exact analysis appear as a sacrilege.

The reader will feel in Mr. Salter's reply the uneasiness caused by our procedure. He invites us to present our opinion,* but he resents a clear statement of our differences.† This statement of our differences may have been emphatic, but I feel confident that it

* Mr. Hegeler in a letter of May 8th, 1890, wrote: "In the last number of *The Open Court* that reached me, I find Dr. Carus has defined our position towards Ingersoll and his followers, and also that towards the Societies for Ethical Culture. I believe the article was written by him already some time ago, and the publication was delayed by our hesitancy to open what I will call civilized war upon you. I have told the Doctor already,—a long while ago,—that it was our duty to do this."

So, also, in a letter of June 4th, Mr. Hegeler wrote: "We ought to clear our differences of opinion for the general good. You are an influential public teacher, and I certainly spend a large amount of money for the same object—and avoidance of waste and also the reduction of mental as well as physical struggle or war to the smallest possible limit (but not the avoidance of the struggle) belongs in my opinion to the essence of Ethics. The energy thereby saved we have to use for a 'building up.'"

To this Mr. Salter replied, on June 8th: "I agree with you entirely that we should endeavor to clear up our differences .... Nothing but preoccupation and lack of time have prevented me heretofore from explaining myself at length to you. Indeed, I hoped that when my book came out, giving my views at such length, I should have the benefit of criticism from you and Dr. Carus. I, by no means, count my present views as final, as indeed I say in my preface. And I wish to learn and assimilate all of positive truth, which you give in *The Open Court*—and I have already gained help from it. So please criticise me in public or in correspondence—and, at least in the summer, I will agree to answer to the best of my ability, and I will *always* attentively read and consider."—[*Published with Mr. Salter's permission.*]

† Mr. Salter says in a marginal note: "I did not invite you to criticize the movement in your public lectures; still you had a perfect right to do so, and I am not sorry."

was not made so as to be offensive, for I have at the same time not concealed my respect—nay, my admiration for the efforts, the seriousness, and the noble ideals of the ethical societies.

Mr. Salter is embarrassed by our criticism, because he neither feels the need of a basis of ethics, nor does he feel urged to have a scientific explanation of it. Ethics regarded as unexplainable, appears to him greater, nobler, and holier than if it were explained. Yet we can assure Mr. Salter that morality will not be degraded by any explanation. On the contrary, it will rise in its purest and holiest dignity.

Mr. Salter considers the demands of the conscience as an ultimate fact; it is to him "the unmovable rock" upon which he bases the ethical movement. He asserts the independence of morality from religion as well as science; he attempts to make morality absolute. If a gardener, in this way, makes the tree independent of its roots, he becomes a wood-cutter; he will deprive the tree of the conditions of its life.

If Mr. Salter would ask himself how he had come into the possession of the ethical stimulus, he would soon be urged to travel the same path with us.

The ethics of mysticism is only the prophesy of ethics based on science. It is the bud's promise of a fruit. It is like astrology which will mature into astronomy. The astrologer has set his heart on the mystic element of his profession; it alone possesses in his mind the charm of beauty, and he watches with great grief how the bud loses that beauty while it ripens into a fruit.

Before proceeding to the main subject of our controversy, which refers to the question of the dispensability or indispensability of a basis for ethics, I shall briefly dispose of a few side issues of less concern. In so far as they are side issues I might pass them over in silence. But it appears that they presuppose principles which are of great ethical significance.

THE ETHICAL IMPORT OF CRITICISMS.

As to the occasion of the three lectures, I am told that my article, "The Basis of Ethics and the Ethical Movement," was not the cause which suggested to the speaker and the Board of Trustees of the Society for Ethical Culture at Chicago, the idea of extending the invitation to me. The invitation was tendered without any special motive, and would have been tendered even if that article had never been written.* I confess that I was under the impression that the society wanted me to explain our views with special reference to their own position. It is a principle of *The Open Court* to solicit criticism, and we expect that the same principle animates every one who is eager to find out the truth. We believe that the truth can be established only by a square fight, where ideas are pitted against ideas in fair and honest controversy. We do not want to intrude upon the world with our private and personal pet theories. We want to bring out the truth. If our views are wrong, we want to be refuted, and if we are refuted, we shall give up those ideas which we have recognized as errors.

Mr. Salter says, "the ethical movement believes that philosophical systems should have a free field and that *that* one should survive whose claims prove the strongest in the struggle for existence, and all within the fold of an ethical fellowship held together by a

*In the present edition of *The Ethical Problem* the words, "In consequence of this article" (p. ii, 1st ed.) have been replaced by the clause "soon after the publication of this article" (see p. ix, present edition).

community of moral aim." Very well then, we act accordingly: we propose a certain view and struggle for it. Yet we do not enter the lists vainly or merely for the sake of controversy. We do not struggle for something which is indifferent, for we maintain that it is *the most important question* with which the members of the ethical societies can concern themselves.

There is, at present, a fashionable tendency to consider every struggle, whatever be its nature, as bad. War, competition, emulation, criticism, are considered as more or less barbaric forms of one and the same principle—the principle of strife; and this principle of strife is denounced as the source of all evil. The abolition of all strife, it is expected, will usher in the beginning of a millennium. Whatever may be true in this view, we see no other possibility of arriving at truth than by struggling for it, and the struggle for truth appears to us as a duty.

The weapon in the struggle for truth is criticism. If we believe we are in possession of truth, let us expose our opinion to the criticism of those competent to criticise. If we differ in opinion, let us compare our opinions and investigate as to which opinion is nearest the truth. The invitation to speak before the Ethical Society, was made with the special understanding that we were to propose *our* view on the ethical problem; and it would not have been proper to ignore the position of the Ethical Societies entirely. I should be sorry to "have taken an occasion, incidentally, to reinforce an earlier criticism"—if that criticism was not welcome. Having stated a difference of opinion, it seemed to me, that a further explanation, a justification was demanded. Could I have acted otherwise since, after all, criticism and counter criticism are the sole means of arriving at truth? And then, our struggle for truth is not a personal fight between our private views in which you or I should hope to come out victorious. Our struggle for truth is rather a co-operation, in which every one of us contributes his share of insight and tries to free himself from the errors that might be mixed up with a partially correct conception of truth.

Mr. Salter is mistaken, when he speaks of "an attitude of antagonism" towards the ethical societies on our part. We do not intend to antagonize the ethical societies; on the contrary, we intend to promote their welfare; and we therefore call attention to that which we consider as their most urgent and indispensable duty. It is their duty to build their house upon a rock, so that it will withstand the rain and the winds. Our antagonism, if our attitude is to be characterized by that name, is an antagonism arising from a common interest, from a religious zeal for the same great cause, from a desire that the ethical societies shall not neglect the one thing that is needed, that they shall have been founded to stay for good, to prosper, to increase, and to conquer.

INTUITIONALISM AND SUPERNATURALISM.

Mr. Salter blames me for "carelessness in treating of ethical theories;" he says, that I identify Intuitionalism with Supernaturalism. Mr. Salter adds:

> "And Paley on the strength of his theology is called an intuitionalist, while he was, in fact, one of the founders of utilitarianism."

Undoubtedly Paley was one of the founders of utilitarianism. His theory is characterized in his own words as follows:

"God Almighty wills and wishes the happiness of his creatures."

Paley is a utilitarian with reference to the purpose and aim of ethics. He is generally characterized as "a theological utilitarian"; nevertheless I do not hesitate to class him among the intuitionalists, "on the strength of his theology" as Mr. Salter rightly remarks.* Professor Sidgwick (in the Encyclopædia Britannica, vol. viii, p. 606) describes Paley's views in the following words:

"To be obliged is to be 'urged by a violent motive resulting from the command of another'; in the case of moral obligation the command proceeds from God, and the motive lies in the expectation of being rewarded and punished after this life."

Intuitionalism if it means anything means that the moral command comes to us in some unaccountable way mysteriously and directly from some sphere beyond. I confess myself guilty of identifying "intuitionalism with supernaturalism." Everybody who maintains that the basic view of intuitionalism is true, is in my opinion to be classed as an intuitionalist. If the sense of duty, the moral ought, the idea of right or wrong of conscience or whatever we call it, is an unanalysable fact, if our knowledge of it comes to us not through experience, but through some mystical process concerning which philosophy and science can give no information, we are confronted with a dualistic theory. We have in that case to deal with a world-

* Whether Paley is represented as an intuitionalist or in the usual way as "a theological utilitarian," does not in the least affect the subject of our controversy. I selected his name, because his works are still read and better known than those of other theological teachers of ethics. I confess openly that I should not have mentioned him as one of "the representative authors of intuitionalism," and have therefore in the present edition of *The Ethical Problem*, suppressed his name by omitting the passage in which it occurs. I do not, however, cease to count Paley among intuitionalists.

conception recognizing the existence of certain facts, which are of a totally different character from all the other facts. Whatever name we may be pleased to give such a conception, it is and will remain supernaturalism or at least extra-naturalism.

I look upon intuitionalism in ethics and upon its philosophical correlative supernaturalism, as a kind of scientific color line. Any one who attempts a conciliation between supernaturalism and naturalism is a supernaturalist, and every one who attempts a conciliation between intuitionalism and other ethical views, is an intuitionalist.

Are not all intuitionalists at the same time utilitarians, in so far as they expect that in the end the good will be rewarded and the bad will be punished? We can reconcile intuitionalism with utilitarianism, if utilitarianism means that in the end the good will be rewarded and the bad will be punished. But we cannot reconcile intuitionalism with any theory that considers conscience as being of a natural growth, so that it can be analysed and scientifically explained.

Utilitarianism is that theory which explains the good in terms of the useful, and thus misleads people to identify the useful and the good. If utilitarianism means that the consequences of good deeds are somehow always useful, (perhaps not useful to ourselves, but useful to somebody, and though perhaps not useful in the present, yet useful in the future,) I shall not hesitate to range myself among the utilitarians, however strongly I protest against any identification of the useful and the good, against making the usefulness of a deed the test of its moral goodness, and still more against defining the good in terms of pleasure.

UTILITARIANISM AND HEDONISM.

As a further carelessness in treating of ethical theories, Mr. Salter mentions the distinction made between utilitarianism and hedonism. Mr. Salter says:

> "Hedonism is treated separately from utilitarianism although every form of utilitarianism has been hedonistic, modern utilitarianism being simply universalistic hedonism."

I have deliberately treated hedonism and utilitarianism as separate theories, because I consider it necessary to make a distinction between them. Hedonism proposes the pleasurable, and utilitarianism the useful as the ultimate test of ethics. These two propositions are in my opinion by no means congruent. Most utilitarians, it is true, (I hesitate to say "all" utilitarians,) define the useful as that which affords the greatest amount of pleasure. I see, nevertheless, sufficient difference between the useful and the pleasurable. The term useful comprehends many things or processes which cause much pain and produce little pleasure.

While we uncompromisingly reject hedonism, we see a possibility of reconciliation with utilitarianism, provided the utilitarians drop for good the principle of hedonism, and exclude from the term useful all those transient advantages (generally considered as useful) which occasionally come to man in consequence of bad actions—for instance wealth gained by fraudulent means. In short there can be no objection to utilitarianism if we limit the term useful strictly to that kind of usefulness which is the inevitable consequence of good actions, provided we agree concerning a further definition of good. Consider, however, that the main motive perhaps of all immoral actions is the presumed usefulness, and so far as the acting individual is concerned, not unfrequently the actual usefulness of the consequences attending immoral actions, and you will confess that it is one of the most important duties of ethics to set us on our guard against the temptations of an imagined utility, and to inform us that what appears useful is not always useful, that what is useful now, may become very obnoxious in the future, and that what is useful to one individual may be detrimental to others. There are many phases of the useful which ethics cannot and does not recommend, and we must have a criterion for that kind of usefulness which is desirable. This criterion alone is the standard of moral goodness; and the character of every ethics depends upon what is to be considered as this criterion.

It is characteristic of almost all utilitarian systems (if they enter into the subject at all) that this criterion is nothing that transcends the usual conception of utility. The criterion of utilitarianism is usually defined as the greatest happiness for the greatest number. Wherever a conflict arises between two or more things that are useful, utilitarians propose to give preference to the greater amount of usefulness: the quantity of usefulness has to decide, not the quality.

Quantity or intensity of happiness, and quantity of usefulness, can as little constitute moral goodness as a majority vote can in moral questions decide as to what is right or wrong. If, however, the quality of different kinds of utility were to be considered as the determining factor of goodness, the useful as such would cease to be the ultimate criterion of ethics, and that quality would have to be considered as the ultimate test of goodness which makes this or that act ethically preferable.

So long as this quality, which gives to one kind of

acts with useful consequences the value we call moral goodness, is not singled out as the characteristically moral feature, I shall continue to maintain that utilitarianism, and most so hedonistic utilitarianism, slurs over the difference between moral goodness and material usefulness.

MONISM AND THE ETHICAL MOVEMENT.

Mr. Salter says:

"What I had at least hoped for, was an exposition of the way in which the monistic world-conception would serve as a basis of ethics, for to me personally at any rate, and I think, to many more, this would have been of considerable interest; but monism is classed along with agnosticism and materialism as one of the thought-constructions of theorizing philosophers."

My lectures on the ethical problem were intended to discuss the principle of ethics and its dependence upon a conception of the world. They were not intended as an exposition of the ethics of positivism or of monism. It is not an exhaustive work on ethics, but a modest pamphlet ventilating the problem of ethics. Nevertheless, the solution of the ethical problem is sufficiently indicated so that the reader can form a clear conception as to the basis, the construction, the plan and the scope of that system of ethics which we defend. But Mr. Salter should not be astonished to find monism classed along with agnosticism and materialism among the world-conceptions of theorizing philosophers. Are there not many philosophies pretending to be monistic? Shall we accept whatever goes by the name of monism? Or is it advisable to warn against all philosophies except our own? Our own view is certainly not exempt from criticism. It has to be classed, and I have purposely classed it among the theories to be criticised. It must be considered as a mere theory, until its character as being a statement of systematized facts is proved.

A distinction must be made between 1) the positive and monistic philosophy that is growing now in the minds of men, and 2) the monism and positivism which we represent. There are a great number of philosophers and scientists who work in the same line as ourselves, and many truths are, with more or less lucidity, pronounced independently by different scholars, sometimes in terms which seem to contradict one another. I am sure that if we did not contribute to the growth of this monistic world-conception, it would nevertheless develop. We do not create it; it is not an invention of ours to which we have any patent right. All we can do is to hasten its development to mature its growth, to concentrate the many different aspirations that tend to the same aim.

Should the special work we are doing in exhibiting our monistic view of the universe happen to be radically wrong, it will pass away. The constructive work we have been doing will in that case be transient, and its usefulness will be confined to having served as a stimulus to thought.

The monistic philosophy that is growing in mankind is an ideal. Our special and individual view is an attempt to work out the realization of the ideal. But the fact that we consider our view as an attempt to realize the ideal philosophy of the future, does not raise our special representation and elaboration of it above criticism.

A similar discrimination must be made between the ethical movement and the ethical societies. There is an ethical movement preparing itself among mankind, and the ethical societies are one important symptom of this movement, but they are not the sole symptom. The ethical movement is perceptible also in the churches; it is perceptible in the Secular Unions and in the political life of our nation. The ethical societies, it seems to me, might become and they ought to become the centre of the ethical movement; and they would become its centre, if they understood the signs of the times.

The ethical movement and the new philosophy of positive monism are closely allied with each other. Indeed, I consider them as the two main characteristic features of the spiritual life of the future. Positive monism in order to be complete, must be practically applied, it must become a religion. It becomes a religion by bringing about an ethical movement which bases morality on the facts of life, so that the ethics of supernaturalism are replaced by natural ethics.

The ethical movement cannot refuse to go hand in hand with the philosophy of the times. It need not commit itself to this or that particular representation of monism, but it must upon the whole recognize the basic principles of the coming religion of positive monism; for if it does not, the movement will be of no avail, and can be of no use to future generations to whom the old and antiquated views have passed away.

Our desire is to make the leaders of the ethical society understand that this is the vital problem of the day. And here we come to the main point of our controversy; viz., the question whether we can have ethics without having a basis of ethics.

THE BASIS OF ETHICS AND THE LEADING PRINCIPLE IN ETHICS.

Mr. Salter says that I confound two questions:

> "[First,] what is the true world-conception, upon which every special science may, in a broad and rather loose sense, be said to be based; and secondly, what is the ultimate principle in ethics itself? The second question might be more distinctly stated as follows: Not what is the *basis of* ethics, in the sense of "a philosophical view back" of it (a theology or philosophy), but what is the basic principle *in* ethics? Ethics, in the popular sense, being a system of rules for conduct, it is necessary, if it is to be treated scientifically, that there should be some supreme rule, by their agreement or disagreement with which all lesser rules should be judged."

It appears to me that I do not confound these two questions; yet I am confident that I see their intimate connection. Our proposition is that the leading* principle *in* ethics must be derived from the philosophical view back of it. The world-conception a man has, can alone give character to the principle *in* his ethics. Without any world-conception we can have no ethics (i. e., ethics in the highest sense of the word). We may act morally like dreamers or somnambulists, but our ethics would in that case be a mere moral instinct without any rational insight into its *raison d'être*.

If there is any difference between morality and ethics, it is this, that morality is the habit of acting in a certain way which, according to our view of the world we live in, is considered as good; while ethics (the science of morality) is the conscious recognition of the reasons which make an action good or bad. A bear that sacrifices her life in the defense of her cubs acts morally according to our view; but her action is mainly

*The word "leading" appears to me preferable to "basic" in this connection.

the result of impulse. The morality of animals appears almost as a blind reflex action when compared to the conscious self-sacrifice of an ethical man who acts deliberately, knowing the reason why.

If I rightly understand Mr. Salter's proposition, the Societies for Ethical Culture should according to my terminology be called "Societies for Moral culture."

Mr. Salter indeed emphasises this idea in the chapter of his *Ethical Religion* to which he calls my attention. He says:

> "The basis of our movement is not a theory of morality, but morality itself." (p. 302.)

Is not Mr. Salter's meaning this? "Practical morality must be the *object* (and not the *basis*) of the ethical movement. Theories have no value unless they are made practical by application." If this is Mr. Salter's theory we agree with him, but we should add: "No practical work can efficiently be done without a theory. The result of the work will greatly depend upon having the right theory."

In another passage Mr. Salter says:

> "We do not propound new views of the Universe. We wish rather a new sense of duty." (p. 292.)

Are not Christian and Jewish preachers constantly at work to make our sense of duty more sensitive? If that is Mr. Salter's meaning, he does the same work that all honest clergymen are doing. David cried for the renewal of a right spirit within him (Psalm LI, 10), and Ezekiel described his work with the words:

> "A new heart also will I give you and a new spirit will I put within you. (36, 26.)

For preaching "a new sense of duty" in the sense of an unceasing moral progress and of a constant renewal of moral purposes, there would have been no need of leaving the churches. Yet if by a new sense of duty is meant an entirely new morality, different in kind from the old morality, how can it be proposed unless the basis of ethics be radically changed at the same time, or at least differently applied? In no case can we ignore it.

I do not doubt but that humanity has made a great moral progress, I do not doubt but that the average morality among our grandchildren will be higher than is the average morality of the present age, but I am also firmly confident that we shall have to preach the same morality over again to later generations. The substance of our morality will not be changed. That which must be changed is our conception of morality, in so far as it is to be based not upon a supernatural authority, but upon the authority of natural laws. We have to free ourselves from the ethics of supernaturalism, we must overcome the mysticism of the intuitionalists' view; we must be led out into clearness. If we understand morality, its natural conditions, its growth and purpose, we shall the better be prepared to obey the moral commands.

The most important moral rules are not to be altered. So far as I can see, some of them will be altered as little as our arithmetical tables can be changed. Our sense of duty may become more enlightened and more sensitive, but its contents will remain about the same. If we read the properly moral injunctions of Confucius, or of Epictetus and Marcus Aurelius, or of the Hebrew prophets, are they not, aside from a few odd expressions due to the speech of their time or to awkward translation, quite as modern as the sermons of a lecturer of the societies for ethical culture? There is the same earnestness, the same impressiveness, the personal tone of fatherly instruction, the appeal to the noblest motives of the understanding and the heart.

How is it, that these old books have remained so modern? Because the subject of their exhortations is ever new, and the same things have to be repeated again to every generation.

Mr. Salter says that the ethical movement is not devoted to antisupernaturalism. Supernaturalists not only believe in a supernatural deity, they also base their ethics on the revelation of a transcendent God. Every attempt at humanizing ethics must from the standpoint of supernaturalism be considered as a superstitious presumption, and I have strong doubts whether any serious believer in supernaturalism will ever join an ethical society. One kind of supernaturalism only can be imagined to be compatible with the views propounded by the ethical lecturers, viz., that in which the idea of God has no practical meaning. He alone, to whom his belief in supernaturalism is ethically indifferent, will agree with Mr. Salter that the ethical societies are not devoted to antisupernaturalism.

Mr. Salter looks upon supernaturalism, and indeed upon any other basis of ethics not as a real basis, but as a mere interpretation of ethics. He speaks of first principles in ethics, but how does he come into their possession, unless he derives them, if not consciously, then unconsciously, from his conception of the world? *The leading principle of ethics must always be the expression of a conception of the world.* This is the point Mr. Salter does not recognize. If he recognized it, he would not so repeatedly complain about a lack of clearness as to what a basis of ethics means.

FACTS, HOW THEY TEACH.

It has been emphasized in the three lectures on The Ethical Problem that ethics must be based on facts. With reference to this principle Mr. Salter says:

> "What then is the scientific world-conception, the true basis of ethics? I confess to having been completely taken aback, when as I read on I discovered that Dr. Carus declined to answer the question, contenting himself with vaguely saying that the true philosophy will be one which is in accordance with facts, which seems equivalent to saying that the scientific system will be a scientific system."

The principle that the new ethics must be based on facts, is certainly so obvious that it must appear as a self-evident redundant truism. So all the most complex arithmetical theories may be shown to be mere equations, they are tautologies which will appear to every one who understands them, just as self-evident as the equation $1+1=2$. And yet it is sometimes quite difficult to analyze and understand such a simple proposition as that ethics must be based on facts.

Although Mr. Salter considers the proposition that "the scientific world-conception, the true basis of ethics," must be based on facts as sufficiently obvious as to be tautological, he makes objection to it as being something in the air. He says:

> "It has long been plain to me that resting ethics on our matter-of-fact wishes or instincts is not establishing ethics, but undermining it and leaving it a something "in the air."

Does Mr. Salter mean that "basing ethics on facts" denotes an exact imitation of the facts we experience? Does he think, that if we witness a murder, we are thereby invited to commit a murder also?

I said (as Mr. Salter declares "in one clear-sighted passage") that

"Ethics is not ready made, it is not the one or the other fact among all the realities of the universe. Ethics is our attitude toward the facts of reality. (The Ethical Problem, p. 18.)

With reference to this statement Mr. Salter says:

"The latter remark seems to imply that the same facts may be looked at from different attitudes; if so how are the facts themselves to decide which attitude we shall take?"

Certainly we can take different attitudes toward facts. But the proper attitude toward facts can be learned from the facts alone. Facts teach us for instance the laws of health. Mr. Salter suggests that any one might say, "I do not care about my health." But in that case the laws of health are not (as Mr. Salter declares,) meaningless to him. He will soon find out the meaning of the laws of health. Facts will teach him to care for his health, and if he does not, nature will soon deprive him of health and life.

I happen to know a sad case of my own experience. A strong and healthy young man, a jovial companion and of social habits, defied the laws of health, and could do so for some time on account of his strength and youth. I plainly remember that he once said to me almost in the same words in which Mr. Salter puts it: "I do not care about the laws of health, nor do I care for a long life. It is not pleasant to grow so very old. I would rather live so as to please myself, even though my life be shorter by ten years." A year elapsed and he fell sick never to recover again. His parents buried him in the bloom of his life.

Facts are not mute; they teach us. Our knowledge of facts is called experience, and from knowledge of facts alone the principles of action can be derived.

Mr. Salter is far from basing ethics upon the solid ground of facts. He combines with ethics the idea that it must be something absolute. In his lecture, "Is There Anything Absolute About Morality?" he says:

> "If by morality is meant only the actual conduct of men, we have plainly to negative our question, and say there is nothing absolute about morality, since the conduct of men has been after any but a fixed, unvarying type." (pp. 83, 84.)

Mr. Salter finds the absolute of morality in conscience. The commands of conscience, Mr. Salter declares, are absolute. But have there not been erring consciences which prove that conscience is anything but an absolute authority? Mr. Salter evades the difficulty by declaring that the inquisitors and other men who committed crimes in perfect faith that they were doing a good work, had no conscience at all. Concerning the barbarous treatment of the Canaanites, he goes so far as to maintain:

> "I doubt if Moses, or one of the heroes of the Israelitish legend ever seriously asked himself, What is right?" (p. 91.)

In a certain sense there is something absolute in ethics, although we should not call it "absolute." We should prefer to say, there is something objective in ethics; and the objective element in ethics makes it possible for ethics to become a science and for morality to be based on science i. e., a systematized statement of facts.

THE MORAL LAW AND MORAL RULES.

For the sake of clearness let us distinguish between the moral law and moral rules. By the moral law we understand a law of nature which is as rigid and objective as are all other laws of nature. By moral rules we understand the formulation of certain commands, based upon a more or less comprehensive knowledge of the moral law.

The moral law operates in nature with the same unfailing exactness as does, for instance, the law of gravitation. If a stone is without support, it falls to the ground whether we wish it to fall or not. If the members of a society infringe upon the moral law, they will reap the evils consequent thereupon. The course of events follows with the same necessity in the one case as in the other, in the realms of inorganic as well as of organized nature.

Organized nature develops feeling, and feeling develops mind. The acts of beings endowed with mind take place with the same necessity in a given situation, as does the fall of a stone under certain circumstances. But it must not be forgotten that, aside from the intensity of impulsive force in the different inclinations for this or that course of action, the intelligence of beings endowed with mind has become the main factor in the determination of their acts. A cannon ball, shot under exactly the same circumstances, will take exactly the same course, and a man of a certain character will be guided by the same motives in exactly the same way. But we must bear in mind, that if the same man happens to come a second time into the same situation, he is no longer the same man. The former experience has modified his character, be it ever so little. He has profited by that experience either for a repetition or an avoidance of the act. And the more he has profited by experience, the freer he will become, i. e., the less will he be dependent upon the situation, and the more decisive will be his intelligence in determining his will.

The method of intelligent action is that of formulating knowledge of natural laws in the shape of commands. All knowledge is a description or systematized formulation of natural facts; and all intelligent action is an application of knowledge. If we pursue certain purposes, how can we, for our own use as well as for the education of others, state our knowledge better than in the shape of rules? The rules of architecture help us in the construction of a house. But these rules of architecture are nothing but the knowledge of building materials and of the methods of combining them to provide people with dwellings. The rules of morality help us in building up our lives, so that our individual existence is not antagonistic to the growth of society; but it furthers the development of humanity in the sphere of our activity, and will after our death continue to be a blessing unto mankind. But the rules of morality are based upon the moral law not otherwise than the rules of architecture are derived from our knowledge of natural facts. The rules we set up, may be right or wrong, they can show a greater or smaller comprehension of the nature of things, at any rate they are ultimately based upon the facts of nature, and alone by an investigation of the facts of nature can we become assured of their truth.

THE GROWTH OF CONSCIENCE.

Mr. Salter in declaring that ethics cannot be based on facts, does not sufficiently appreciate the truth that experience actually teaches man. Man is educated in the severe school of natural facts, ruled by the unalterable law of cause and effect. Man's whole existence and also his moral existence, his conscience is a product of this education.

Is conscience truly beyond the pale of science? If it were, we should have to accept the mysticism of its existence. Let us see how man's conscience originates.

A child observes the behavior of his parents, he listens to their instruction. He imbibes almost unconsciously with his first impressions the ethical nature of his mother. He notices the disdain of his father, for instance, when somebody told him a lie, he witnesses the contempt with which the liar was alluded to or thought of. All these many experiences are implanted into the soil of an inherited disposition which has come down from ancestors, swayed by the same motives and acting in a similar way.

Whenever a temptation arises to tell a lie, all the memories of former experiences that are of a similar nature will be more or less dimly awakened. Not the moral injunctions of his parents and teachers alone will be awakened, but also the evil examples of his bad comrades. There is perhaps one among them who lied and he succeeded with his lie: he extricated himself by a lie out of an awkward situation. Such instances are dangerous, for they corrupt the souls of the weak. Yet there is most likely also another instance of some one who heaped shame upon himself; the lie was found out and his plight was changed from bad to worse. In addition to these reminiscences other considerations awaken, such as: Even if the lie be not found out, I should in the future have to class myself among liars!

Conscience is by no means a simple and unanalyzable fact; it is not at all one single voice. Conscience is the combined experience of innumerable lessons, taught us by our teachers' injunctions and by observation of surrounding events.

Conscience is as little a faculty, having a special seat or organ in the brain as is for instance memory, imagination, or will, or any other abstract concept designating a special attitude, phase, or quality of the mind. The term "conscience" is an abstraction which covers a special group of psychical activities. Conscience in any other sense is a ghost, and to believe in it is a superstition. It does not appear that Mr. Salter adopts the ghost-idea of conscience, but it seems to me that he fails to see what conscience actually is. By conscience we understand the sum-total of all those impulses which serve for the regulation of human action. But there is no conscience that demon-like lives as a mysterious being somewhere in the abodes of the soul.

If man's life consisted of single and isolated moments, he would have no choice but to obey the impulse of the moment. Since his life consists of moments that are coherent forming all together a unity, and since before obeying an impulse that prompts to action, man can and will have to take into consideration other impulses, a choice is offered and he will naturally choose to follow that impulse which promises the greatest amount of pleasure. This is the beginning of rational action. Man's life, however, is not only a complex unity of many coherent moments, it is also interwoven with the lives of his fellow-beings. His actions affect others; and in whatever way he affects others, they will again affect him. The principles of his conduct are brought home to him. He may try to evade the consequences of his actions. Exceptionally he may apparently succeed, but not in the long run. He can as little escape the consequences of his actions as he can annul any law of nature. His life is intimately bound up with the lives of all his fellow beings; and sooner or later the truth will dawn upon him that his life is only the part of a greater whole. He will die, but the greater whole will contiue, and the worth of his life will have to be judged in the end by that which remains of his actions after death. He will hear the men praised whose lives were a blessing to mankind, he will see their deeds continue working good and perhaps preserving their individual memory. He will learn to detest the man who leaves an inheritance of curses. The examples of the one as well as the other are most impressive and will contribute much in forming the conscience of man's soul.

Conscience does not well up from a mysterious source, but it grows from natural conditions, and for that reason it is not at all infallible. The conscience of a man well instructed and surrounded by noble examples, is different from the conscience of the uneducated. The conscience of a savage is often grossly mistaken. The most shameful acts are performed often against all natural inclinations not for the sake of gaining some personal advantage but solely because they are erroneously considered as "right."

In a certain sense it is proper to proclaim that man should obey the behests of his conscience; but conscience is not one special voice in man. It cannot be compared to a person, although figuratively we may call it the God in us, the prophetic soul, or the judge of our actions. It is not rounded off as are individual beings; but consists of many thoughts, the meanwhile accusing or excusing one another (Rom 2, 15).

One most essential part of man's conscience must be the sincere desire to criticize the different propositions of conscience. Conscience must not be blind, but its principle feature must be that of examination. And exact examination is not possible without knowledge. Thus it is an essential principle of a well directed conscience to aspire for more knowledge, for more light, so as to be able to judge the better. A healthy conscience is constantly growing.

It cannot be denied, that upon the whole the voices of conscience, i. e., those impulses which lift man above the transient advantages and the petty egotism of his limited individual interests, naturally tend to preserve his soul; they find approbation by his fellow men and let him partake of the superindividual life of humanity. According to natural law the immoral element of humanity is constantly discarded as unfit to survive. However, the moral aspirations that tend to bring man into harmony with the conditions of his existence especially with the social relations of mankind, preserve his soul, and must in this way very soon acquire a greater strength than the lower desires of his animal nature.

The impulses of man's animal nature, hunger, thirst, acquisitiveness of all kinds, i. e., the impulses arising from the wants of his individual existence, appear to originate within himself, they are considered as expressions of his individual existence. But the superindividual voices of his conscience seem to come to him from the outside of his surroundings. They teach him to restrain the animal impulses and to set himself in accord with those conditions which are more comprehensive and more lasting than his individual existence. They bring him in union with that greater whole of which his individual existence is but a small part and a transient phase.

In this way the many promptings to action in the soul of man are mainly divided into two classes: the first we call egotistic motives; they urge man to follow his natural appetites; and the second we will call the superindividual aspirations; they keep man's natural appetites in check and teach man regard for the greater whole to which he belongs. The former appear to him as expressions of his individual will and the latter as manifestations of an outside power higher, nobler, and stronger than himself. The latter alone form that which is generally called conscience. Conscience, accordingly, is justly considered as invested with authority and its promptings appear naturally in the shape of commands.

The recognition of this authority for the purpose of regulating conduct in accordance with its laws, is the beginning of all ethics; and thus it is this authority which represents the basis of ethics.

The authority which finds expression in man's conscience, however, is by no means beyond the scope of science. We can investigate it and we must investigate it. The more we understand its origin, the better we shall be able to judge of its importance and the less we shall be liable to be guided astray by an erring conscience.

SCIENCE AND ETHICS.

TO BASE ethics on facts, to derive the rules of our attitude toward facts from experience, to shape our ideals, not from the airy stuff of something beyond the ken of science, but in accordance with laws derived from reality, this is (as I said in my first lecture) the line of demarcation between the old and the new ethics. Mr. Salter by rejecting science places himself upon the antiquated ground of intuitionalism. I know that he rejects the old fashioned supernaturalism, but indeed his view (if expressed with consistency) ought to appear as supernaturalism. He says:

> "Conscience is not knowledge,—for knowledge is of what is, and conscience is the thought of what ought to be."

And in other passages (p. 304):

> "These moral laws of our being are so close and constitutional to us that the very existence of virtue is bound up with a recognition of them."
>
> "Who can give a reason for the supreme rule? Indeed, no serious man wants a reason. The supreme command appeals immediately to the human mind; it is an assertion of the human mind."
>
> "Amiel, 'the sweet-souled Genevan mystic,' says: 'It is not history which teaches righteousness to the conscience; it is conscience which teaches righteousness to history. The actual is corrupting; it is *we* who rectify it by loyalty to the ideal.'"

Might these expressions not occur in any work of an intuitionalist? Is not in this way, by considering conscience as something that lies beyond the pale of science, beyond the knowable realm of natural facts, mysticism introduced as an essential element of morality? And indeed, Mr. Salter does not approve of it that "morality is thought to be without mystery." There is a dualism lurking in Mr. Salter's ethics, as if the moral order were something radically different from the order of this world:

> "Though it [morality] warns us and commands us, it does so in that supreme act in which we warn and command ourselves; it is the utterance of the God in us, of the 'prophetic soul' in which we all share, and signifies that we are part and parcel of another order of things than that which we can see and handle, and are rooted in somewhat firmer than the earth, and more ancient, more venerable than the heavens."

There is no objection to defining morality in poetical terms as "the utterance of God" (i. e., the immanent God) or as the "prophetic soul," but it is not another order of the world. Morality is based upon, it is creating a better state of things by conforming to the order of this very same world in which we live.

The moral law is not considered by Mr. Salter as the highest natural law, higher than other natural laws; but it is said to be above or outside of nature. Mr. Salter says:

> "The moral sentiment dwarfs Nature, it goes out to that which is beyond Nature."

In consistency with his view that the moral sentiment goes out to that which is beyond nature, Mr. Salter rejects science as a basis of ethics. He says:

> "Agnosticism is no more than a confession of the *limitations* of our knowledge. But what we do not know is hardly a basis for action. . . . Nor is science, teaching us positively what we do know, a sufficient guide for us. I will yield to none in my admiration and wonder before the world which science has revealed to

us. How has space widened and time grown infinite, and how does one law seem to hold in its grasp the mighty movements of systems and the least tear that trickles down a child's face! It is a *uni*verse, majestic, solemn, in the midst of which we live, and it would seem to suggest to us great and solemn thoughts as to what our own lives should be.

"But when I turn from Nature to consider human life and the order of human society, my reverence in one way lessens rather than grows deeper. The science that reports faithfully, philosophically the varied facts of our human existence is not altogether a pleasant page to read. History, which is one branch of the science of man, tells of animalism, of brutal selfishness, of towering wrongs, of slow-returning justice, often of a blind infuriated justice, that punishes the innocent and leaves the guilty free. And observation—statistics, which is nothing else than scientific observation—reveals almost as many things that ought not to be as things which should be. Statistics of crime are just as much science as would be statistics of peace and order,—statistics of prostitution as truly scientific as those of family purity, of poverty as truly as those of comfort and competence.

"What science teaches must invariably be accepted as fact, but it may none the less provoke moral repulsion and rebellion. We may say to some of the facts, 'You have no right to be!' Yes, the very end of our scientific observation may sometimes be to render such observation in the future impossible,—that is, to destroy the facts. Plainly, then, science is not ultimate. It tells us simply what is; it tells us nothing of what ought to be. What ought to be,—that is reported to us by a higher faculty than that of scientific observation; it is an assertion, a demand of the conscience.

"Here, then, is to my mind the true basis of our movement,—not the old religions; not religion itself, in the popular understanding of that term; not agnosticism, though as matter of fact some of us may be agnostics; not science, though the facts of science, every one of them, should have our recognition. It is something deeper and more ancient, I might say, than any of these: it is the rock of conscience, the eternal laws that announce themselves in man's moral nature. . . . Conscience, in a word, ushers us into an ideal realm."

The ideal realm is nothing that stands in contradiction to the facts of life. Ideals which do not conform to the laws of nature derived from facts, are mere dreams.* Ideals must be based on science, in order to be realizable; and ideals that are unrealizable, impossibilities, are mirages, but not ideals.

Mr. Salter has a wrong and too limited conception of science; he takes science to mean knowledge, viz., a mere understanding, of facts, but he excludes from his definition "our judgment upon facts." He says:

"In the strict sense of the word, science—the science of man as truly as any other—knows nothing of right and wrong, but only of what is; of facts, and the law of their connection. To the pure understanding, virtue and vice do not exist. These notions arise in virtue of our judgment upon facts; and the organ of that judgment is other than that by which we learn of and explain the facts themselves: men call it Conscience."

The sole purpose of science is the application of science. As Mr. Salter rightly says: "For man is not only to know, but to do and to achieve." We study nature, and science exists for doing and achieving. In order to do and to achieve we must know. Knowledge is the basis of any achievement, not only in practical business for manufacturing, invention etc., but also for moral life. There is no conscience without knowledge, there is no *Gewissen* without *Wissen*. Conscience is not a faculty that exists prior to knowledge of facts, but it develops from a comprehension of facts, from a knowledge of the consequences of human action. Mr. Salter says (p. 37):

"It is strange, when we bear in mind the ideal nature of morality, to hear that morality must be based upon facts. Morality is not really a question of facts, but of the right of facts to be, of their correspondence with a standard of the mind. . . .

* See above, pp. 19 and 23.

Base morality on facts? Which facts? There are innumerable facts, an induction from which would only give us immorality. The good facts, then? But plainly, this is moving in a circle. In truth, there is nothing on which to base morality. We do not so much find it, as demand it in the world.

Can anyone derive from evils and the consequences of evils, rules of iniquity? The facts that ought not be, speak loud, very loud; they speak with no uncertain voice, and morality is preached mainly on account of such facts as, like the innocent Abel's blood, cry out to heaven! Suppose that a murderer has no conscience to guide him, will not the results of his crime teach him a most impressive lesson? The results of his crime will set him thinking, so that he will ask himself: Was it right to slay my brother? The evils of immorality and the consequences of these evils are a most powerful stimulus for asking the question what is right and what is wrong? Man has to face the facts of life and has to find out the right way of salvation by experience. His experience appears first as a dim instinct, often erring and sometimes hitting upon the right thing. Yet there is no other guide, no supernatural revelation, no intuitional faculty (in the sense of intuitionalism), no direct commands that might 'appeal immediately to the human mind.'

Mr. Salter may not call himself an intuitionalist, but he takes the standpoint of intuitionalism. He does not call his world-conception supernaturalism; but it is supernaturalism. While the Unitarians, following Theodore Parker, are seriously at work to "rationalize religion," while many Jewish rabbis recognize the truth of monism and therewith ackowledge the immanence of God, the leaders of the ethical societies remain upon the dualistic standpoint of extra-naturalism.

It is true the leaders of the ethical societies have dropped the old fashioned terminology of super-naturalism. Yet their ethics is as supernatural as the old conception of an extramundane deity. The idea of God is replaced by the ethical command, but the latter has remained as mysterious and transcendent, extramundane and extranatural as was the Jehovah of old-fashioned dogmatism.

THE AUTHORITY OF THE MORAL LAW.

CONSCIENCE is not so much an authority itself, as it is representative of an authority. It represents the authority of the moral law in the world, which is no less a reality than all the other natural laws. Mr. Salter in a most enthusiastic lecture on the higher law containing much that is true, asks the question :

> "Whence comes the authority of this law that is within and over us ?"

Mr. Salter continues :

> "The ordinary answers seem to me here entirely to fail . . . . the last answer as to the sources of the authority of the higher law fails as truly as the first. In fact there is no answer ; there are no sources for that supreme authority."

The Israelites conceived the authority of the moral law, the power that makes for righteousness, under the allegory of a powerful ruler of nature, as a great, personal being, as a legislator who had revealed his wise orders to Moses. And through the mouth of Moses, the God of the Old Testament is said to have characterized himself in the following words :

> "I the Lord thy God am a jealous God, visiting the iniquity of the fathers upon the children unto the third and fourth generation of them that hate me ; and showing mercy unto thousands of them that love me, and keep my commandments."

That God is jealous means he is intolerant. He enforces his will and suffers no one to live who attempts permanently to resist his will.

The God of Science is just as jealous, just as intolerant as the God of the Old Testament. The laws of nature are firm, unalterable, irrefragable, and omnipotent. The will of God is described to be "steadfast forever," and his dominion over the world* is proclaimed to be eternal. It is only by obedience to the immutable laws of nature that we can live. The Psalmist says:

> "Unless thy law had been my delights, I should then have perished in mine affliction." (119, 92.)

Who can doubt that nature enforces her laws rigorously, that she ruthlessly punishes him who does not regard them, but that, on the other hand, (to use the poetical phrase of the Bible,) she is "plenteous in mercy" to him who loves her, who studies her secrets and obeys her commandments? Certainly, the laws of nature are not deities, and the moral order of the world is not a person. But they are, nevertheless, objective realities just the same.

We have ceased to believe in Demeter, but we have not ceased tilling the ground. And if we ask, Who is it that taught man to till the ground? we do not hesitate to answer, "It is experience; the facts of life have taught man to sow and to harvest the fruits of the earth." The myth of Demeter is not wrong, it is simply an allegory; and the myth of a personal God having spoken to Moses out of a fiery bush contains great truths, but we must bear in mind that the truths contained in the Mosaic religion are wrapped in poetry. And science can just as much explain ethics and the moral law, and the authority of moral obligations, as it can derive the rules of agriculture from the facts of nature.

* Daniel 6, 26.

It is true as Mr. Salter says, "Science teaches us that which is, but Ethics that which ought to be." But that which ought to be, must be based upon that which is; else it will not stand.

What is the ought? The *ought* is that into which the *is* has the tendency to change. It is the *is to be*.

A Unitarian friend of mine compares in this respect ethics to obstetrics. Ethics cannot at individual pleasure create ideals of morality, all it can do is to find out the tendency of life and to assist in bringing the *is to be* to birth. The authority upon which ethics is based, he says, is not a person, but we can represent it as a person. We can symbolize its activity as if it consisted of personal actions, and that is the method by which the various religions teach ethics.

In fine, the authority according to which moral ideals must be shaped, is not subjective, but objective. It is not to be sought for in the realms of absolute principles, but must be modeled in conformity with existing facts and with the eternal laws that science abstracts from existing facts.

Ethical ideals that are not based on facts, are like the mirage in the desert. The mirage may be more beautiful than the oasis, but he goes astray who ventures to follow it.

THE THREE PHASES OF ETHICAL DEVELOPMENT.

There are three phases or periods in the ethical development of mankind. Like all phases of evolution they are not sharply divided; one passes over into the next gradually. Their development is nevertheless sufficiently marked to be noticeable.

The first period begins with the dawn of civilized

life and culminates in the establishment of authoritative dogmatism. The transition to the second period is marked by the breakdown of this authoritative dogmatism. The second period is the substitution of the individual conscience in the place of dogmatism. It culminates in the recognition of the sovereignty of the moral ought, and of the freedom of conscience. The transition to the third period is the result of the conflicts produced by the arbitrary nature of the various conceptions of duty.

If man's conscience is to be considered as the ultimate court of appeal we can have no objective standard of right and wrong. That which is wrong according to my conscience, may be right according to the conscience of others. How shall we decide? It is obvious that we want an objective standard of morality. Without an objective standard of morality we shall sink into moral anarchy, where the will of the individual is the sole test of what is right or wrong.

Accordingly ethics is in need of an authority to decide the conflict between two consciences or the conflict between two different commands in the conscience of one and the same man.

Must we return to the old dogmatism of the first period? We shall not; for we have outgrown mythology, and shall never return to the creeds of the old religions. But we need not think of returning to the old views, we can progress to a higher view. We have now better means than our ancestors had for recognizing the authority upon which the moral ought rests. Our knowledge of nature and of the laws of nature has grown sufficiently for us to be able to account for the necessity as well as the natural growth of morality. The authority upon which the moral commands are

based can be scientifically investigated and explained no less than the other facts of nature.

The first period is represented by the Mosaic law, by Roman Christianity, and similar institutions of authoritative dogmatism. The second period is represented by certain phases and ideals of the Reformation, the overthrow of Roman authority, and the recognition of the liberty of conscience. The third period is the religion of the future, which is near at hand. It is the basing of ethics upon the firm ground of facts. It is the recognition of an authority the nature of which can be explained by science. It is the establishment of the religion of science.

This religion of science is not only the fulfilment of the old religions; it is also the realization of that ideal which has been called natural religion. If the societies for ethical culture had been founded to represent this view, they would grow like the mustard seed; the seed would soon be the greatest among herbs and become a tree so that the birds of the air would come and lodge in the branches thereof.

Mr. Salter does not approve of what he calls "setting up a standard of philosophical orthodoxy." He says:

> "Dr. Carus, I am sorry to see, has not outgrown the sectarian principle of the churches, and would apparently give us another sect as 'exclusive' and 'intolerant' as any of the past, though (Gottlob) it will slay with the sword of the spirit and not with the arm of flesh."

It lies in the nature of ethics to establish an authority, and every authority is in a certain sense exclusive and intolerant. An ethical teacher, in my mind, cannot help being "exclusive" and "intolerant," if "intolerant" means the confidence that there is but one truth. Or shall any kind of ethics have the same right? Can anybody violate a law if only his conscience impels him to ignore that law? and can truth be tolerant of error? or can we have different kinds of truth which, although contradictory among themselves, may be of equal value?

The ideal of tolerance (as the word is commonly used) means that we use no other weapons in the defense of our opinion than the sword of the spirit, but it does not mean that any and every error has the same right as demonstrable truths.

It would be intolerant to make a certain belief the condition for being admitted to a religious society; but it is not intolerant for anybody, neither for societies nor for individuals, to have a definite and outspoken opinion. Nor would the leaders of the Ethical Societies commit themselves to intolerance and exclusiveness by declaring what they understand by ethics. We maintain that they cannot properly teach ethics without knowing what ethics means. In order to know what ethics means, they must define the idea of moral goodness, and they cannot define the idea of moral goodness without proposing a basis of ethics. If that is intolerant sectarianism, they have in our opinion to become intolerant sectarians. But definiteness of opinion is neither intolerance nor sectarianism, so long as an opinion remains exposed to scientific criticism, so long as in the struggle for truth its upholders slay only with the sword of the spirit and not with the arm of flesh. To have no opinion and to declare that officially the Societies for Ethical Culture do not intend to have an opinion, is not tolerance, but indefiniteness.

Conventionalism may be a sufficient *raison d'être*

for formalities, ceremonies, and customs; but it is not a sufficient basis for ethics. And a reformatory movement such as the Societies for Ethical Culture aspire to inaugurate, cannot take deep root if it is planted on the stony ground of conventionalism.

The intolerance of the first period is an intolerance of assumed authority, but the intolerance of the religion of science—if intolerance it can be called—is the sovereignty of demonstrable truth. Truth is one from eternity to eternity, and there is no other truth beside that one and sole and immutable truth. Truth is that Deity which suffers no equal. Like Jehovah in the Decalogue, Truth pronounces as its first commandment:

"Thou shalt have no other gods before me."

CONCLUDING REMARKS OF THE DISCUSSION.

I

REJOINDER BY MR. W. M. SALTER.

NOTHING but extreme pre-occupation has hindered my noticing earlier Dr. Carus's replies to my comments on his book (*The Ethical Problem*). I do not doubt his sincerity in wishing to come to an understanding, and with this desire in my own mind I offer the following remarks.

Dr. Carus says that the Ethical teachers agree that what he calls the basis of ethics is not needed. Now all that we are agreed about is that such a basis is not to be laid down as a necessary part of the Ethical movement—as something to which all members of the movement pledge themselves. But any individual in the movement can hold to such a basis, can feel the need of it and even maintain that without it there can be no rational ethics. This opinion may be held; the only requirement is that there shall be tolerance of other opinions. If one does not feel that he can belong to a society with others who think differently (whether as to the specific basis or as to the need of a basis in general) he of course leaves the society—or does not join it in the first place. For example, I myself believe that a true world-conception is of great importance, though I could not call it "a basis of ethics," as Dr. Carus does; I am in search of such a conception, and what elements of it I have already gained, those who hear me know; but I can respect others who are following different lines from my own and am glad to call them my brothers in an ethical fellowship.

Dr. Carus says that the Ethical lecturers do not acknowledge the 'reason why,' presented by orthodox theology. By this 'reason why' he means the will of God. But any of us might regard whatever is right as the will of God, if he chose to. The opinion of any member to this effect we should have no right to challenge.

Basing the right on the will of God is, however, another matter; and I think Dr. Carus is unjust to orthodox theology in assuming that it does so. Many are the theologians who regard God's will as identical with what is right; the few are those who regard God's will as the author of it. Can Dr. Carus instance another theologian of repute, besides Dymond, who did so? There may, of course, be others, but I do not happen to know of them. But even so extreme an opinion we should not have the right to exclude, so long as it did not injuriously influence actual conduct.*

Hence my own controversy with Dr. Carus will be hereafter purely in my personal capacity. It would be thoughtlessness and arrogance for me to allow all the windings, questionings, hesitancies, affirmations of my own mind in a controversy like the present one to be regarded as representative of the Ethical movement. In speaking of the aim and nature of the Ethical fellowship, I do speak for the movement and am answerable to it; but in discussing questions of Ethical philosophy I speak solely for myself and am answerable to no one.

Dr. Carus says that I know no 'reason why' for my moral law (as he is pleased to term it), and that I imagine that to give a reason why "would be not to explain but to degrade morality." With all wish to be charitable, I cannot acquit Dr. Carus of a misuse of my language in this connection. A 'reason why' in the sense of an ultimate standard of right and wrong I have expressly admitted to be necessary. But after the standard has been found and, by the use of it, the right in a concrete case determined, the question is sometimes asked, why should we do the right, which is equivalent to asking why should our will be regulated by any 'ought' whatever? My answer was that we should do the right out of reverence for the right and it appears to me that Dr. Carus's language implied the same view. 'Reason why' is ambiguous;

* Dr. Carus thinks that our societies should be called "Societies for Moral Culture." I have sometimes thought that I should myself prefer such a designation, simply because it sounds less technical. But Dr. Carus's distinction between morals and ethics appears to me arbitrary; no unthinking, conventional, or merely reflex action can properly be called moral. Again, Dr. Carus sees no need for our leaving the churches, in case it is duty simply that we are concerned for, since the churches also are concerned for the same thing. But is not Dr. Carus aware that almost no Christian church would receive a person to membership on the strength of a moral aim and purpose alone, that besides this, requirement is made of a confession in some theological creed?

it may refer to standard and it may refer to motive. A motive is always, in one sense, a reason, but in a very different sense from that in which a standard is a reason. A motive is a feeling, a desire; a standard is an object of thought. Now there is what I call a properly moral motive—the desire to do what is right or to live in harmony with one's reason or to obey one's highest thought; these are but different expressions for the same feeling. In its fullness the moral motive is beautifully expressed by George Eliot, in her description of Dorothea (in *Middlemarch*): "She yearned toward the perfect right, that it might make a throne within her and rule her errant will." Asking for another motive beyond the moral motive practically means, what shall I gain by right action, what selfish advantage shall I have from it?—but action under such motives is not moral action at all, and appealing to such motives (i. e., furnishing such reasons) is not explaining morality, but degrading it. Hence Dr. Carus's language as to my 'mysticism' is wide of the mark. He thinks that like other enthusiasts, I regard "science and all close scrutiny with suspicion," and that "the relentless dissections of an exact analysis appear as a sacrilege." I am actually amused at these words; for it is just the absence of close scrutiny into his ideas and exact analysis of them that I thought I observed in Dr. Carus. The clear distinction of things that differ, the avoidance of vague and ambiguous language are surely the first (or at least an indispensable) step towards the scientific understanding of any subject.

This inexactness still appears in Dr. Carus's use of the term "Intuitionalism." "This view," he says, "if it means anything, means that the moral command comes to us in some unaccountable way, mysteriously and directly from some sphere beyond." Not so. Intuitionalism, as used by Professor Sidgwick (to whom Dr. Carus refers and than whom there is no better authority) does not refer to the source of the moral command at all, but to the immediate way in which we are supposed to know that certain things are duties. The obligation, to tell the truth, for example, is regarded by Intuitionalists as a matter of direct perception, not as an inference or deduction from some other obligation. Intuitionalism is not necessarily theological or supernaturalistic; and on the other hand utilitarianism even egoistic utilitarianism may be supernaturalistic, as it was in the hands of Paley. Yes, the evolutionary theory of Dr. Carus, if we give this name to the view that progress, and not happiness, is the supreme end, is just as capable of being ultimately interpreted in a theological or supernaturalistic manner; the rule, work for progress, for the development of human-soul life, may be interpreted as a Divine command as readily as any other rule. In fact, almost all the Ethical theories may be "intuitionalist" in Dr. Carus's vague use of the term.

As to the distinction between Utilitarianism and Hedonism, I acknowledge that Dr. Carus has the right to make it, if etymology and not scientific usage are to determine such matters. The useful and the pleasant are certainly two distinct conceptions. Utilitarianism has always said that the useful was determined by its relation to the pleasant; but abstractly speaking, anything is useful, which serves an end, whatever that end may be. I have not called myself a Utilitarian, but I have been accustomed to say that I sympathized with Utilitarianism so far as it opposed the claim of Intuitionalists to settle special duties by means of ready-made intuitions; but not in so far as it made happiness or pleasure (whether individual or general) the final end. Practically, as I think Mr. Hegeler was aware, I regard progress as a better standard than happiness. Whether it be an ultimate standard is another question, and I think it can hardly be that, since progress (if it be more than mere movement) implies some idea of a goal in the direction of which progress takes place. Utilitarianism, however, as every moral theory worthy of the name, distinguishes between moral goodness and material usefulness. Only a theory which sunk ethics to the level of mechanics would fail to do this. Bentham himself says: "Beneficence apart from benevolence is no virtue; it is not a moral quality—it belongs to a stock or stone, as well as to a human being."

Failure to think out the implications of what he says seems to me to mark Dr. Carus's assertion that the stern facts of life teach us what desires should be suppressed and what wishes should rule supreme. I do not question the value of such experience as a teacher—but all on one condition, namely, that we wish to live, and more than that, that we wish others to live. Apart from such a wish, immorality is as consistent with the "stern facts of life" as morality. The fundamental problem of ethics is deeper than Dr. Carus imagines; and it is because he does not seem to me to go to the roots of things, that his ethics appear to be "something in the air." So far as I can see, it is a purely hypothetical or conditional morality that he gives us; if, for example, we wish for health, he says in substance we must regard the conditions of health—and aside from such a wish obligation has no meaning. The facts are, of course, the same whether we so wish or not; I do not question that many a "jovial companion" has been "buried in the bloom of life." The real question is, was there any obligation upon such an one to care for his life—not did he feel it or even could he be made to feel it, but did it (the obligation) *exist?*

Dr. Carus does not make a careful statement of my views as to the absoluteness of morality. I do not say that conscience is absolute. It appears to me necessary to distinguish between conscience and the moral law, just as we do between science and the facts and laws of which science takes cognizance. I fully admit the "facts of an erring conscience" to which Dr. Carus alludes. So physical science has varied and often erred in the past; but we do not therefore conclude that there have been no unvarying physical laws. Why is it not possible to allow that conscience is a development and by no means infallible, and yet hold that there is an unvarying objective moral law? The real absolute of morality is in the objective principles, not in conscience or the subjective sense of them. This I have brought out in the very lecture from which Dr. Carus quotes, and which perhaps he had not time to read to the end (vide pp. 94 to 101 of *Ethical Religion*). Yet by the moral law I have in mind something quite different from a mere formulation of natural sequences (though I agree with Dr. Carus in holding them to be necessary and unvarying); I mean a commandment, a rule, an imperative—and the special moral rules are so many applications of the fundamental rule to the various special departments and situations of life. I have recently given my views on the important distinction between physical law and moral law in *The New Ideal* (Boston), June and October.

Dr. Carus recognizes the distinction between the leading principle *in* ethics and the philosophical view *back of* ethics. He however holds that such a leading principle must be derived from the philosophical view. This, so far as the words go, is perfectly clear and consistent. But before I can be sure of what they *mean*, I feel that I need an illustration of how the derivation takes place. It was because I thought that Dr. Carus would give us such an illustration that I took up "The Ethical Problem" with such interest. I have already recorded my disappointment; since not only did he not derive his ethics from his "monism," but he classed monism as one of the many "thought-constructions of theorizing philosophers," to which it was not wise for an ethical movement to commit itself. If then, as Dr. Carus says, "without a world-conception we can have no ethics," it is difficult to avoid the conclusion that he has not given us any ethics himself. Will he not try to show in what way the principle of "truthfulness" or that of "the development of human soul-life" is to be derived from Monism—that is, in what way different from that in which it could be derived from Theism or from Materialism?

As to the "ethical stimulus" in my own case, I have not the slightest doubt, and acknowledge it reverently, that whatever I have of it is largely due to the influences of home and of the religious faith in which I was nurtured. But that faith did not include the view that God was the author of right and wrong; and so when my theistic confidence was disturbed, the foundations of morality were not shaken. The Divine will was one with whatever was right, according to my early teaching—and such a view made it perhaps easier to do the right, just as it is often easier for a child to do some task, if the parent askes it; but duty was not made to rest on the Divine will. At bottom the faith in which I was brought up was an ethical faith (just as prophetic Judaism was an ethical faith). I mean that it was a view of the universe dominated by ethical elements. Apart from the idea of a *just, righteous and loving* God, this view would have had little ethical value and imparted little ethical stimulus. It was justice, righteousness, love that had my central reverence, that have it still.

II.

ANSWER TO MR. SALTER BY DR. P. CARUS.

The basic difference between Mr. Salter's and our own position will be pointed out in the Concluding Remarks to our discussion. I refrain here from answering Mr. Salter's reply in a detailed exposition. Mr. Salter repeats his objections, and in order to be explicit we should have to repeat the arguments set forth in former articles. We shall confine ourselves to a few concise remarks on six points:

1) We not only believe that 'a basis of ethics is needed,' but also that it has to be laid down as a necessary part of any ethical movement, that is started for preaching morals. No system of morals can exist without a basis. And who will preach morals without a clear and a systematic conception of ethics?

2) Mr. Salter distinguishes between two theological conceptions the one "basing the right on the will of God", the other re-

garding "God's will as identical with what is right." The distinction appears to us irrelevant, and has no connection with our present discussion.

3) Mr. Salter accuses me of a misuse of his language where I refer to his speaking of 'the reason why' of the moral law. After a careful consideration of the case, I find that the misrepresentation of Mr. Salter's view is entirely due to a lack of clearness on his part. The passage in question runs as follows:

"In fact, Dr. Carus gives no 'reason why' in the sense of a motive beyond the moral motive; and is well aware that to do so would be not to explain but to degrade morality."

I interpreted this sentence in the light of another passage of Mr. Salter's:

"Who can give a reason for the supreme rule? Indeed, no serious man wants a reason."

Mr. Salter in his present article explains the passage under consideration in the following way:

"A 'reason why' in the sense of an ultimate standard of right and wrong I have expressly admitted to be necessary. But after the standard has been formed....the question is sometimes asked, Why should we do the right?" etc.

What Mr. Salter understands by this second Why, which rises after the first Why has been settled, he explains in this way:

"Asking for another motive beyond the moral motive practically means: What shall I gain by right action, what selfish advantage shall I have from it?"

We admit that to ask the question "What selfish advantage shall I have from ethics?" would not be to explain but to degrade morality. But we must confess that this idea never occurred to us. Thus in the passage under consideration, we had no idea that Mr. Salter could understand by 'reason why' an exclusively egoistic motive. If he meant that, he should have said so. With all due appreciation of Mr. Salter's charitableness, we do not feel the need of it, because we are confident that if there was any misuse of language, it was not made by us, and we are not to blame for it.

Aside from the question of priority in the misuse of language, the objection we have to make against Mr. Salter still holds good, in so far as Mr. Salter maintains in other passages, especially in his book, that there is no reason for the supreme rule in ethics. He actually and repeatedly declines to derive the moral ought from the facts of experience, and thus he imagines that that something from which morality grows lies outside the pale of science.

We maintain that no standard is ultimate. Every standard of right and wrong has to be derived from the facts of reality. We investigate the laws of nature, of social development, of a healthy evolution of the soul, and our standard of morality is nothing more or less than conformity to these laws.

If the question is asked of a moral teacher, "Why should we do the right," this in our mind can mean only, "Why should we obey those rules which you lay down as right ?"

Mr. Salter says : "We should do the right out of reverence for the right." Of course, we must have reverence for that which we should do. That which we should do, must be regarded as the highest we can think of. What we wish to do, must not be suffered to be taken into consideration where it conflicts with that which we should do. But considering the fact that we call that which we should do "the right", the prescript "to do the right out of reverence for the right" appears from our standpoint, as tautological.

4) I do not at all deny that the Intuitionalist considers conscience as "a matter of direct perception"; yet at the same time I maintain that the Intuitionalist considers the moral sense, the ought, duty, conscience, or whatever it may be called, as "a fundamental notion, ultimate and unanalyzable". This is the very expression of Professor Sidgwick. Science, it is supposed, cannot analyze conscience, it cannot explain its origin, and thus its existence must remain a mystery to us. See Professor Sidgwick's latest article on the subject, "Some Fundamental Ethical Controversies" in Mind, October, 1889.

5) I read Mr. Salter's article "Obligation and the Sense of Obligation" in *The New Ideal*, where he compares duty with the physical law. Mr. Salter fails to make a distinction between the objective moral law in Nature, on the one hand, which is a physical law as much as gravitation, and duty on the other hand ; the latter being the subjective formulation of our obligation to conform to the moral law. Mr. Salter says :

> "Duty is like gravitation in that it is objective and yet unlike it, in that it (duty) is an ideal, rule, or command, and not a necessarily acting force."

The question arises, What is objective and what is subjective in duty. Mr. Salter says :

> "The *sense* of obligation is just what appears to me to need to be clearly distinguished from the *reality of obligation itself*."*

* The italics are Mr. Salter's own.

This "reality of obligation itself" is an unclear idea; yet I find that it appears in Mr. Salter's book under different names again and again. So long as Mr. Salter feels satisfied with this idea, he will naturally think that the cause of all our differences lies in a failure on my part to think out, as he says, the implications of my assertion that ethics must be based on facts. Mr. Salter's "reality of obligation itself" is a something that is not found among and cannot be derived from facts.*

6) Mr. Salter again expresses his disappointment at my treatment of the Ethical Problem. He says:

> "Not only did he not derive his ethics from his 'Monism' but he classed Monism as one of the many 'thought-constructions of theorizing philosophers to which it was not wise for an ethical movement to commit itself."†

I have purposely avoided the terms "Positivism as well as Monism" because it is not these particular "isms" we fight for, but the ideas that generally go by these names. The word Monism can help nothing. It is not from a name that we expect salvation.

It would be ridiculous to demand that our presentation of Monism or of Positivism should be adopted either by the Ethical Societies or by any one without critical examination. Accordingly we class monism among those systems that have to be examined. But we demand that certain truths be recognized which considered as philosophical principles are generally known as positivism and monism. Positive ethics I have briefly characterized as "the principle of truthfulness." Truth is agreement with facts. We must base our conduct unswervingly upon a correct conception of facts. This implies on the one hand that we should shirk no effort, trouble, or struggle to comprehend truth, and on the other hand that we should never attempt to belie either ourselves or others. The ethics of Monism urges us to heed the most important truth in the realm of facts, namely, the oneness of all-existence. The ethics of Monism teaches us to consider man as a part of the whole universe. The moral man aspires to conform to the All and to the laws of the All; he longs to be one with the power in which we live and move and have our being. In obedience to this impulse man's soul grows; it becomes more and more a microcosm within the macrocosm.

* For a further explanation see the end of the Concluding Remarks to our discussion.

† My answer to this objection is given in the article: "The Moral Law and Moral Rules," p. 117 supra.

SUMMARY.

Making a call of late on Mr. W. M. Salter, I enjoyed with him a conversation, in which we tried to understand one another, in order to arrive, if not at an agreement, yet at a clear statement of our differences. Mr. Salter complained of my presentation of the case, that I did not make distinctions which were necessary to properly comprehend his position and that of the societies for Ethical Culture. He did not object to "a basis of ethics." Whereupon I said that the leaders of the Ethical Societies are perfectly right in not wanting to pledge their members to any religious or philosophical belief, yet they must themselves have a ground to stand on ; they cannot preach ethics without a basis of ethics, for every ethical rule is the expression of a world-conception. By implication then, an ethical movement after all rests on a philosophical basis.

On my saying that the ethics of a spiritualist, of a materialist, of a believer in theism, of an Agnostic, of a Christian, a Jew, a Mohammedan and a Buddhist, actually differ, and that they must differ, Mr. Salter replied that " it was true, they might differ, but it was very possible that *im Grossen und Ganzen* they might agree.

We take exception to this. Even the different denominations of the same religion, for instance Protestants and Catholics, have different ethics. I do not deny that certain ethical rules are regarded as binding by all the religious teachers of the world ; there is a "common conscience," (to use Prof. Adler's term,) developing in mankind, but is not this common conscience, so far as it is not a mere incidental concurrence, the expression of a common world-conception ? A common world-conception (viz., a positivism or a systematized statement of the facts, founded upon scientific investigation) is preparing itself in humanity and together with it we can observe the evolution of the ethics of positivism, viz., of ethics in agreement with facts, an ethics that can be analyzed and comprehended by science.

But this kind of ethics (positive ethics) is found insufficient by Mr. Salter. He maintains that the ethical problem lies deeper than scientific inquiry can reach. "Granted that the knowledge of facts is the basis of ethics," he said, " there is a basis below this basis. In studying facts, we are influenced by a purpose ; we have some end in view, and we study facts and conditions in order that we may know how we shall attain that end. The deeper question is, then, What is the true end ? And the bottom obligation is to regard and seek this end, when it is once rationally determined. What are our matter-of-fact wishes is a secondary matter."

Before answering the question as to this so-called deeper obligation I would ask and answer another question. What is meant by "obligation?" Obligation is simply a statement of ours; it is the formulation of facts for special practical purposes, very appropriately put in the shape of a prescript. The obligation formulated with reference to the facts of our existence, and the conditions of our existence, is already the bottom obligation; there is not a second bottom beneath it.

In that case Mr. Salter says, "your ethical commands are hypothetical; they are conditioned by the wish to be in harmony with society; the wish to be in conformity with the conditions of nature; the wish for life."

Certainly, the ethical rules are in this sense conditioned; for all we can say about the ethical ought is to state the facts as they are: the man who does not care for being a useful member of society, or who does not care for his physical, mental and moral health, who does not care for going to the wall and whose actions are expressions of this indifference, he will do harm to his fellow-beings and he will be doomed to perdition. His soul so far as it is possible will be blotted out, and his life will become a curse to humanity. These are the facts and the moral ought is a statement of such and kindred facts for pastoral purposes, or as a help for self-education.

Here, it appears, lies the ultimate divergency between Mr. Salter's view and our view. Mr. Salter finds, or believes he finds, an obligation of absolute authority beyond facts and beyond the realm of science. We cannot see that an obligation outside of the province of positive facts, the obligation of an absolute authority has any meaning.

This ethical view will naturally appear to him who holds it, deeper than positivism and broader than monism. To the monist however it must appear dualistic, to the positivist metaphysical, to the man of natural science, supernatural. The former standpoint recognizes a profundity where the latter finds a vagary.

THE OUGHT AND THE MUST.

BY JOHN MADDOCK.

Dr. Carus, in his book on the ethical problem, truthfully states that "ethics must have a basis to rest upon." What is true of everything else in the universe is true of ethics—there is a foundation for ethics. As there is but one basis for all things from the standpoint of monism, moral fruit has the same basis as material fruit. If the tree is good, its fruit is good. But the basis of the fruit is not the tree; neither is the basis of morals the man. The basis of both is that subtle power which resides in every atom, in every form. Both are rooted in the "All." Morals are not acquired, they are evolved; and to affirm to this truth is to establish the doctrine of Monism upon a scientific basis.

The conflicting ideas which are expressed upon the ethical subject are caused by not reasoning from the right premise. Philosophers have reasoned from the tree instead of the root. All things in nature are the results of certain combinations. Material fruit is the result of the combined influences of the rain, the earth, the sun, and the specific nature of the tree. All these have their roots in natural law. Moral fruit is the result of the combined influences of the Church, the State, and the intelligence and power of the individual; and all these have their roots in natural law—in the

"All," they all proceed from one. There are different influences exerted in and upon men, but they are maintained by the same power, so that no man can boast of his morality any more than the vine can boast of its grapes. "Ought" is not the word from the standpoint of evolution and monism; whatever degree of moral quality is in a man, he *must* express it according to the combination of organism and environment.

There is no alternative; the laws of nature make no mistakes. With the basis of fire and gunpowder we have nothing to do, but we can play a part in the combination of an explosion when some circumstance demands it. So of ethics; we have nothing to do with the basis, but we become a part of the combination for moral evolution when we are consigned by natural law to our specific places. We do not bear the root, but the root bears us. The hands of the clock do not move the works, but the works move the hands. From the standpoint of evolution and monism, we stand in the same relation to the "All," as the hands do to the works of a clock.

Monism and evolution must not be confounded by separating man from the universe, and giving him self-determining power. This may do for religion, but it will not do for science. By religion man has been condemned; by science he is justified. Ethical societies are not possible [except] when a number of persons desire to organize for the purpose of creating an environment in which they will enjoy themselves the most, and influence one another to "live justly and walk uprightly." The best people, therefore, will be found there. Instead of artificial morality—the product of the whip and threat of religion—there will be real, natural morality according to the principles of science.

The basis of an ethical society is a number of good people, and the basis of good people is the powerful "All" which reigns in all things. As a safe cannot be unlocked until the right combination is found, so ethical societies will not be in a flourishing condition until the natural combination is complete. There must be affirmation; due credit must be given to the power in the universal "All." Scientific affirmation must take the place of the superstitious.

THE OUGHT AND THE MUST.

SCIENCE knows of no arbitrariness in nature; science meets with dire necessity everywhere. Indeed, science is possible only in so far as the laws of nature are irrefragable and immutable.

The scientist who makes the facts of human morality the object of his investigation, can make no exception. He also must recognize the rigidity of law in the actions of man, and if he does not, he is no scientist.

Suppose there were no law in human action, but arbitrary irregularity, so that the same motives affecting the same character under exactly the same circumstances need not result (as from the standpoint of science we must assume that they do) in a definite action, or the inhibition of an action, but might produce results entirely undeterminable even to an omniscient spectator who knew every secret spring, every cog and wheel in the soul-mechanism of man: Suppose there existed any freedom of will in the sense of such an arbitrariness (a view which is generally called indeterminism): in that case, there would be no science of morality; ethics as a science would be an impossibility. But if science is true and if monism, the unitary conception of the world is true, man's activity can form no exception in the great household of nature. Man also must be considered as a part of nature, and man's activity, his moral actions no less than his immoral actions, as strictly determined by law.

Mr. Maddock (taking his standpoint on the ground of science, which is strict determinism,) is perfectly justified in declaring that "we do not bear the root, but the root bears us. The hands of the clock do not move the works, but the works the hands."

Accepting the principle of determinism as correct, must we at the same time accept Mr. Maddock's conclusion that "*ought* is not the word . . . ; whatever degree of moral quality is in a man, he *must* express it according to the combination of organism and environment."

Nature's laws are rigid. The crystal forms itself, if no disturbing influences interfere, with minutely exact regularity. And furthermore, every disturbing influence alters the formation of the crystal in exact agreement with law. This is no exception to the law, it is a confirmation of it. The evolution of feeling beings is also regulated by law. The development of the soul of mankind shows the same necessity of natural law as does the formation of a crystal, and every disturbing influence affects the growth of humanity with precisely the same regularity as in the lower domains of natural processes. Man has become a rational being of necessity—of the very same unavoidable necessity by which, for instance, the shape of the fixed stars and their planets becomes spheroidal.

Having become a rational being man can comprehend his situation, he can understand the laws of nature, and with the help of his knowledge of the laws of nature, he can forecast the result of processes that take place around him. The knowledge man acquires thus becomes the most important factor of his existence; and the great advantages which accrue to man from making a more and more extensive use of knowledge, become a stimulus to develop strongly the tendency of obeying the rational advice which we can derive from experience. It is knowledge which discloses to man that in his individual existence he is only a part of a greater whole, and that he individually can live and prosper only when the community to which he belongs is in a state of health. The life of human society carries and nourishes the life of the individual; the part derives its existence from the whole, as the single cells of our body are sustained so long as the whole organism is vigorous and healthy. Knowledge accordingly creates the *ought*, and the *ought* is nothing that supersedes or stands in contradiction to the *must*; it is a comprehension of the *must*, and this comprehension finds expression in the ethical command of an *ought*. The formulation of the *ought* accordingly is in the course of nature the necessary result of comprehension becoming a factor in the further development of man.

The *must* of nature is not suspended by the *ought*; yet it is utilised. The curse only that under unfavorable conditions attaches to the *must*, is taken away. Man as a rational being, learns to avoid the disturbing influences in the formation of his soul, and human society can attain to a higher perfection. The *ought* of ethics accordingly must be based upon the *must* of science. A careful investigation of the *is* will give us information about the *is to be*. The ethical teacher on the ground of his comprehension of the *is to be*, formulates the stimulus working in the right and desirable direction in the moral command of the *ought*, and raises his warning voice to call attention to the evil consequences

LEADING PRINCIPLES IN ETHICS.

BY F. M. HOLLAND.

THE declaration of the editor of *The Open Court*, (see supra p. 111,) that "The leading principle of ethics must always be the expression of a conception of the world," is so true and important, that I wish to indicate what sort of a conception is needed for this great purpose. And I am particularly glad to take up the subject in a paper whose editor holds with me, that the true test, which is to enable us to tell what is right or wrong, must be sought in the idea of usefulness, rather than in that of pleasure.

It has seemed to me for many years that Utilitarians, while doing much to place moral laws upon a firm scientific basis, above all vagaries of individual caprice and vicissitudes of sectarian dogma, have attributed far too much ethical value to man's desire for pleasure and happiness. The tramp would say, "I am much more happy than if I were hard at work; and I make no one less happy, for people like to be generous." The lazy and licentious savages on the Sandwich Islands seemed perfectly happy. Who of us would follow all the ways to make ourselves happier, which our neighbors would recommend? The cannibal's happiness is not like the missionary's; neither is the book-worm's like the prize-fighter's; nor the school-boy's like his grand-mother's; nor the art critic's like the trapper's; nor the rake's like the philanthropist's. Human ideas of happiness differ so widely, that it is as hard to bring them together into one theory as to make a rope out of sand.

* * *

The Utilitarians are right, however, in looking for the leading moral principle in the relations of man to man. Whatever duties the individual has towards himself and towards the lower animals, are included in those moral laws which originate in his relations to other human beings. This is proved by such facts as that, "moral" and "ethical" are derived from the Greek and Latin words for "customary." The same is the case with the word translated "just" and "righteous" in the New Testament; "justice" comes from the Sanskrit verb "yu" to "bind," and "right" from the Aryan verb "rag," or "rak," to "make straight"; "virtuous" originally meant "manly," "honest," "honorable," and "wicked" "like a witch". Morality got not only its name, but its power from the fact that men have insisted on its observance from the beginning, as the necessary condition of social existence.

Men and women cannot exist except in society; and society cannot exist without some observance of moral laws. Any community would go to pieces, if the members did not respect each others' rights, relieve each others' necessities, and abstain from provoking each others' passions. Thus justice, benevolence, and self-control are conditions of social existence; and thus they become primary virtues, which all men and women desire to have practiced towards them, and which they know they ought to practice themselves. As Leslie Stephens says, (*Science of Ethics*, chapter viii, sec. 39,) "The moral law being, in brief, conformity to the conditions of social welfare, conscience is the name of the intrinsic motives to such conformity." I might add that both the strength and the disinterestedness of conscience may be readily accounted for, when we consider how long these conditions of social existence have been observed, and how earnestly their observance has been insisted upon by priests, heads of families, and other rulers.

* * *

What I wish particularly to point out, however, is that the idea of social existence, while having the advantage of being more definite than that of happiness, labors with it under the disadvantage of insufficiency. It is correct as far as it goes; but it does not go far enough to furnish all the highest moral ideas. The suppression of tramps and drunkards has not been found absolutely necessary for the preservation of social existence, even in the United States; and the natives of the Sandwich Islands might have kept up their filthy habits for thousands of years, without dying out. It is easier to point out this difficulty than to remove it, but I hope I shall be able at least to suggest a method of solution.

These natives, and other savages, are actually dying out; and the reason is that they cannot stand competition with races which are more faithful to what I would call conditions of social progress. I mean, in the first place, such advanced forms of justice, benevolence, and self-control as go beyond the mere requirements of social existence, and improve perpetually under the stimulus of competition. Thus, civilized nations recognize sobriety and veracity as necessary parts of self-control and justice; and benevolence has but recently been so far enlarged as to include humanity to lower animals. Not even agnostics doubt, as Paul did, whether men have duties towards oxen.

* * *

In the second place, I mean some moral ideas which are of later origin than the three primitive ones, but almost as old as human history. Here I would place chastity, patriotism, and physical culture, qualities which have done much to make one community more fit to survive than another, ever since competition began. The advantage of having little children cared for carefully is so great as to cause all nations that have risen above barbarism to insist on matrimonial fidelity; and the tendency of unchastity to weaken virtue and encourage vice has been fully recognized by Christianity. This religion did not pay so much respect as its predecessors to patriotism or physical culture, but modern thought insists that care for health and love of country are as necessary for individual perfection as for social progress.

* * *

The third and highest group of virtues is peculiarly modern, except in so far as two of its members, mental culture and love of personal liberty, were exalted in pagan Athens to a place which they lost after the establishment of Christianity. All that can be said of their value, in promoting chastity, patriotism, physical culture, self-control, justice, and benevolence, is equally true of another great virtue, whose importance has been sadly ignored by teachers of religion and morality. Study of the tendency of indolence and extravagance to produce crime, and of the aid given by industry, economy, foresight, and enterprise to the development of qualities universally acknowledged to be highly virtuous, justifies my giving thriftiness a place among our most sacred duties. All other virtues have become easier and commoner, as life has been made more comfortable than ever before, especially for the poor. These latter now enjoy comforts and luxuries which were, until recently, beyond their reach; and this gain is due, partly to other men's increasing thriftiness, and partly to the help given them by practical philanthropists. Philanthropy differs from benevolence in requiring the assistance of mental culture. Love of liberty, thrift, mental culture, and philanthropy characterize our most advanced civilization, and guarantee future progress. And by progress I mean movement from the primitive condition of mankind toward our present civilization and thence onward in the same direction.

A TEST OF CONDUCT.

BY F. M. HOLLAND.

In a previous article I tried to show that a practicable and accurate test, to show what is right or wrong, may be found in the conditions of social existence and progress. In other words, I hold that actions which tend to help mankind to exist and advance are morally right, that those which tend to destroy the existence of our race, or even to check its progress, are morally wrong, and that those which have no tendency either way, are neither right nor wrong. Motives, of course, are virtuous or vicious, according as they are meant to produce actions by which social progress is promoted or checked; no action which does not proceed from virtuous motives can be right; but an act which is so prompted may be morally wrong, as is the case with persecution, not to mention other conscientious errors which will soon be pointed out.

Calling this test practicable does not mean that it ought to be substituted for conscience as a daily guide. When conscience bids us be generous, chaste, or honest, it is morally safer, as a rule, for us to obey promptly and disinterestedly, than for us to sit down to calculate the probability that this particular action will prove conducive or detrimental to social progress.

And so, when I want to know what time it is, I usually prefer looking at my watch, to making the journey necessary to consult a clock regulated by the Cambridge Observatory. When I happen to pass such a clock, however, I am very glad to see whether my watch differs from it; and I always know which is in the wrong. So if we feel any doubt whether we ought to feed a tramp, or help wreck a liquor saloon, or resist force with force, or take a vow of celibacy, we cannot be sure that we are acting virtuously, unless we choose some guide less subject to be perverted by passion and prejudice, than conscience.

The test I propose does not justify the encouragement of mendicancy by thoughtless charity, or the wanton disturbance of the public peace. It permits both nations and individuals to defend themselves; but it condemns wars of conquest, as likely not only to retard the general progress, but to curse the conquerors with retaliation from abroad and despotism at home.

Thus this test shows its accuracy by censuring nothing universally acknowledged to be virtuous, and sanctioning nothing generally considered vicious. What I claim most confidently for it, is its capacity to furnish a full code of duties. As I repeat the list already given, I will try to arrange them in the order justified by their fitness to promote social progress. And first, should come a virtue which has been insisted upon by all rulers and teachers from the very beginning, which is still required peremptorily of all the members of society, and which has also the peculiar merit of not being liable to excess. All this is true of no virtue but justice.

The only danger about recognizing the rights of

others is that of failing to do so fully. If I give my neighbor more than his due, I act unjustly towards myself or some other member of society. Whatever is just is obligatory; and whatever is not just is unjust.

In the same way, when we enlarge the definition of justice so far as to include veracity, we find not only that whatever is not true is under condemnation because it is false, but also that, when I tell my neighbor all he is entitled to hear, and nothing more, I comply fully with the requirements of social progress, as well as with those of the law of justice.

It may be noticed that I agree more closely with ancient than modern moralists, in placing justice above benevolence; but I am inclined to think that this last virtue is so liable to be carried to excess that it ought to stand lower than justice, though among other duties which are constantly obligatory on all the members of society, within the limits marked out by the conditions of social progress.

Thriftiness is so liable to be carried to excess, that it has been regarded with little favor by Christian moralists; and its cultivation ought to be kept in strict and constant subordination to that of justice. It must, however, be remembered that one of the most uniform characteristics of criminals is incapacity for success in business or even for steady work, and also that thrifty nations have been highly virtuous in all other respects, as well as very successful in making progress. The states in our own Union which have a peculiarly industrious, frugal, and enterprising population can show the largest amount of benevolence, patriotism, and scholarship, as well as the smallest taint of lawlessness, dishonesty, drunkenness unchastity, and other gross vice. An honest and thrifty nation, family, or individual, is so much more likely than a thriftless one to be virtuous, and not vicious, that I should place thriftiness second in the scale of duties; while the danger of excess will be sufficiently guarded against by keeping justice high above it, and giving the next below to benevolence, a virtue absolutely necessary to social progress, if only to provide adequate care for young or temporarily disabled members of society.

This reason also makes the maintenance of the family tie so important, that we may give the fourth place to chastity, which has the farther advantage of greatly promoting the culture of all other good qualities. This last is also true of the kindred virtue, self-control, especially when we define it as including temporance.

Having thus filled five places, we must certainly give the next one to physical culture. Utter neglect of this duty would soon make it impossible to practise any other; and it is hardly necessary to say that healthy people are generally much more thrifty, benevolent, honest, patriotic, intelligent, fond of liberty, and capable of self-control than invalids are. The care now given by civilized governments to make all the surroundings of daily life healthy, for the poor as well as the rich, ensures not only rapid progress in civilization, but steady moral improvement.

Then last come duties which are not required of all the members of society, but are highly obligatory on those men and women who are capable of performing them. Here, in order of relative importance, may be placed love of liberty, mental culture, patriotism, and philanthropy. All four are very liable to be carried to excess; and their manifestation should be carefully restricted by the claims of higher duties, especially justice.

First among these four, I put love of liberty, because lack of this virtue was the main cause of the decay of classic civilization. The capacity of vigorous rulers to promote social progress, and the liability of anarchy to check it, are so great as often to cause the establishment of despotism; but this has always been found, sooner or later, to be incompatible with further progress. The most highly advanced communities need most to have their influential members love liberty with a zeal ever on the watch against oppression.

Mental culture seems to be somewhat less important, and not so necessary as physical culture, self-control, and other qualities which must always be added in order to make it permanently useful, and which have proved extremely beneficial where it has been utterly lacking. I cannot insist too strongly on the fact that the life and strength of society lies mainly in its thrifty, honest, and healthy members. All its members ought to do their utmost to belong in this class; but all cannot be scholars, patriots, or philanthropists.

Patriotism is much more generally obligatory at election times in this country than during the rest of the year; and there are many countries which scarcely permit its manifestation in time of peace, as well as some rulers who give it no opportunity of legitimate exercise, except in insurrection. Those of our own citizens who are constantly in charge of our national interests are under so great moral responsibility, that patriotism rises for them to a very high place in the rank of duties.

The same may be said of philanthropy for the few who are able to practice it successfully; but it must be remembered that this requires not merely wealth, leisure, and earnestness, but also sound judgment, high business capacity, and thorough acquaintance, not only with the evils actually existing in society, but with the actual working in times past of various institutions and reforms. There are few ways in which one can do so much good as in philanthropy, or so much mischief.

Those who ignore the claims of justice, self-control, thriftiness, love of liberty, and mental culture, cannot attempt philanthropy except to its discredit and to the public injury. There is no space left to dwell on what may be done by wise and just philanthropists, especially in diminishing poverty, which has been dangerously increased by thoughtless and lavish benevolence. Highest in honor among the men and women who carry society onwards and upwards are these philanthropists.

A CRITICISM BY PROF. FRIEDRICH JODL.

In your work "The Ethical Problem" I have read much with the heartiest approval, and with admiration of your frequently so happy, popular style of expression. Other things there were, however, that neither met my approval, nor were intelligible to me.

As the two points in your views with respect to which this was most the case, let me cite your polemical attitude towards Hedonism, and your reference to nature as a moral standard. What you oppose as Hedonism may deserve, indeed, your attacks; but I know of no author since La Rochefoucauld and Helvetius that has advocated such a hedonism.

The principle of general welfare as a criterion of the ethical value of character and acts, has, so far as I can see, been entirely neglected by your criticism. And how we can hope to overcome the old orthodox conception of ethics, without representing the new scientific ethics as eudemonism, I do not know. Let man, in his most virtuous conduct and in his most heroic acts, seek his happiness, on condition only that it take place in a manner and with means that are qualified also to promote the happiness of others. The whole question simply is, to teach men to seek happiness in the right way. Happiness itself need not therefore be eliminated from their thoughts. And this conscious striving after happiness is the very characteristic also that distinguishes human conduct from all natural phenomena. Nature is wholly disregardful of individuals; she merely creates, produces in the greatest possible abundance, and thus maintains herself in equilibrium. What sacrifices this may cost, the destruction caused by it, is of no consequence. Her procedure is the type of what we may characterize as colossally brutal immorality. But her human victims gradually came to speech and thought: the whole history of morality is to me nothing but a growth of nature out and beyond itself, an aspiration to replace natural laws by the laws of rational will, to win for every living being his rights to put into the blind-mechanical play of natural forces the soul of a purpose—eudemonism. How much have we already won, how much yet remains? Reason and will, however, are still too feeble, we still copy too much "our good mother nature," confide ourselves only too willingly to her guidance, and we constantly have to experience that what she wants and what we want are two wholly different things.

There are many passages in my *Geschichte der Ethik* which represent my views perhaps more precisely and fully than I have done here. Yet I state them here again, because our common cause, it seems to me, demands unity on this very point.

IN ANSWER TO PROFESSOR JODL.

Prof. Friedrich Jodl advances two points in which he cannot agree with the views presented in *The Ethical Problem.* First he criticises my polemical attitude towards Hedonism, and secondly he declares that Nature cannot be considered as a moral standard. Concerning the latter point, I have to say that the demeanor of Nature (if we use the poetical licence of personifying her) cannot be and I suppose never has been proposed as a model for imitation. Nature is neither moral nor immoral, but Nature and Nature's laws are that immutable power conformity to which makes man moral. In this sense alone can Nature be said to be the moral standard, and ethics must be grounded upon our knowledge of Nature.

What we say of Nature holds good also for the theological conception of that power in which we live and move and have our being. There is no pleading with God (Job 16, 21); no entering into judgment with him (Job 34, 23); no multiplying words against him (Job 34, 37). The apostle says: "O man, who art thou that repliest against God? Shall the thing formed say to him that formed it, Why hast thou made me thus?" In short God is neither moral nor immoral; he is the standard of morality. It would be a poetical licence to speak of God as being moral, for morality is obedience to his commands, or conformity to his immutable will.

Professor Jodl says:

> "The whole history of morality is to me nothing but a growth of Nature out and beyond itself; an aspiration to replace natural laws by the laws of rational will."

It appears that Professor Jodl has a different conception of Nature from what we have. I see no possibility of replacing natural laws or growing beyond Nature. Says Shakespeare:

> "Yet nature is made better by no mean,
> But nature makes that mean; so, over that art,
> Which, you say, adds to nature, is an art,
> That nature makes . . . . . .
> . . . .
> . . . . This is an art
> Which does mend nature—change, rather; but
> The art itself is nature!"—*Winter's Tale.*

Concerning our objections to Hedonism, Professor Jodl says:

> "How we can hope to overcome the old orthodox conception of ethics without representing the new and scientific ethics as eudemonism, I do not know."

This passage corroborates my conviction that hedonism and utilitarianism were put forth in opposition to the old orthodox conception of ethics, which declares that the ethical motive in man, conscience or the sense of duty, is of supernatural origin. The orthodox as well as their antagonists believe that the pursuit of happiness alone is natural; the natural man seeks pleasure and shuns pain. The presence of higher motives, accordingly, is considered by the orthodox believer as a proof of supernaturalism, while his adversary feels constrained to deny their existence.

It appears to me that the old orthodox conception of ethics (religious ethics) contains a truth which the hedonistic ethics (irreligious ethics) does not contain. The old orthodox conception of ethics, although represented in mythological allegories, is nevertheless based upon the facts of life. It has grown naturally; and its main mistake is that it represents some natural facts the origin of which it did not understand, as supernatural interferences; it misinterprets facts; it has not as yet developed from the phase of a belief in magic into a scientific conception.

Hedonistic ethics, on the other hand, must appear as artificial. It represents ethics as eudemonology, i. e. the science of attaining the greatest possible maximum of pleasure over pain, and it goes on to explain that the peace of soul following the performance of duty is a satisfaction much greater than all the pleasures of the world. True, but it is this kind of explanation which appears artificial to me.

Brutus condemned his sons to death and had them executed, because he considered it as his duty. We may doubt whether it really was his duty, but he certainly did it because he considered it as his duty; and who will deny that it was a most painful duty which gave pleasure to nobody and contributed nothing to the general happiness of Rome; it only tended to preserve that spirit of Roman sternness which made the Romans fit not only to conquer but also to rule the world, and to evolve for the first time in history an international code of laws and a standard of justice. The Romans suffered much from the impulse natural to them; and I am inclined to believe that they never attained a greater happiness than other nations. If happiness is the ultimate test of morality, Cyrene was superior in morality to Sparta, and Sybaris to Athens.

Can we say that the Spartans, or the Romans were

prompted in their actions by a desire for pleasure, that sternness was a pleasure to them? I should say that we cannot. Is the fighting cock impelled to fight by a desire for pleasure, and does the pleasure of fighting really outweigh in his opinion the pains of his wounds and the fear of danger when confronted with superior enemies? It appears to me that in animals as well as in man there are many impulses the motives of which rise from the nature, from the character of the creature, which cannot be explained as a pursuit of happiness. The fighting cock must fight under given circumstances because it is his nature. Certain structures are in his brain that impel him to fight. Does the stone fall to the ground because it gives it pleasure, or doesn't it rather fall because it must fall in agreement to its nature? How often does it happen that a man follows an irresistible impulse, although he knows that it will give him pain. Thus it happens that men of good intentions commit evil actions, and rascals sometimes act morally, in spite of themselves; not at all with the desire to avoid pain or to gain pleasure, but simply because the impulse to act in this way lives in their soul. It is a part of their nature, and under given circumstances they cannot help letting that impulse pass into act, even though they know that they will have to regret the effects of the deed. It will in many persons take a long time and much exercise of will till this knowledge acquires sufficient strength as a motive for prohibiting actions which will be regretted.

Every science deals with a certain province of nature or it limits its inquiries to a special abstraction. Thus mechanics deals with motions. Purely mechanical motions do not even exist. The mechanical aspect of motions excludes many properties which are inseparably connected with the things in motion. But the method of abstraction is a limitation, indispensable to science; it is the method by which alone we can comprehend the world. Ethics, it appears to me is no less limited to a peculiar aspect and to a special province, than are for instance zoölogy, botany, or mathematics, geodesy, etc. Ethics deals with all those impulses of the soul which in the popular expression are comprised under the name of duty, conscience, the ought, or moral sense. Obedience to these impulses is sometimes pleasurable, sometimes painful; yet whether they are accompanied with pleasure or pain is of secondary importance in ethics. The pleasurable and painful elements in man's actions do not belong to the abstraction of ethics. They need not and they cannot be excluded from ethics, but they are of secondary importance and do not constitute the properly moral element. We might just as well speak of colors when discussing mechanical laws. We may say that yellow gold will outweigh an equal mass of white silver. But the yellowness of gold and the whiteness of silver have nothing to do with the weight. Thus pleasure and pain are qualities which are inseparably connected with moral actions, and it is certainly advisable to consider their relation to the strength of motives. Yet to search in them for the standard of morality would be as wrong as to set up yellowness as a unit of weight.

The investigations of modern psychology, it appears to me, throw much light upon the mechanical apparatus of soul-activity. An impulse placed into the mind of a man by suggestion prompts to action with the same necessity as, for instance, a wound-up spring exercises a pressure and sets a clock in motion.

For example a hypnotized subject receives the suggestion to stab one of the physicians present; a piece of card-board is given her instead of a dagger and she commits the deed with the imaginary weapon. The stabbed physician pretends to be dead, and the woman is asked why she committed the murder. "He was a bad man," she answered. "But is that a sufficient reason to kill a man?" the woman was asked. "In this case it is," she said, "for he attempted to assault me." The action is done because the impulse exists; the motives are often invented afterwards; and the attempt to explain all actions as intended to pursue happiness appears to me as such an after-invention. A scientific explanation should show how the different impulses, and especially how the ethical impulses, that which we have defined as superindividual motives, develop. If we are to define the feeling attending the performance of something that could not be avoided, not only as satisfaction but even as happiness, in that case only should we have to concede that all ethical aspirations are pursuits of happiness. The Buddhist monk who does not believe in personal immortality, and inflicts most cruel tortures upon himself to atone for the sin of existence would in that case have to be said to pursue happiness. Pursuit of happiness would then be identical with any kind of action.

If the happiness attained or attainable were to be considered as the standard of measurement for the morality of actions, we should have to call the preparation for a ball extremely moral. Likewise, if the utility of an act were to be considered as the standard of measurement, the invention of the sewing machine would as such be a moral act. I do not deny that the wish to spread joy and also the aspiration to make oneself useful are moral; but neither the happiness nor the usefulness attainable by this or by that act constitutes the properly moral element. The properly moral element is an entirely different kind of abstraction. It consists of those motives or impulses to action which regulate conduct, not from the egotistic standpoint, but from the standpoint of a greater whole, to which the person who acts belongs.

Is there any doubt about progress being a law of the development of the human race? It can fairly be assumed that all the aspirations which serve the progress of the race, are to be considered as moral impulses. Nevertheless, it is very doubtful whether progress will bring more happiness. One thing is sure: Progress will bring more comforts, and together with an increase of comforts, it brings more wants. Life having more wants causes greater troubles in satisfying the wants. If there is any increase of happiness, there will certainly be a greater increase in sensitiveness to pain; and the condition of a savage who feels no need to cover his nakedness, is enviable in comparison to the wretchedness of a civilized man, if he fails somehow in his struggle for existence. If happiness is to be considered as the standard of measurement for morality, I doubt greatly whether it would not be more moral to keep humanity in a state of childhood and ignorant innocence. Pessimism indeed, as represented by Schopenhauer and his followers, considers the development of individual life as the original sin, as the initial *faux pas*, the first wrong step of the "will to live." Sin, according to Germany's neo-Buddhistic philosopher, is individual existence, and the meed of sin is all the evils of individual existence, pain, old age, and death, and the happiness aspired for is a mere illusion.

If happiness, or joy, or pleasure, were indeed the standard of morality, I am inclined to say, that it would be better if the All were a mere play of unfeeling forces, developing and dissolving again solar systems in their luminous grandeur without evolving feeling and thinking beings on the surface of planets. The problem in ethics, however, it appears to me, is not how to set up a standard of morality of our own in contradiction to the laws of nature, but how to conform to the laws of nature. Science leads to Monism, and Monism teaches us to consider ourselves as a part of nature. The standard of morality cannot be derived from man's likes or dislikes ; it cannot be based upon the separateness, the individuality, of his existence. Ethics can rest only upon the recognition of natural laws. We must know how nature operates in the universe, how nature produces us, how she moulds us, and we must comprehend that all our individual actions are acts of nature.

If God is defined as the All in so far as it is a cosmos of orderly laws, we shall find that the old orthodox morality contains more truth than might appear from the standpoint of an unbeliever. Hedonism, Utilitarianism, Eudemonism, or any other system that has arisen in opposition to the old orthodox ethics of the dogmatic religions, represent an important phase in the further evolution of ethical ideas, but for the mere sake of overcoming their adversary they discard together with the errors of supernaturalism, the valuable truth that is contained in the ethics of the old religions. The merits of these ethical systems of opposition should not be underrated ; but it appears to me that they have not solved the problem. We must search for a solution of the ethical problem in a higher synthesis of the old ethics of orthodox religion, and the oppositional ethics of all the different happiness-theories. It is this higher synthesis which we have attempted to present in our solution of the Ethical Problem.

RELIGION AND SCIENCE—THEIR INCONGRUITY.

A CRITICISM.

BY ROBERT LEWINS, M. D.

"To say I have changed my opinion, is only to say I am wiser to-day than I was yesterday."—*Pope*.

HAVING recently read, with much interest and profit, Dr. Carus's *Fundamental Problems* and *Lectures on Ethics*, I am desirous, with his sanction, and in accordance with the noble sentence which closes the preface to the latter work: "Criticisms are solicited from all who dissent from its views; wherever any one will convince me of error, he will find me ready to change my opinion and to accept the truth whatever it be,"—to offer a few but crucial objections to his in many respects harmonious world-scheme. I shall be very brief as the points at issue are quite simple and self-evident.

I base all I have to say on Positive Science, which, in our *fin de siècle* age at all events, entirely eliminates "Spiritualism" of every shade, and brings us face to face with the purest (its gainsayers term it crudest) Materialism, or Somatism. I think a very little reflection ought to convince all who have overcome prejudice and superstition to see that the interaction between an immaterial and material entity, from their incompatibility, is logically unthinkable.

Spirit or *Anima* was to the Ancients really material, being prefigured as a thin vaporous substance like the hypothetical ether of modern chemistry and physics. Plato insists that our souls are made of the same material as the fixed stars, which alone is Materialism unmasked. So that when Greek Philosophy speaks of animism, it can note something quite different from what our Religion labels "Spirit."

My position is that the union or *eirenicon* of Science and Religion is impossible. Just as that of Matter and *Anima*. And that where Religion is Science and Reason are not, and *vice versa*.

I prefer arguing the point in dispute on physiological *data*, the offspring of the century, now verging to its close, in which we live. At one fell *coup* we thus, in the simplest and most *naive* manner, get entirely scot-free of the dual distinction between soul, which is only another word for life, like *Psyche*, and body. Dr. Carus appears to me to make too much use of the compound epithet "Soul-Life," which at best is only tautology. Define Life, as Medicine, now the science of human nature itself, does, as the sum of the organic functions, and a consistent Monism, unifying Self and the Cosmos, *i. e.* subject and object, is the self-evident result. It is the identification of Being and Thinking, only reached by a short cut as compared with the Kantian, Hegelian, or all other Metaphysics. Kant denying *Ding an sich* exactly hits the mark. Only he is not consistent with his principle. Indeed it is difficult to make out his real meaning, for *ehrlich* as, in general, he was, he still practised a certain mental reservation, as he himself during his most energetic period, confesses in a letter to Moses Mendelsohn. As Goethe says, *Gefühl ist Alles*, and *Gefühl* and *Bewusstsein*, or Consciousness, are synonymes. Till an object is subjectived by entering the sphere of consciousness, it can have no rational value and is as non-existent to a sentient being after it has sown its intellectual wild oats.

And this *apodeixis* alone proves my case that there is, and can be no other "outer" world than our senses, of which Thought is a mode made for us. We are thus at once both *creator* and *creation* in the only sphere, relational or phenomenal, to which we have access. Religion haunts the Absolute sphere, and that is quite out of our lines as utterly inaccessible to human thought. The mere fact that all percepts and concepts are produced in a human mind (brain) ought to convince us that higher than humanity and ultimately Egoity, Man and the Ego cannot range. God therefore, like every "thing" (concept) else, must be a brain-made phenomenon and the only noumenon, if we care to use these now familiar terms which is non-essential, is *Ourself*.

Pope, in the fourth book of the *Dunciad*, is very severe on this lapse from Absolutism. And yet it is really his own theory in his *Essay on Man*, when he traces Heaven to the passion of pride and Hell to that of spite. I could argue this question in other ways, indeed have done so in former years *ad nauseam*. Even on transcendental grounds from the Omnipresence of Deity, which as Pantheistic practically forecloses all Personal Divinity, or form of Divine Worship. But the above argument seems all-sufficient. Regard Life as organized function and Death as its exhaustive and cessation and the immemorial fallacy of the impossible interaction of soul, or mind, on Matter is dissipated at one blow as by a thunderbolt. Nothing ever really dies but only changes its form—and the constituents of our present bodies are as eternal as are Suns and Planets. No real distinction differentiates Time and Eternity, Space and Immensity. And both Concepts, like all others, have no other source that we can hope or fear to reach, than *Ourself.*

It is clear from modern Chemistry that no partition separates the organic and inorganic worlds. And therefore, putting aside all the modern sciences, we reach the physiological (non-spiritual) result equally well on the *data* of Newtonian cosmology. The eschatological colophon of the Attraction of Gravity is to make matter active, not passive and inert. No foreign factor or "Spirit" is therefore needed to "*animate*" what by an inseparable *Vis Insita* is already capable of doing its own work. And Deity *inter alios omnes* is thus an illogical superfluity, must be so if Self be all in all.

Natural Religion, of which Voltaire and other sceptics of the eighteenth century were votaries seems a retrogression from the higher "revealed" ones, which were evidently the well-meant, but to us now-a-days, futile and immoral attempts of humanitarian enthusiasts like Christ and Mahomet—to supplant the cruel "God or Law of Nature" by a Being with whom, on certain terms fatal indeed to human dignity and progress a *modus vivendi* became possible.

Mr. Darwin traces all the different species of animals and plants from a few originally called into being by a Creator. But, in a letter to Sir Joseph Hooker, he subsequently retracts that rash assertion and expresses lasting regret that he had ever so far truckled (*sic*) to vulgar opinion as to have broached so unscientific a *genesis* of living beings. It conflicts entirely with the real Principles of Evolution—as does Mr. Spencer's cryptic Agnosticism of the *Unknowable*.

SCIENCE AND RELIGION.

IN ANSWER TO DR. LEWINS'S CRITICISM.

BY DR. PAUL CARUS.

DR. ROBERT LEWINS is one of the most original thinkers of the present day; but being original he uses a terminology of his own, and it may sometimes be difficult to understand his meaning. He characterises his view as Hylo-idealism, which appears to me similar to Monism to the extent that it has been invented for the purpose of combining the truths of idealism as well as realism.

The soul, certainly, can no longer be considered as a material being. Yet "soul" is not quite so identical with "life" as Dr. Lewins declares. We cannot think of a soul without its having life. Similarly we cannot think of matter without its being mass. Soul and life, matter and mass, are abstractions, different in kind, each of which in a certain sense covers the same sphere. The physicist may very well speak of the mass of a certain piece of matter and the life of a certain soul. Soul is not life and nothing but life. Soul is life of a certain kind. We can speak of soul-life with the same propriety that we speak of the movement of a mechanism, though a mechanism is movement of a special kind. If life is as Dr. Lewins says, "organized function," would it be wrong to speak of the functions of an organism?

The application of Goethe's words "Gefühl ist Alles," as made by Dr. Lewins, is very ingenious, but scarcely redeemable. He says: "Till an object is subjectived by entering the sphere of consciousness, it can have no rational value, and is as non-existent to a sentient being after it has sown its intellectual wild oats." Can, for instance, bacilli so long as they do not "enter the sphere of consciousness," be regarded as non-existent to sentient beings?

Dr. Lewins understands by religion the absence of science and reason. He says: "Religion haunts the absolute sphere, and that is quite out of our lines as utterly inaccessible to human thought." Similarly philosophy was formerly supposed to haunt the realm of the absolute. The religion of the absolute has been given up just as much as the philosophy of the absolute, but philosophy and religion will not perish on account of religious and philosophical errors. Far from considering religion as antagonistic to science, we understand by religion the practical application of science; it is the regulation of life in accord with our conception of the world.

MR. GOLDWIN SMITH ON MORALITY AND RELIGION.

Mr. Goldwin Smith discusses the ethical question in an article in the *Forum*, entitled "Will Morality survive Religion?" He presents no definite solution but sufficiently indicates one, and that is a denial of the question; between the lines we read the answer, Morality will not survive Religion. He says:

"The withdrawal of religious belief must, however, one would think, have begun to operate, and some observers may be in a position to say what the effect is and how far philosophy or science has been able to fill the void. As the twilight of theism and Christianity still lingers, nobody expects a sudden change. Least of all does anybody expect a sudden outbreak of immorality among philosophers, whose minds are elevated by their pursuit and in whom the coarser appetites are sure to be weak; so that the sensitiveness which men of this class are apt to show, whenever a connection is suggested between religious and moral agnosticism, is out of place."

Mr. Goldwin Smith illustrates his position vividly by presenting to us "some specimens of the moral as well as of the religious agnostic." The murderer Birchall is described in the following words:

"As he was the son of a clergyman and had been well brought up, he must have been thoroughly enlightened, and cannot have been led into crime by anything like the brutal ignorance of moral law which is often the heritage of the gutter child. Nor does it seem that evil passion of any kind was overpoweringly strong in him. The attempts of the enemies of capital punishment to make out a case of moral insanity were in this case more faint than usual. It even appears that there was an amiable side to his character. His college companions liked him. He seems to have been a loving husband, and there was something touching and almost heroic in the effort which he successfully made, while he was awaiting execution, to master the fear of death and to write his autobiography for the benefit of his wife. The autobiography, it is true, is nothing more than the vulgar record of a fast undergraduate's life at an inferior college ; but this does not detract from the nerve shown in writing it, and in illustrating it with comic sketches, beneath the shadow of the gallows. He only happened to have occasion for his friend's money. It is possible that if Birchall, instead of being sent to college—where a youth of his stamp was sure to be idle, and, being idle, to become dissipated—had been set to regular work in an office under a strong chief, he might have gone decently through life, though he would have been a very selfish man. But he was a thorough-going agnostic in morals as well as in religion. Evidently he felt not a twinge of remorse for what he had done. No doubt he cursed his own carelessness in having, when he was destroying all the proofs of identity on the corpse, overlooked the cigar case, the name written on which gave the fatal clew ; but the recollection of having killed a confiding friend for his money evidently gave him no more concern than as if he had slaughtered a bear for its skin. Bred a gentleman, he admirably preserved his dignity and impressiveness of manner when standing at bay against his pursuers, and he showed the same qualities for the two months during which a whole community was staring at him through the bars of his cage, when the least sign of weakness would have been at once proclaimed. When he was sentenced, he remarked, with a philosophy which appears to have been genuine, that life is short for all, and that there is not much difference between a term of a few months and one of a few years. He might have added that he would make his exit from life more nearly without pain than ninety-nine men out of a hundred."

A similar striking case is found in the person of William Palmer, the Rugeley murderer, who also, Mr. Goldwin Smith says, "was evidently a perfect moral agnostic. He behaved at his trial as if he had been watching a game of chess, showed not the slightest sign of remorse, and met death with perfect apathy, if not with Birchall's genteel composure."

Mr. Goldwin Smith adds:

"As moral agnostics these men were low specimens of a character of which the great Napoleon was the highest. . . . He (Napoleon) was simply 'The Prince' of Machiavelli, that prophet of moral agnosticism."*

The present situation is described in the following words:

"Religious agnosticism is gaining ground, not so much perhaps in America as in Europe, because America is less speculative than Europe and because free churches do not provoke sceptical criticism so much as establishments; but everywhere religious agnosticism is manifestly gaining ground. Are we to expect a corresponding growth of moral agnosticism? We shall not have a crop of Birchalls and Palmers, still less of Napoleons; but may we not have a crop of men who will regard morality as a superstition or a convention, and will do what suits their own interest?

*I beg to differ in some respects from this view concerning Napoleon's character. Napoleon's success is not due to his unprincipled egotism and unscrupulousness; it is due to the actual services he rendered to his nation and to humanity in general. He may be considered as a "scourge of God" but even as such he was the most indispensable man of his era. He was a scourge to Germany, but his achievements in having swept out of existence so many antiquated institutions and principalities, especially in having broken to pieces the old rotten Roman-Teutonic Kaiser-humbug, so as to make a regeneration of Germany possible, alone made his career a great blessing to Germany which outweighs all the innumerable injuries and suppressions he caused her. Let us not look to the vices of a man to explain his success. I am inclined to declare *a priori* that a successful man must have some virtues which are the causes of his success, and if he has great vices, it is, to say the least, probable that his virtues will eclipse his vices. The effects of the virtues will remain, the effects of his vices will disappear in time.

Does Mr. Goldwin Smith believe in Machiavelli? I do not believe in Machiavelli. The great king who wrote the "Anti-Machiavelli" has refuted, not only in words but also in deeds, the theory that unprincipled rascality is the best policy for a king to maintain himself upon a throne. It is due to Frederick the Great's maxim that "the king is the first servant of the state" which proved a live presence with almost all his successors, that a scion of his family now occupies the imperial throne of Germany.

Greece, after the fall of her religion, had the moral anarchy depicted by Thucydides and ascribed by him to that fall. She had the moral agnosticism of the Sophists. Rome, after the departure of the religious faith to which Polybius, in a famous passage, ascribes her public morality, had the immorality of the Empire. On the decline of the Catholic faith in Europe, ensued the moral agnosticism of the era impersonated in Machiavelli. In each case, into the void left by religion came spiritual charlatanry and physical superstition, such as the arts of the hierophant of Isis, the soothsayer, and the astrologer—significant precursors of our modern 'medium.'"

We feel inclined to say, this is a very pessimistic diagnosis of the future, but we are told:

"There is nothing pessimistic in this; no want of faith in the future of humanity, or in the benevolence of the power by which human destiny is controlled. The only fear suggested is that society may have a bad quarter of an hour during the transition, as it has had more than once before."

A 'bad quarter of an hour' for humanity may mean the ruin of nations! Was the pessimism of Tacitus unjustified because other nations arose in a grander glory after the ignominious ruin of Rome that followed its moral decline? Pessimism means to us that we ourselves and our nation will see this 'bad quarter of an hour,' and if it comes it will be terrible to all concerned. It will come like a deluge to sweep away the innocent and the good together with the guilty.

Pessimism in any other sense is not justified. The world is such that if the nation to whom by natural advantages the future of humanity seems to be entrusted, shows herself unwilling or unable to fulfil her mission, other nations will arise and take her place. We Americans especially are more inclined than others, and I do not deny that in some respects our hope is justifiable, to consider ourselves as the children of promise. But at the same time we are apt to forget that our mission implies duties. It is not enough to say, "We have Abraham to our father." The children of promise must be worthy of their duties; if they are not they will be rejected. Yet as to the whole, as to the evolution of mankind, there is no need of being pessimistic. "For I say unto you that God is able of these stones to raise up children unto Abraham." Evolution will not be checked because we prove unfit to carry the torch of progress. We shall, in that case, go to the wall and the torch will be handed to others.

And here we come to the point of disagreement with Mr. Goldwin Smith. He says:

> "Evolution is not moral, nor can morality be educed from it. It proclaims as its law the survival of the fittest, and the only proof of fitness is survival."

Evolution, it is true, is in a certain sense, "a quasi-mechanical and necessary process"; it "will fulfil itself without effort or sacrifice" on my part, or on your part, or on the part of any individual. Yet in another sense, evolution is not a merely mechanical process;* nor can it fulfil itself without the effort or sacrifice of mankind. The question is not whether my help is indispensable for evolution to fulfil itself, the question is whether my soul will enter into the evolutionary movement, or to use a biblical term, whether I shall enter into life eternal, as an element representing an

* Every motion is mechanically explainable, or in other words, every motion can be described in mechanical formulas, i. e. there is a uniformity of motions which can be formulated in the laws of mechanics. Evolution considered as a movement sweeping onward over the life of mankind is a mechanical process. But the mechanical aspect of natural processes is only one side; it does not cover the whole of reality. Not even the fall of a stone can be considered as a purely mechanical process. See the author's remarks on the subject in "Fundamental Problems" (p. 115 et seqq.), "Can the World be Mechanically Explained?" and his article "Some Questions of Psycho-Physics," *The Monist* No. 3, p. 401.

upward or as one representing a downward pull. To speak of a single individual as helping evolution is something like helping God in governing the world. The individual does not come into consideration at all from an ethical standpoint, but that alone which is represented in the individual.

Mr. Goldwin Smith still recognises, particularly with regard to the gentler virtues, the influence of religion upon our code of ethics. He says:

> "There is no saying how much of theism, or even of Christianity, still mingles with the theories of agnostics. When the agnostic assumes that the claims of the community are superior to those of the individual, when he uses such a term as 'conscientious,' and even when he speaks with reverence of an 'eternal source of energy and force,' careful scrutiny of his expressions might discover a trace of theism."

Certainly, there is a trace of theism in any kind of morality, even if the expression "the *eternal source* of energy" be rejected. We at least do most emphatically reject it as a dualistic and a meaningless phrase. Nevertheless, morality means obedience to some law higher, grander, and nobler than our individual interests. The recognition of the authority of this law is the kernel of all religion, it is also the truth contained in the idea of God.

Mr. Goldwin Smith says:

> "The saying that if God did not exist it would be necessary to invent him, was very smart but very silly. Nothing can be done for us by figments. Whosoever will be saved, before all things it is necessary that he keep his allegiance to the truth."

With this we perfectly agree. Nothing can be done for us by figments. But if all the nations that cease to believe in, and at the same time also cease to obey, the authority of the moral law, irredeemably go to the wall, can that moral law be considered as a figment?

We may consider the personification of the moral law as a figment, and we have good reason to do so, but if by God is understood that objective reality in the world which by the penalty of extinction enforces a certain kind of conduct, we may expect no serious contradiction when we maintain that the existence of God can be scientifically proved.

It is a matter of course that the God of science is not like the God of the heathenish religions, not even like the good Lord of pagan Christianity who can be bribed by flattery and prayer, and still less like the benevolent and philanthropic God Father of Deism. He is an inflexible law, immutable, irrefragable, eternal; stern toward transgressors and kind toward those who keep his commandments. If Mr. Goldwin Smith will consider God in this sense as a natural law, or rather as *the* law of nature, as that in nature which is as it is, in the Pentateuch called by the expressive name *Javeh*, as that which we cannot model at pleasure, but to which we must model ourselves in order to live and to continue to live—he will find that God is at the bottom of evolution also; he will find that morality indeed can and must be educed from it. It is true that evolution proclaims as its law the survival of the fittest. But who in the long run of millenniums are the fittest if not those that conform to that stern authority, to the law of nature, to the order of the cosmos, to that all-power of which we are a part which has created us and still maintains our life,—to God.

If Mr. Goldwin Smith means to say that ethics without religion is a failure and will remain a failure, we agree with him perfectly. He says:

> "With misgivings, conscious or unconscious, about religion, came the desire of finding a sanction for morality independent of theology; in other words, moral philosophy."

He adds that all those moral philosophers "whose philosophy has been practically effective, from Socrates downward, have been religious and have regarded their philosophy as the ally and confirmation of religion." This, I grant, is true if religion is used in the broad sense we use it, and not in the sense of a creed which declares that religiosity consists in a blind belief of traditional dogmas.

Mr. Goldwin Smith quotes approvingly a passage from his late friend Mr. Cotter Morison, whom he calls "the most thorough-going of agnostics." Mr. Morison says:

> "Virtue may, and possibly will, bring happiness to the virtuous man; but to the immoral and the selfish, virtue will probably be the most distasteful or even painful thing in their experience, while vice will give them unmitigated pleasure."

This is true, and being true it suffices to explode any kind of hedonism which would fain make us believe that happiness is the consequence of virtue, and that virtue must be explained as that which gives pleasure or produces happiness. The quotation is valuable because it comes from an agnostic. Agnostics not being able to found ethics upon something which they do not know and which they consider as unknowable, have attempted to explain morality as that which is conducive to happiness. If ethics cannot be deduced from happiness or that which causes happiness, how can we explain it?

Mr. Goldwin Smith calls attention to the fact that all other attempts of teaching or explaining morality contain religious elements, and he is right. He says:

> "Where they take as their foundation the authority of conscience, the categorical imperative, or the command of nature, it is clear that they are still within the circle of theism."

He adds these two propositions which, it appears, he believes to be equivalent: "Nature," he says, "is an unmeaning expression without an author of nature, or rather, it is a philosophical name of God." The former proposition we reject as a decided *non sequitur;* the latter we accept. As soon as we consider nature, the world-order, the laws of the evolution of life in their moral importance, we are confronted with the true kernel of religious truth; their recognition is the kernel of the God-idea, for God if it means anything is the moral authority whose will must be done.

Agnosticism is an untenable and a practically useless philosophy. Mr. Goldwin Smith says, "The profession of safe acquiescence in ignorance may sound very philosophic." But it is not; and he has our full assent when he says:

> "The generation after next may perhaps see agnosticism, moral as well as religious, tried on a clear field. By that time, possibly, science, whose kingdom seems now to have come, will have solved in her own way the mystery of existence; at least so far as to provide us with a rule of life, personal and social."

We also believe that the kingdom of science seems now to have come. But if it comes, in what way and by whose authority does it come? It comes in the ordinary course of evolution by the authority of the God of the religion of science. It comes after all as a survival of the fittest in spite of Mr. Goldwin Smith's denunciation of the law of evolution. This is so palpable that no words need be lost about it. Yet Mr. Goldwin Smith's argument is so strong that we shall have to add a few further explanations.

Mr. Goldwin Smith says:

> "The tiger has been as much evolved as the lamb; and the most noxious of human beasts, if he can hold his own in the strug-

gle for existence, at whatever expense to his fellows, has as good a right to existence as Socrates."

Here we have to make two objections.

First we have to repeat what we have said again and again on other occasions: that this famous comparison so often employed to contrast the immoral evil-doer with the moral martyr does not correctly represent the nature of the problem. The tiger is not more immoral than the lamb; on the contrary, if the tiger represents the active energetic fighter who in the struggle for existence holds his own, while the lamb represents the passive sufferer who is too weak-headed to face his foe, the tiger is more moral than the lamb and it serves the lamb right that he succumbs to the victor. There is no morality in ovine indolence. Morality is not, as it is often supposed to be, merely the omission of certain grosser or more refined crimes, of different sins, bad habits, and pecadilloes; true morality is not passive, it is active, it consists in the achieving and doing of that which is our duty to do for ourselves and for mankind, which latter is only a wider range of our nobler self.

Our second objection to Mr. Goldwin Smith's argument is that "human beasts" can *not* hold their own. They are constantly being eliminated by the natural selection of evolution.

We agree with Mr. Goldwin Smith when he says: "It is absurd to say that a life of self-denial and endurance, ending in martyrdom, is happiness"—for the law of morality cannot be educed from man's yearning for happiness—and in a certain sense we also agree to the clause he adds—"unless there is a compensation beyond." Morality as a factor in life and in evolution, as a law of nature, cannot be understood unless we rise above the sphere of the individual. Egotism is not morality, and moral actions are those which are consciously or unconsciously performed with an outlook beyond the narrow interests of the individual in time and space. Moral motives are superindividual. I purposely do not call them altruistic, because altruism does not seem to me the proper moral view; it simply replaces the interests of the own ego by those of other egos. The superindividual aspect however makes humanity and its ideals, the natural laws of social justice and the moral law of the world, parts of the individual and it is not the individual but these superindividual parts of his soul which will survive.

Mr. Goldwin Smith is not yet free from the individualism of our time. He seems to expect that morality and happiness shall be doled out to the individual in equal proportions. He introduces the following instance:

> "A man acquires a great estate by fraud, enjoys it wisely, uses his wealth liberally, makes himself popular, takes good care of his health, lives long, dies respected, and leaves healthy offspring. Freed by his opulence from wearing toil and injurious exposure, he exhibits all the energy, vivacity, and sociability which are held out as the rewards of a right course of living. Morality says that he is miserable, but how can evolution condemn him?"

Evolution does condemn him. Evolution will in the long run eliminate such types as he is, as certain as it will eliminate the tigers from off the surface of the earth.

Mr. Goldwin Smith continues:

> "Evolutionary philosophers give excellent precepts for healthy and comfortable living; but these precepts apparently the man fulfils, and thus he fulfils all righteousness. They may talk to him, indeed, of a more perfect state of society to be some day brought about by ethical science, in which he would be out of place; but he, having only one life, takes the world as he finds it,

and makes the best of it for himself. Why should he sacrifice himself to the future of humanity?"

Why should he sacrifice himself for the future of humanity? Because the future of humanity is his own future. Why shall a boy sacrifice the hours of his childhood for the future days of his manhood? Why! Because the man is the continuance of the boy. The objection may be made that the comparison does not hold good; the future generations of mankind are not we ourselves, while the adult man is the same person as the boy. What, however, does "the same person" mean? The word "person" represents a history, a continuance, nothing more. Persons are not unchangeable units; there is not one atom of the boy left in the man. Materially considered the adult man is as exactly as much and not more different from himself when he was a boy, as the present generations of mankind are different from the past generations, for in both instances the continuity is preserved in exactly the same degree and measure.

It is said that a man "having only one life takes the world as he finds it, and makes the best of it for himself." The truth is man has *not* "only one life."

> "The soul that rises with us, our life's star,
> Hath had elsewhere its setting
> And cometh from afar."

Man's life, his humanity, does not consist of the material particles of his body. The properly human in man consists almost entirely of his relations with other men. His very language is superindividual, and if we could cut out the superindividual from his brain, there would remain a mere brute. There is a great truth in the idea of immortality, although there need not be an immortality either of bodily resurrection or in a purely spiritual heaven beyond.

THE PRINCIPLE OF WELFARE.

BY PROF. HARALD HÖFFDING.

I.

If we wish to discuss ethical problems in a fruitful manner and form just judgments of ethical theories, we must always bear in mind the fact that there is not merely one single ethical problem, but many. With the solution of one of these problems the solution of the others is not necessarily given, and thinkers who have treated a single problem have not, in dealing with that problem, always determined their position with reference to the others. At all events, it will be an especial and separate task to investigate the relation to each other, the reciprocal dependence or independence, of the different ethical problems. When we speak of *the* ethical problem as an especial philosophical problem, we must not forget that upon closer examination it resolves itself into a number of different problems.

The reason of this tendency to regard the ethical problem as simple and indivisible throughout, may be partly sought in the fact that philosophical ethics did not develop until the positive religions had lost their undisputed control over the minds of men. Religious ethics is simple and indivisible by virtue of its principle. It is founded on authority. Its *contents* are the revealed commands of authority; the *feeling* which impels us *to pass ethical judgments* is the fear or reverence or love with which men are filled in the presence of divine authority; the same motives impel man to follow in his conduct the commands of the authority; and the principles of the education of individuals and of the order of society are just as immediately given by definite relation to this authority. It is upon the whole the peculiarity of positive religions and the cause of their great importance in the history of mankind that they grant man satisfaction in a lump for *all* his intellectual wants. The true believer has concentrated in his belief his whole mental life; his belief is at once the highest science, the highest virtue, the highest good, and the highest æsthetics. Philosophical ethics has sought too long to retain the simple unity which is peculiar to religious ethics. The mistakes of the greatest philosophical ethicists may be in part traced to this source. A criticism of Kant and Bentham would more fully illustrate this. The fundamental error—one so often found in the science of the past—is too great a love of simplicity.

I shall try, in the briefest possible manner, to give an outline of the most important ethical problems.

Ethical judgments, judgments concerning good and bad, in their simplest form are expressions of feeling, and never lose that character however much influence clear and reasoned knowledge may acquire with respect to them. An act or an institution that could awaken no feeling whatsoever would never become the object of an ethical judgment, could never be designated as good or bad. And the character of the judgment will be dependent upon the character of the feeling that dictates the judgment. From the point of view of pure egoism the judgment of the same act will be wholly different from what it is when regarded, say, from a point of view that is determined by motives of sympathy embracing a larger or smaller circle of living beings. An ethical system, accordingly, will acquire its character from the *motive principle of judgment* upon which it builds. This motive principle is the power that originally and constantly again gives rise to ethical judgments.

If our motive principle is to operate with clearness and logical consequence it must set up a definite standard. A *test-principle of judgment* must be established that will furnish guidance in individual cases by enabling us to infer consequences from it in instances where simple, instinctive feeling fails. The natural course will be that the test-principles will correspond directly with the motive principles at their base. The relation between the two may, however, be more or less simple. If we fix upon the feeling of sympathy as our basis, regarding it as the main element of ethical feelings, it follows of itself that the criterion we adopt must be the principle of general welfare, that is the principle that all acts and institutions shall lead to the greatest possible feeling of pleasure among living beings. This principle merely defines with greater precision what is unconsciously contained in the feeling of sympathy and in the instinct that springs from this feeling. The same test-principle (as Bentham's "Deontology," for example, shows) may also be accepted as valid from the point of view of pure egoism, only in this case the relation between the motive principle and the test-principle is more indirect. We must in this case endeavor to prove that the happiness of others is a necessary *means* to our own happiness. Our own happiness is then the real end, but in order to reach this end we must take a roundabout course, and ethics is the presentation of the system of the courses thus taken. Kant arrives in a different way again at establishing the happiness of others as an end of ethics. It would be the business of a special investigation to determine the extent to which this varying motivation of the principle of test must influence the consequences derivable from it.

A third question is, By what motive shall an individual act be determined? The *motive to action* is not necessarily the same as the motive that dictates judgment. The man who is animated with love for his fellow-creatures has reason to rejoice that ambition and the instinct of acquisition constitute grounds of action of so very general a character; in that results become thereby possible which,—for such is the unalterable character of human nature,—would otherwise remain unaccomplished. A special investigation would have to point out whether cases occur in which motive of action and motive of judgment must coincide if the act is to be approved of, and whether there are not motives to action which would rob the act of all ethical character.

Different from the problems already mentioned is the pedagogic problem: How can the proper and necessary motives be developed in man? This problem arises as well with respect to the motive principle of judgment as with respect to the motive principle of action. It is clear that between points of view that rest upon entirely different psychological foundations, (the one, for example, starting from egoism, the other from sympathy, and the third from pure reason,) the discussion can be carried only to a certain point. The person who with conscious logic makes himself the highest and only aim can never be refuted from a point of view which regards every individual as a member of society and of the race, and therefore not only as an end but also as a means. If an understanding is to become possible, the emotional foundation adopted (the motive spring of judgment) must be changed; but the change is not effected by mere theoretical discussion: a practical education is demanded in addition thereto which life does not afford all individuals, although our inclination to make ourselves an absolute centre is always obstructed by the tendency of society to subject us all to a general order of things. There is an education of humanity by history the same as there is an education of single individuals in more limited spheres. This education demands its special points of view, which are not always directly furnished by general ethical principles. The same is true of the motive to action. For pedagogical reasons it may be necessary to produce or to preserve motives that do not satisfy the highest demand, because such motives are necessary transitional stages to the highest motives. Thus, ambition and the instinct of acquisition may be the means of attaining to true ethical self-assertion. Reverence for authorities historically given can be of extraordinary effectiveness in the development of character, since only thereby are concentration or fixity of endeavor as well as the power of joyful resignation acquired,—without our being able to see in such reverence the highest ethical qualities. A ground-color in fact must often be laid on before the final, required tint can be applied. The law of the displacement of motives operates here which in ethical estimation generally is of the utmost importance.

There must still be mentioned here finally the socio-political problem. This problem has reference to that particular ordered arrangement of society which is best adapted to a development in the direction of ethical ideals. As the former problem leads inquiry out of the domain of ethics into that of pedagogics, so this one leads us from ethics into political economy and political science.

Although in the present discussion I intend to occupy myself only with a single one of these problems, I have nevertheless mentioned them all in order that the light that I shall attempt to throw upon the problem I deal with may be seen in its proper setting. As will be observed from what follows, the principle of welfare will be misunderstood if the problem to whose solution it is adapted is confounded with any one of the other ethical problems. The systematism of ethical science is still so little advanced that it is necessary to draw out a general outline before we pass on to any single feature. The value of systematism is namely this, that we are immediately enabled to see the connection of the single questions with one another as well as their distinctive peculiarity. In ethics we are not yet so far advanced.

II.

1) If we accept the principle of welfare as our test or criterion in judging of the value of actions and of institutions, these are then good or bad according as in their effects (so far as we can trace them) they produce a predominance of pleasurable feeling or a predominance of painful feeling in a larger or smaller circle of sentient beings. Every action may be compared to a stone thrown into the water. The motion

produced is propagated in large or in small circles; and the estimation of its value depends upon whether it produces in the places it strikes predominant pleasure or pain. Just as theoretical science explains the single natural phenomenon by its connection with other natural phenomena, so ethics tests the single feeling by its relation to other feelings: the satisfaction of a person acting over the accomplishment of the act is only then to be called justifiable or good when it does not create a disturbance in the pleasurable feeling of other beings, or when such a disturbance can be proved to be a necessary means of a greater or more extended pleasurable feeling. This principle, as a principle of test or valuation, corresponds directly with sympathy as motive of judgment. The extent to which it is possible to accept this from other points of view I cannot here investigate in detail.

The act of estimation, the testing, does not stop at the outer action but goes down to the motives of the person acting, to the qualities of his character, to the whole inner life from which the act has sprung. This has its ground in the nature and significance of the estimating judgment. Ethical judgments, in fact, are in their original and simplest form spontaneous expressions of feeling. But the great practical significance of such expressions of feeling lies in the fact that they operate decisively upon the will (upon the individual will and that of others) and produce motives of future action. Logically, accordingly, they must be directed towards the point at which an altering effect on the power that produces the act is possible, and this point lies precisely in the inner life, in the character of mind of the person acting. For this reason feelings and impulses, disturbances and desires, are also judged of according to the tendency which they have of producing acts and effects that will increase pleasurable feeling or avoid unpleasurable feeling in more extended or more limited circles.

Only by its effects do we know the power. We form by inferences our conclusions as to what takes place in the mind of a man, his motives and his capacity. Goodness or greatness that never expressed itself in action could never become the object of ethical approbation; it would not even exist in fact, but would rest upon a self-deception, upon an illusion. At least some inner activity, a longing and endeavor in the direction demanded by the ethical principle must manifest itself. The individual in self-judgment must often take refuge in this inner activity, and any deep-going, unpharisaical ethical estimation will have to follow him there;* but just here do we have a beginning of that which is demanded by the principle of welfare, except that in consequence of individual circumstances its prosecution is impossible.

Equally important as the principle that we can know the power only from the effects is the other principle that the effect need not appear at once. When good and great men are so often mistaken by their contemporaries the fact is explained by the circumstance that only a very wide-embracing glance can measure the significance of their efforts and activity. Their goodness and greatness is founded in the fact that their thought, their feeling, their will, comprehend far more than their short-sighted and narrow-minded contemporaries see. A long time may elapse before it is possible for them to be generally understood, and

* Compare my article "The Laws of Relativity in Ethics" in the *International Journal of Ethics*, Vol. I. p. 37, et seqq.

for what they have done to be assimilated. It is therefore by no means implied in the principle of welfare that people are to direct their conduct so as to be in accord with impulses and wants which men have at the moment. The principle of welfare demands in very fact that we should not shrink from the battle with prejudice and with inertia. The best thing, often, that we can do for others is to make them feel that they stand on entirely too low a level in their wishes and wants and do not make adequate demands generally. Thus, to take a single instance, the great artist often treads a solitary path ununderstood or even mistaken by the great mass. Yet in so doing he follows, perhaps without being aware of it, the principle of welfare,—if he rigorously observes the demands of art. He increases the mental capital of the species, and gives it a power which later on can operate in broad spheres. Only a short-sighted conception and application of the principle of welfare stops with the need of the moment and dismisses the consideration of the permanent conditions of life and the permanent sources of new life and new activity.*

2) The principle of welfare simply furnishes a norm which may be laid at the foundation of the testing of all classes of actions. But it by no means demands, as has at times been supposed, that consideration for welfare should also be the ground and motive for every act. We have recourse to general principles only in order to be able to set ourselves aright in cases in which direct judgment, instinctive feeling cannot determine the question presented, that is in cases of doubt, or when we have in view a systematic treatment

* This last argument is taken from my *Ethics* (Danish edition, P. 94, German edition, p. 110.

of ethical questions. The ethical feeling may operate quite involuntarily and without real ratiocination, in that we can be moved directly by the act (whether possible or real) as it appears to us, just as in our æsthetical feeling we may without æsthetical reasoning be struck by the beauty of a work of art or of a landscape. Or, we follow with confidence the "unwritten laws" that are contained in custom, in tradition, and generally in so-called "positive morality." And in agreement precisely with the principle of welfare, is immediacy of this kind to be recommended and maintained, so long as it does not lead to the neglect of real problems and questions. It is the state of innocence out of which no one dare be wrested unnecessarily. Abstract principles become necessary aids when direct reliance fails; but frequently they can only be applied to individual concrete cases by the employment of a great number of complicated intermediary steps, and do not easily acquire a practical influence upon the will. Indeed, the principle of welfare may even demand quite different motives from ethical feeling or devotion to the requirements of positive morality. It is in fact most beautiful and best that a man should care for his wife and children because he loves them and not because his ethical instinct requires it. Where conscious duty has to be invoked in the innermost relations between man and man, it is as a rule a sign of an unfortunate state of affairs. Perfect love dispels not only fear but also duty.

In his "Ethics," at page 339, Wundt advances the following objection to the principle of welfare: "It is conceivable that a person should sacrifice himself for another; it is conceivable that a person should yield up life and possessions for definite ideal ends, for his country, for freedom, for religion, for science. But it has never come to pass, and never will, that people shall renounce a thing solely to increase the sum of happiness of the world." This objection overlooks the fact that the principle of the valuation of an act that is regarded as good need not be the motive to this act. The thought and feeling of the person acting may stop very properly at country, freedom, or any other ideal object, without the person's instituting any formal reflections whatsoever with regard to the reasons of the value of the ideal ends for which he sacrifices himself. But in systematic ethics or in practical cases of doubt we inquire what value and importance love of country, freedom, poetry, and science possess for human life. If, for example, freedom were not a good for a people, the individual would do wrong to sacrifice his life for it. It is never of course a question of the abstract notion of welfare of and in itself, just as in a single theoretical problem it is never a question of the abstract idea of cause. But in ethics we lay down the principle of welfare and in the theory of knowledge the principle of causality; endeavoring, thus, to go back through analysis to the final assumptions of our practical and theoretical intellectual activity.

3) It is no argument against the principle of welfare that pleasure must be so often bought with pain. Pain is in that case only the necessary transitional step, and the significance of the principle of welfare is precisely the requirement it makes that the duty of demonstration shall rest on those who maintain the necessity of such an intermediary step. Any infliction of pain must be supplied with a motive, whereas the feeling of pleasure in and of itself (that is if its causes do

not at the same time produce additional painful effects) is justified. The principle of welfare simply says: Produce by thy conduct as much pleasure and as little pain as is possible! The degree to which it is possible to realise this demand, of this the principle in and of itself says nothing. A principle is not subverted by the difficulties of its application.

As experience teaches, there is a happiness that is not bought too dearly with pain. Clara's song in Goethe's "Egmont":

> "Himmelhoch jauchzend, *zum Tode betrübt!*"

has been cited in disproof of the principle of welfare. But let us hear Clara to the end and note the last line of the song, in which she gives the result of the entire train of her emotion. She says:

> "*Glücklich* allein ist die Seele die liebt!"

The phenomenon is this. There is a movement of the heart and mind, a life of feeling, which are joined with a satisfaction so deep and great that the powerful oscillation between pleasure and pain does not destroy the total feeling of happiness, but strengthens it. Two psychological factors co-operate here. The one is, that the pain (the dis-pleasure or grief), unless it transcends a certain degree, forms the background of the pleasurable feeling and is thereby able to intensify the latter. In this very fact a sufficient motive lies to choose conditions of this sort in preference to such as do not stand so high in intensity but are nevertheless conditions of more unmixed pleasure. The other factor is, that there can be an element of attraction even in grief, simply because intense life, powerful movement, and the straining of faculties that come with it, produce of themselves satisfaction. All exertion of power which is not out of proportion is connected with a feeling of pleasure. The feeling of pleasure that accompanies grief and anxiety asserts itself in the fact that we do not *wish* to be transported out of it. An important element here is also the organic process connected with every powerful state of mind (the effect of the condition of the brain on the circulation of the blood, on breathing, and on the organs of digestion), granting that it is not the whole cause.

When Auguste Comte lost the woman who exerted so decisive an influence on the direction of his mind in the last period of his life, he said once in an outburst of sorrow evoked by her memory: "I owe it to thee alone that I shall not leave this life without having known in a worthy manner the best emotion of human nature. . . . . Amid the severest pains that this emotion can bring with it I have never ceased to feel that the *true condition of happiness* is, to have filled the heart—though it be with pain, aye with bitterest pain."

Auguste Comte and Clara are accordingly quite in agreement, and the ethics of welfare is in agreement with them both. If we desire to be wholly secure against pain and anxiety, then we dare not love anything. But what if love were the greatest happiness, even though it brought as much sorrow again with it! With powerful action and great fulness of life come also great costs, great contrasts, and great vibrations. Yet who has said that the highest was to be had for little expenditure?

The feeling of pleasure is the only psychological criterion of health and power of life. That which in all its immediate or remote effects in all the creatures that it touches produces only pleasurable feeling, cannot possibly be condemned. Welfare, therefore, in the sense of permanent pleasurable feeling, is the final test-principle of action. Pain is everywhere the sign of an incipient dissolution of life.* This is exhibited in the simplest manner in the "physical" pain that arises through the tearing of organic tissue. But it also holds true of the "mental" pain that arises from anxiety, doubt, or repentance. It points to a disharmony between the different forces and impulses of the mind, a disharmony that can lead to the dissolution of consciousness. If pain is a necessary intermediary step, the fact is partly founded in the two psychological laws above mentioned, partly also in the circumstance that it means the dissolution of something in us that impedes a more free and more varied development of life. Childbirth is accompanied with pain because the new life can only come into the world at the cost of the old. Analogously the knowledge of truth is often gained with pain because prejudices and illusions must first be shattered. In the pain of repentance a lower self is dissolved in order that a new and higher self may develop.

4) A circumstance that has especially fostered the opposition to the principle of welfare is undoubtedly the tendency to think exclusively, in connection with the expression "pleasurable feeling," of the most elementary sensual forms of pleasure. The latter are not excluded by the principle of welfare; the principle, however, takes all the aspects of human character into consideration, maintaining that permanent pleasurable feeling is not to be established with certainty if an essential aspect of this character is neglected. The de-

* Compare my *Psychology* (Danish edition, pp. 315-318; German edition, pp. 343-347).

fect of elementary feelings of pleasure is that for the great part they correspond to only momentary and limited relations.

A being whose feeling is of a purely elementary kind can maintain itself as long as the simple conditions of life to which it is adapted do not change. Thus some of the lowest animal forms like the infusoria and rhizopods appear to have existed throughout infinitely long periods of time in exactly their present condition. Here the adaptation to the given conditions is as good as perfect. The same may be the case with beings that at an earlier stage of their development have possessed more developed organs and forms. Animals that live free in their youth, afterwards however as parasites, lead a purely elementary life and lose all the nerves and muscles that do not directly subserve this form of existence. This is also true of man. Of the Fuegians, whose wretched existence (wretched in our eyes) he portrays in vivid colors in his "Journey Around the World," Darwin says: "There is no reason for believing that the Fuegians are diminishing in number; we must therefore assume that they enjoy a sufficient measure of happiness (of whatever character this may be) to give life value in their eyes. Nature, which makes habit an irresistible power and its effects hereditary, has fitted the Fuegian to the climate and the products of his wretched country." Primitive peoples of a higher type even (and not only primitive peoples) afford examples of an adaptation to conditions which excludes all motives to change and progress. It is dire necessity that has brought man into the path of progress. Where such a compul sion does not operate human emotional life is conditioned by a narrow sphere of relations only and is therefore itself narrow and restricted. Perhaps more complete, more unmixed satisfaction can be obtained here than would be possible under more manifold and more complicated circumstances. A small vessel may be fuller than a large one although it holds less.*

It might perhaps be objected to the principle of welfare, that we should really be obliged, in consistency with it, to make ourselves all little vessels, and that agreeably to the principle an existence limited to the primitive necessities of life and to purely elementary feelings, would stand just as high as a life taken up with intellectual labor and the activity of culture, or even higher, since an existence of the latter kind could scarcely be accompanied with so unmixed and secure a well-being, but would be united with trials and efforts constantly renewed and with unrest ever recurring. If—as it might be suggested—an existence like that of the Fuegians appears poor and wretched to us, since they often suffer from scarcity and want, let us take another example. Alexander von Humboldt came across a tribe in South America that lived from banana trees,—trees so fruitful that an acre of land planted with them would supply food for fifty human beings. The trees require no real expenditure of labor; only the earth about their roots must be broken with implements once or twice a year. The consequence is that the tribe is stupid and uncivilised. But the wants that it has are satisfied.

That which would make such a life unendurable for us, *the strong desire for activity, development, and progress*, this desire does not exist at such stages. It

* Fieri potest, ut vas aliquod minus majore plenius sit, quamvis liquoris minus contineat Cartesius, Epistola iv, Ad principem Palatinem de sita beata.

is,—a fact that must be remarked,—*itself a consequence of development and progress.*

Whereas Lamarck assumed an inner, innate impulse to development in all living creatures,* Darwin maintains, on the ground of experience, that development is invariably introduced by the influence of external causes. It was a difficulty to Lamarck how the very lowest forms of life could continue their existence, why they had not long since developed to higher stages. In Darwin's theory, which takes into consideration the external conditions of development, there is no difficulty on this point. A development that is favored *in no way* by external circumstances is simply impossible. As regards human beings, the anthropologist Th. Waitz has clearly proved, that the impulse and desire of development is itself a product of development. To this effect he speaks in his treatise "The Indians of North America," page 69: "A people without intercourse and not in competition with other peoples, a people which supplies its natural wants with relative ease or only by overcoming long accustomed difficulties regarded as inevitable, directly from its natural environment, and that feels satisfied therewith and lives a happy life: from such a people it is not to be expected that it will make any endeavors to civilise itself. He that has what he needs and therefore feels satisfied in all respects, will not work; people do not civilise themselves voluntarily in following some noble instinct of the heart. Is it different in fact in our modern society? Is not a long period of schooling and culture previously necessary to instil in man an interest for work as work? How many are there among

* The theory of Lamark is made the sublect of an interesting criticism by Herbert Spencer in his *Principles of Biology*, Part iii, Chap, 3.

the so-called learned and cultured that make endeavors in behalf of the education of themselves and others without they are required!"

It is peculiar to the state of nature in contrast to the state of civilisation, (in so far as a distinct contrast may be asserted,) that in the former the impulse to change of manner of life and thought must come from without, whereas in the latter an impulse to progress operates which be it now powerful be it now feeble never ceases entirely to operate. This difference is analogous to that that prevails between inorganic and organic existence. It is the peculiar character of an organism that the play of forces is preserved in it with a certain independence of the effects of the moment and of its immediate environment. So in civilised peoples an impulse is aroused to change life in all directions, to differentiate, to shape it, and to bring it to a point in every single direction. Spiritual antennæ are grown which are in never ceasing movement. Through this a new species of feeling also is possible, *a feeling that is determined not only by the definite ends that are attained but which links itself with the work, with the activity itself which is requisite to the acquisition of these ends.* Man is thereby become more independent and more free, and his mental life, especially his emotional life, has gained in depth and intensity, it now being no longer determined merely by the external world, but essentially by the forces that are awakened in the inner world. Now ideal, and not merely elementary feelings act, and higher demands are made in life.

What I wish to maintain here is that *the rise of the impulse to development is in perfect accord with the principle of welfare.* That stability of the "state of nature" which now appears to us wretched now paradisian, is itself dependent on the stability of external conditions. Absolute stability, however, is not found in nature. If the immediate surroundings do not change, changes yet occur in other localities of nature and among other creatures, and the struggle for existence then either causes them to perish or to change in a corresponding manner. The beings that have changed by adaptation will obtain a decided advantage in the struggle for life over those that have remained stationary. This is the fate of many primitive peoples, or indeed civilised peoples, that have remained stationary or in a low state of culture. Extinction awaits them when a higher civilisation approaches.

What is true of peoples and races also holds good for individuals. A perfect adaptation to limited circumstances always involves a danger,—the danger that the individual when its conditions of life are changed and its horizon is enlarged will lack the inner conditions necessary to self-assertion. Childish *naïveté*, dreaming phantasy, sensual enjoyment, have each their rights, but they easily lead to a condition of somnambulism; security and happiness are always precarious here, and on awakening the greatest helplessness may take their place. Here, let us add, we leave entirely out of consideration the fact that such a condition often exists only at the cost of other individuals.

Welfare, accordingly, cannot be conceived as a passive state of things produced once for all and that is not itself in turn the point of departure of new and progressive development. Welfare, in the highest conception of it, must consist of a condition in which power is gathered and rich possibilities gained for the future, and which generates an impulse to frame new ends and to begin new endeavors. It is a condition that is desirable in and of itself as well as one that contains the germ of new desirable conditions,—a condition therefore that is not only an end but also a means, that has value not only as effect but also as cause. The feeling of pleasure is here directly bound up with activity, work, development, the unfolding of forces themselves, and not merely with the result that is obtained by the employment of the forces. Where such feeling of pleasure is possible there much suffering is endurable that at a lower stage would be the sign of the dissolution of all life. Expectation and longing, privation and disappointment will not be lacking; they will accompany with definite rhythmical alternation the joyful advancement toward the aim that man has set himself; but amid all oscillations the fundamental direction and the fundamental activity will be asserted. We will not work to live, we will not live to work; but *in* work will we find life.

This is the ideal that the principle of welfare holds up to us when thoroughly reasoned out. In how far it can be realised is a question that can only be answered experimentally for the time and the individual in question. It demands not only a change of the nature of individuals but also of the relations of society. The essential thing however is, that we here have a criterion by which we are able to test actions and institutions. This criterion corresponds to a tendency that leads throughout all organic nature, in that pleasure as a rule means life and progress, pain, retrogression and death. The principle of welfare asserts the right of life: every creature has the right to exist, to develop, and to obtain its full satisfaction, unless greater pain is thereby produced to itself or to others. The ethics that builds upon the principle of welfare seeks accordingly to continue the evolution of nature in a conscious and harmonious manner. It demands that means be found which the unconscious development of nature have not supplied, and it strives to mitigate or to exclude the unnecessary pain which the struggle for existence brings with it. It embraces a series of problems from compassionate alleviation and assistance up to the highest social, intellectual, and æsthetical endeavors. It is the business of special ethics to treat these questions in detail.

5) From the fact, however, that welfare, properly understood, consists in activity and development, it does not follow that *vice versa* activity and development are always joined with welfare or lead to welfare. Because limitation of wants does not always lead to the aim set, unlimited variety of wants is not necessarily the proper state. Civilisation can assume forms and enter on paths that do not harmonise with the principle of welfare. We find in history accordingly, at times, distinct and decisive warnings against existing civilisations. Thus it was in Greece on the part of Socrates, the Cynics, and the Stoics, in the eighteenth century on the part of Rousseau, and in our day on the part of Leo Tolstoï. The opposition of such great minds should surely make us watchful.

I leave out of consideration here the question in how far that which we call civilisation can be imparted to a people forthwith. The capacity for civilisation has, it is true, been prematurely and overhastily denied many primitive peoples.* But it is not therefore necessarily a good thing for a people to give up the forms of life that it has developed by its own for-

* Compare my article in the *International Journal of Ethics*, No. I. p. 60.

tunes and endeavors to allow itself to be regulated in accordance with forms and ideals that have been developed under entirely different circumstances. Thus directly, even the best-founded and most perfect civilisation cannot be communicated. Waitz who expressly maintains that no proof has been brought forward of the Indian's incapacity for civilisation, praises nevertheless the Indian chieftains who oppose the obtrusion of civilisation on their people, for their love to their people and their just comprehension of its true well-being.

The reason why conflict can arise between civilisation and welfare lies in the restiveness and restlessness of the aspirations of civilisation. It is the same with it as with that spontaneous, involuntary impulse to movement that leads to the use of forces and of the members merely because sufficient energy is present, without their use being guided by the consideration of a more valuable end, so that the results are accidental. The effort that goes with civilisation may lead in part to over-exertion, to an overstraining of forces; in part (in the case of extreme differentiation) to a one-sided direction of effort; and partly to isolation, to the fragmentary elimination of individual activities. In the single individual certain faculties are fostered (in the one intelligence, in the other physical power for work) at the cost of other faculties; the harmony, the capacity of feeling oneself as totality and unity is lacking. By such one-sidedness the individual becomes of value only as a wheel in a great machine: he serves merely as a means, not as an end. And such a one-sided individual development is connected with a one-sided social development. The suppression of certain features of the nature of the individual goes hand in hand with the suppression of single estates and classes of society. If we identify civilisation and ethics, without qualification, and regard progress as a safer criterion than welfare, we should overlook the fact that there exists also a *social question.* The social question is an ethical question and at the same time a question of the correction of civilisation,—both by means of the principle of welfare. Would it be right that the products of material and ideal civilisation should only fall to the share of a small minority, while all the rest should not be able to participate therein? This would clash completely with the ideal of society that flows from the principle of welfare. For the greatest welfare is present when every single individual so develops himself in an independent manner that just by this independent development of his own he assists others to a similar development from their point of view. Then does there exist *a harmonious society of independent personalities.* The idea of such a society is the highest ethical idea that flows from the principle of welfare. Every individual is then a little world for himself and yet stands in the most intimate reciprocal connection with the great world of which he is a part. The individual serves the race and the race serves the individual. Every position of isolation, every inequality in the distribution of possessions and of employments must be founded in the demands of the various circumstances and problems of life, and the faculties and impulses of each individual shall be developed as fully and richly as is compatible with the conditions of life of the whole race.

6) It follows from the considerations presented, that it is by no means always easy to apply the principle of welfare in individual cases. The particular relations of the affairs in question can be so compli-

cated that we are not able to take a broad survey of them and foresee the results of our interference. We cannot deduce *a priori* from the principle of welfare any system of particular acts, any determinate order of society, any civilisation. Its value (like that of the principle of causality in the theoretical field) is to present and to formulate problems, and to serve as a guide to their treatment. It is regulative, not constructive. It presumes the immediate involuntary life of the individual and of society, and its function does not begin until the conscious discussion and treatment occurs of the value on the one hand of that which has thus been developed, and on the other of the manner in which the development shall be conducted in the future. All ethics thus acquires an *historical* character. We never—either in our own individuality or in society—commence from the very beginning, but are always obliged to start with a definite foundation and to work our way further under the guidance of the principles and ideals that spring from our nature.

III.

1) In the previous remarks I have essayed a discussion of the principle of welfare which may perhaps make clearer what was not so distinct in my former expositions ("Ethik," Chapters III and VII). The difficulty always occurs in the enunciation of a principle, that a direct demonstration of its validity cannot be given. Of so much greater significance is it then if an indirect proof can be adduced by showing that the very ones who contest it are themselves forced to employ it and actually to employ it without being aware of it.

I maintain now that Dr. Paul Carus in his book

"The Ethical Problem," in which he combats the principle of welfare, has not been able to avoid giving such an indirect confirmation of the validity of this principle. Before attempting to show this in detail I shall make a few remarks concerning the criticism of my "Ethics" which Dr. Carus wrote in the first number of *The Monist*, and which in an abbreviated form is also embodied in the treatise above mentioned.

Dr. Carus thinks that I have practically surrendered the principle of welfare when I define welfare to consist in activity. His words are:

> "If welfare is to be interpreted as activity, work, development; if this kind of active welfare is the greatest good, whatever admixture of pain and whatever absence of pleasurable feeling it may have; if the greatest amount of a state of continuous pleasurable feeling is not welfare in an ethical sense, what becomes of the utilitarian definition of welfare as pleasurable feeling? If, however, welfare is 'the state of a continuous pleasurable feeling,' how can we declare that the life of a pessimistic philosopher is preferable to that of a joyful fool?"

To this I answer, that *if* it could be proved that increasing pain followed necessarily on *all* advancement of civilisation (without this pain being compensated for, as Clara's philosophy demanded, by new and proportionately greater feelings of pleasure), in that case it would be impossible to combine civilisation and welfare. But only a pessimistic dogmatism—which is just as current in the atmosphere of to-day as optimistic dogmatism—could assert this. What experience teaches us is this, that we find ourselves amid a development, in a line of tendencies the final results of which we cannot foresee but which hitherto have evoked at many points new forces and have thereby opened new sources of satisfaction. Everything that arouses our greatest and most permanent pleasurable feeling has arisen within this development. This justifies our courage and our hope in behalf of further progress, although conflict and pain will as we may foresee not be wanting, and although the way leads through many deserts. Experience alone can show how far we shall be able to get. I agree with Dr. Carus that "this world of ours is not a world suited to the taste of a pleasure-seeker," if we understand by pleasure passive sensual enjoyment, an enjoyment which is not united with the rest and nourishment with which not only an immediate pleasurable feeling is connected but whereby power is also gathered for continued endeavor. If so many pleasure-seekers go through life without having their eyes opened to its true significance and purpose, this fact is precisely one of the things that clash with the principle of welfare, for the latter claims all faculties and powers, and demands that they that sleep be awakened,—that is if they really possess useful faculties. For perhaps the "joyful fool" cannot accomplish more than he does. Wherefore then disturb him, if his pleasure harms neither himself nor others and if his awakening will only lead to unrest and pain for himself and perhaps also for others? I pointed out the fact in my "Ethics,"* that we can determine by the principle of welfare alone in what cases we are to destroy a state of equilibrium or shatter an illusion.

I have admitted the *possibility* of a conflict between civilisation and welfare. Wherever such a conflict arises, there, according to my conception, appears an ethical problem, which must be determined by the principle of welfare, since any order of things or any development that brought with it permanent and ever-

* Danish edition, p. 94. German edition, p. 109.

lasting pain would be in effect a dissolution of life itself. Such pain, however, (as even pessimistic philosophers are optimistic enough to hope,) would destroy the will to live. If we live in spite of pain it is because there is always a surplus of satisfaction.

I give the idea of welfare no arbitrary extension when I deny that it should be limited to denote a passive condition produced once for all time. For our nature is at no stage wholly complete; no one condition can stand therefore as definitive. The future, and the new horizons opened, will make new demands on our capacities and our will, and in the testing of any state of things it must accordingly be a necessary point of view to establish whether in addition to the direct satisfaction which it probably affords it at the same time prepares the capacities and the possibilities of a continued development answering to the new relations. It may be necessary to choose some arduous employment which later necessarily brings with it long continued rest and inactivity. Darwin's struggle with his feeble health is a good example. The man who from love of country or to save a fellow-being risks his life, prefers the active satisfaction of a single moment (the satisfaction, namely, which he feels beforehand at the thought of saving his country or a human life) to the passive joys of years and years. It was such a moment in which Faust saw himself living in mind

"Auf freiem Grund mit freiem Volk"

and which thereby made life of value to him, which all the earthly gratifications that the demon was able to obtain for him could not accomplish. In the face of the pleasure that such a moment can produce the thought of pain and death vanishes. Thus alone is self-sacrifice psychologically intelligible.

2) While I cannot see that Dr. Carus has pointed out a contradiction in my theory of welfare, I may further assert that he himself cannot without a self-contradiction escape recognising the principle of welfare. Dr. Carus indeed, in a certain sense, himself enunciates this very principle. He says, in the preface to "The Ethical Problem," page iii, "The aim of ethics is neither the welfare of self nor that of other individuals, but of those interests that are superindividual." The aim therefore is to be welfare, not however the welfare of individuals but of "superindividual interests." This strange expression is defined in certain subsequent passages of the book. Dr. Carus speaks, namely, later on, of "that superindividual soul-life which we call society."* It is admitted in this, that when we speak of welfare we speak impliedly of soul-life. But how can we give to society as such a soul-life that is different from the soul-life of the single individuals that have their existence simultaneously and successively in that society? This is merely a mythical and mystical personification of society, which may have arisen in the comparison, in many respects instructive, between society and an organism, which however can possess at best a poetical, but no scientific, value. The idea of society, if it is to be scientifically employed, must always be so applied that at every point the definite group of individuals which it represents may be established. The great importance of this idea consists in the fact that it expresses the common and permanent interests of individuals simultaneously and successively existing, in opposition to the interests of single individuals, or of a smaller group, or of a limited period of time. Ethical percep-

* Pages 33, 38, and 40.

tion, (unless it starts from the point of view of egoistical individualism,) must apply its test from the point of view of society. It leads in this case to the consideration of our own and others' actions not only with respect to our own individual circumstances but *sub specie æterni* so to speak, that is with respect to their relation to the great whole of which not only we, but also other human beings are parts. Along with the educative power of authorities, it is due to the sympathy in virtue of which the individual causes to re-echo in his own bosom the feelings of others, that ethical ideals have been formed in the human mind. But as soon as it is made impossible to transpose the idea of society into the idea of individuals that live under certain definite conditions, this idea contains no instruction for us in ethical respects. No ethical norms can in this case be deduced from it. Emotional mysticism takes the place of ethical thought and volition.

Such a mysticism has of course its value. Powerful emotion leads naturally to a state in which all definite ideas recede, the mind becoming entirely occupied by emotional feeling. It will furthermore be difficult to represent by any adequate conception the great multitude of human characters on which our conduct in given circumstances can acquire decisive influence. The expression "society," or "race," characterises very well the unconcluded and the unsurveyable in so many of the consequences of human methods of action and order of life, and it will therefore not be possible to dispense with it. But transposition into concrete conceptions must always be possible. A welfare that at one or another stage is not the welfare of definite individuals is a self-contradiction, and any act that at one period or another does not lead to the welfare of definite individuals has no value.

In Wundt's "Ethics," pages 429 to 431, the same line of thought is found as this of Dr. Carus. Public well-being and progress, according to Wundt, do not consist in the well-being of the greatest possible number of individuals: for the individual is ephemeral! "However richly blest and however perfect the individual existence may be, it is but a drop in the ocean of life. What can individual happiness and individual pain mean to the world?" I should say to this: Yes, it is true, the ocean does not exist for the sake of the individual drops; but what is an ocean that does not consist of drops? And is not the whole ocean clear if every single drop is clear? And only then is it *wholly* clear.

Just as there are people who cannot see the woods for the trees, so there are also people who cannot see the trees for the woods. In ethics this method of conception leads to the consideration of human aspiration as the means of superhuman ends. Every ethics that seeks to stand on a basis of experience and remain within the possibility of progressive verification, must cling to the standpoint of "man with men." It need not for this reason overlook the fact, that ethical conduct, like all unfolding of power, is connected with the universal world-process.

3) Dr. Carus also approaches the principle of welfare upon another, less mystical path. He maintains, with great emphasis, that ethics must be based on facts, on insight into the real, the actual, order of nature. Our ideals—this is the opinion of Dr. Carus—arise through the wants which the relations of reality awaken in us, and must be realised by the means which the relations of reality supply.

"The new ethics is based upon facts and is applied to facts" (p. 18).

"Man wants something, so he conceives the idea how good it would be if he had it. . . . Only by studying facts will he be enabled to realise his ideals" (pp. 19 and 20).

"If you wish to exist, obey reason. Reason teaches us how to regulate our actions in conformity with the order of natural laws. If we do regulate them in conformity with the order of natural laws, they will stand; otherwise not. In the former case they will be good, they will agree with the cosmical conditions of existence; in the latter case they are bad, they will not agree with the cosmical conditions of existence; therefore they will necessarily produce disorder and evil" (pp. 31, 32).

It appears to me clear from this, that the reason why we must regulate our actions to conform with natural laws, must be the fact that otherwise they cannot "stand," which is explained more in detail in what follows, to mean that they are constituted to produce "disorder and evil,"—which in its turn must be surely understood as meaning that disorder is itself an evil. If disorder were no evil, and if no further evils resulted from actions which are not "in conformity with the order of natural laws," what foundation would Dr. Carus in that case be able to give his ethics? I wholly agree with Dr. Carus that our conduct if it is to be ethical must support itself upon as profound a comprehension of the relations of reality as physical science, psychology, and social science alone can furnish. But *this requirement can only be made good through and by the principle of welfare.* It has validity only for the person who wills that his conduct shall "stand" and produce no evil, either in extended or in limited circles. If pain and death were not evils, this requirement would have no validity.

To judge from his somewhat indefinite expressions one might suspect in Dr. Carus here a votary of egoistic hedonism, were it not that a number of other passages in his book exclude this suspicion.

However, it seems quite clear to me that his final criterion must coincide with the principle of welfare. His ethics is an ethics of expediency, in that his ultimate criterion is the influence of actions on the life of mankind.

4) Dr. Carus justly emphasises the relation of ethics to our world-conception at large. But this connection does not mean that ethics can be derived by deduction from a philosophical system previously given. Ethics is an independent discipline which starts from its own peculiar assumptions (which cannot of course stand in contradiction to other established assumptions), although it is obliged to make much use of the results furnished by other sciences. Ethics has an independent foundation in the laws of feeling and volitional life, just as the theory of knowledge has its foundation in the laws of sensations and perceptions. In conformity with the law of economy, (which must prevail in science even though it should not prevail in nature,) we must restrict the established postulates of the single sciences to the least possible limit. If after doing this agreement between the single sciences finally occurs, this result will be all the more valuable.

According to Dr. Carus ethics is to be derived now from a philosophical total world-conception, as according to his view ("The Ethical Problem," p. 71) it originally arose through the influence of the positive religions.* Very weighty objections can be made in my opinion against this latter assumption. It is a fact

* Dr. Carus expresses himself differently in *The Open Court* (1890, p. 2549) where religion and ethics are called twins; whereas in *The Ethical Problem* the latter is the daughter of the former.

that the lower a religion stands the less ethical character it possesses, and the very lowest religions it is probable possess no ethical value whatever. The question then arises how religion gradually acquired its ethical character. The ethical ideas which were perceived in the nature of the deity must have had a natural origin, and this origin can be sought only in the life of man with men. The ethical norms and ideas developed themselves here spontaneously and have been just as spontaneously projected or hypostatised as the attributes of divinity. In the history of the religion of Greece we can see clearly exhibited the development of gods as powers of nature to gods as the expression of an ethical order of nature. Compare for instance, the Dodonæan and the Homeric Zeus with the Zeus that appears in the ideal belief of Æschylus. The experiences are made in human life that lead to the formation of divine ideals. Gods grow better and more gentle according as men themselves grow better and gentler. Religious conceptions are idealised experiences. If religion is a factor in the development of ethics it is because man conceives and represents his essential ideals in a religious form. The movement proceeds therefore from experience to experience; that which acts on nature is, as Shakespeare says, always an art that has been produced by nature itself. How could man understand the meaning of the ethical qualities attributed to his deities if he were not acquainted to some extent with these qualities through experience?

That which distinguishes philosophical from theological ethics is not the fact that the former is constructed on the basis of some philosophical system and the latter upon ecclesiastical dogmatism, but the fact that philosophical ethics brings out into full consciousness the psychological basis upon which ethical life has actually always more or less indirectly builded, and draws all the consequences implied in this. In this it furnishes an independent contribution to a philosophical system.

5) It seems to me to be perfectly justified, that the distinguished men who lead the Ethical Societies keep these institutions as independent as possible not only of all definite dogmatic tendency of thought but also of all unnecessary philosophical hypotheses and speculations. With respect to what concerns the first principles of ethics itself, it is not necessary for the practical ethicist to occupy any definite point of view, although it would be very fortunate if he were acquainted with the discussion of these principles and could take part in an independent manner in the same. He who proposes to teach applied mathematics or employ it in practice need not begin with a definite position with respect to the nature and origin of mathematical principles. So also in ethics there is a complete group of ideas and endeavors which are independent of the manner in which the first principles are conceived. The essential thing for the Ethical Societies is, (as Dr. Stanton Coit has said in his beautiful book "Die Ethische Bewegung in der Religion,") agreement as to the methods of development of character and as to the type of character to be developed.

Dr. Carus can have really nothing to object to in this method of conception, inasmuch as it is his conviction that in the passage from the supernatural to the natural establishment of ethics the "substance of our morality" will not be changed. In an article in *The Open Court*, at page 2575, he says: "The most important moral rules are not to be altered. . . . . Some of them will be altered as little as our arithmetical table can be changed." In this passage less importance for the *contents* of ethics is attributed to the various points of view than I should be obliged to assign. Yet all the sooner should Dr. Carus really admit that the Ethical Societies have added to their other services that of holding a proper course between the different dogmatic and philosophical systems.

6) This last dispute it appears to me also testifies to the expediency of distinguishing between the different ethical problems. By so doing Dr. Carus would also have been more just in his position with regard to utilitarianism. The latter has not arisen so much from the impulse to supply a *motive* for ethical conduct as from the impulse to acquire an absolute criterion. It is true the powerful influence of Hobbes and Locke brought it about that many of the later utilitarians embraced the egoistic theory; but by their side marched another group of utilitarian ethicists (among the earlier, Bacon, Cumberland, Shaftesbury, and Hutcheson) who did not subscribe to this theory. So far as I know, Hutcheson was the first with whom the furmula occurs: "The greatest happiness of the greatest number." These very historical facts show how important it is in the treatment of ethical problems to apply the maxim "Divide et impera!" I have therefore prefaced this my apology for the principle of welfare by calling attention to the relative and mutual independence of ethical problems.

THE CRITERION OF ETHICS AN OBJECTIVE REALITY.

I. TWO DEFINITIONS OF GOOD.

WHILE Mr. Herbert Spencer in his "Data of Ethics," may be considered as the most persuasive and popular, Prof. Harald Höffding, it appears to me, is the most scholarly and learned expounder of that ethical theory which bases morality upon the principle of the greatest happiness for the greatest number. *The Monist* No. I contained (pp. 139–141) a criticism of mine on Professor Höffding's Ethics, and Professor Höffding's article which originally appeared in No. 4 of *The Monist* is in part a further exposition of his views, and in part an answer to my criticism, which is here reproduced as follows:

Harald Höffding, Professor at the University of Copenhagen is a representative thinker among ethical scholars. Unhesitatingly he takes his stand upon the real facts of life and attempts to construct a system of ethics which shall be a science among the other sciences. Professor Höffding says in the preface of his ethics:*

"If we see the snow-covered peaks of a mountain range from a far distance, they seem to hover in the air. Not until we approach do we discover plainly that they rest upon solid ground. It

* The pages of the quotations refer to the German edition.

is the same with ethical principles. In the first enthusiasm one imagines that a place should be assigned to them above the reality of nature and life. On further reflection and after a long experience, which must perhaps be dearly bought, we discover that the ethical principles can regulate life only if they have really proceeded from life."

Professor Höffding is in a certain sense a utilitarian. The influence of utilitarian systems upon his mode of thought can be traced throughout the whole work, and it is this influence perhaps to which the Danish Professor owes his positive standpoint as well as the scientific method of his procedure. Nevertheless he differs from the ordinary utilitarian school and prefers to characterise his system as an ethics of general welfare. He says:

"The so-called utilitarianism,—that ethical conception which has been founded mainly by Bentham,—has the merit of having for the first time energetically propounded the principle of welfare. Yet Bentham has detracted from his cause by proceeding from a psychological theory which considers consciousness as a sum of ideas and feelings, and dissolves society into a number of individuals. The import of pleasurable and painful feelings for the continuous and general welfare cannot be established by a mere process of calculation." (P. 37.)

Professor Höffding opens the first chapter of his work with the following sentence:

"Ethical judgments contain a valuation of human actions. . . . The criterion of the ethical valuation is the contents of ethics."

If life consisted of isolated sovereign moments, every one of them would have an equal right, and no one would be obliged to resign in favor of any other moment. No valuation, no discrimination would be required. But the life of each individual, as well as the life of society, makes up a "life-totality," and we possess a conception of this life-totality. "If the state of feeling in a single moment agrees with the conception of the life-totality, a new feeling arises which is determined by this mutual relation. . . . The ethical valuation is conditioned by this feeling." (P. 27.) Taking this ground, Professor Höffding defines good and bad in the following way:

"'Good' accordingly becomes that which preserves the life-totality and gives fulness and life to its contents; 'bad,' on the contrary, that which has more or less the tendency to dissolve or to limit the life-totality and its contents. Bad accordingly is the single moment, the separate impulse in its revolutionary isolation from the rest of life. . . ." (P. 29.)

"The Bad, therefore, is egotism in its various degrees and various forms. And the verdict about it will be the severer the more conscious this egotism is."

Utilitarianism as a rule has been hedonistic. Utilitarians have proposed as the criterion of an ethical valuation the consequences of an act; if the consequences give more pleasure than pain, it is said to be good; if they are attended with more pain than pleasure, it is said to be bad. In the above quoted definitions by Professor Höffding there is no trace of hedonism, and I should consider an ethical system based upon these definitions as being in strong opposition to hedonism. But Professor Höffding appears to have been so strongly biased by the influence of hedonistic utilitarianism, that he introduces again its fundamental idea, which identifies the good with the pleasurable. Although he objects to employing the terms "utility" and "happiness," "because they are liable to lead to misunderstandings and have indeed done so"; although he declares that "momentary feelings of pleasure and pain are no sure criterion for the total state" (p. 37); although for such reasons he proposes the word welfare, saying, "by the word 'welfare' I think of everything which serves to satisfy the wants of human nature in its whole entirety"; still Professor Höffding again returns to hedonism by limiting the idea "welfare" to the hedonistic conception of goodness. He defines welfare as "a continuous state of pleasurable feelings." (P. 98.)

Thus we are presented with two definitions of what constitutes the criterion of an ethical valuation: (1) that which promotes the life-totality, and (2) that which produces a continuous state of pleasurable feeling.

These two definitions are in many respect harmonious, but on the other hand they may come into conflict; and if they come into conflict, which of the two is to be sacrificed? Supposing that a contemplation of the evolution of organised life should teach us that the development of a "life-totality" is not at all a pleasurable process; that on the contrary it is attended with excessive and innumerable pains. Inorganic nature so far as we can judge is free from pain. The isolated atom, we may assume, exists in a state of indifference. Supposing now that pain could be proved to increase, the higher we rise in the development of a life-totality; supposing that the growth of a life-totality had to be bought with pain, what would be the consequence? I will not here enter into the subject, but I may mention that this supposition is not at all without foundation. Assuming that it were so, would not, in such a case, the good be as Schopenhauer, Hartmann, and Mainlaender propose, that which destroys the life-totality of consciousness and with it the whole world of civilised humanity, built up of the innumerable consciousnesses of individuals?

Professor Höffding has seen this difficulty, which arises from a conflict of the two criteria of ethical valuation (1) the hedonistic principle and (2) the principle of progress, i. e. the constant evolution of a higher life-totality. He says:

"John Stuart Mill has declared that it is better to be a dissatisfied man than a satisfied pig, a dissatisfied Socrates than a satisfied fool. He bases this assertion upon the fact that even if the pig and the fool were of a contrary mind, their opinion would have to be rejected, since they possess no knowledge of the higher point of view from which man and Socrates consider life, whereas man knows the needs of the pig and Socrates fathoms the fool. We must be regulated by the judgment of those that know the two kinds of needs in question and that are consequently able to institute an estimation of the value of the same.

"But I feel obliged to put in a word for the pig and the fool. The difficulty is greater than Mill imagines. Man, it is true, knows all the wants of the pig, and it would not be difficult for a Socrates to comprehend those of the fool. But man does not have the wants of the pig, nor Socrates those of the fool, as his *sole and only dominant* wants. And yet this is the very circumstance that determines the matter. Man cannot transform himself into a pig without ceasing to be a man, and a Socrates will hardly be able so to identify himself with a fool as to lose completely his Socratic wants. If, now, the pig can attain the *complete* satisfaction of all *his* wants, is not his happiness greater than that of man whose desires and whose longings are never wholly satisfied? And the fool, who does not nourish many thoughts and makes no great demands upon life, is he not happier than Socrates who spends his whole life in striving to know himself and to stimulate others, only finally to declare that death is really preferable to life?"

Professor Höffding's solution of the difficulty is summed up in the following paragraph:

"Welfare is an illusion if we understand by it a passive condition of things, created once for all. It must consist in *action*, work, development. Rest can only mean a termination for the time being, the attainment of a new level, upon which it is possible for a new course of development to proceed."

Thus it appears that Professor Höffding decides in favor of the second principle. The evolution of the life-totality is considered higher than a continuous state of pleasurable feeling. Nevertheless Professor Höffding adds:

> "On that account, however, we are not obliged to retract our first definition of welfare as that of a continuous state of pleasurable feeling. That which must be rejected is only the notion of a passive state."

Truly, as Professor Höffding says, "the difficulty is greater than Mr. Mill imagined." The difficulty is great enough to undermine the whole basis upon which welfare is defined as "a state of continuous pleasurable feeling." If, as Professor Höffding declares, welfare is to be interpreted as activity, work, development; if this kind of active welfare is the greatest good, whatever admixture of pain and whatever absence of pleasurable feeling it may have; if the greatest amount of a state of continuous pleasurable feeling is not welfare in an ethical sense, what becomes of the utilitarian definition of welfare as pleasurable feeling? If, however, welfare is "the state of a continuous pleasurable feeling," how can we declare that the life of a pessimistic philosopher is preferable to that of a joyful fool?

Must not the ultimate reason of this conflict be sought in Professor Höffding's statement that—

> "The proposition of a purpose presupposes in the subject which makes the proposition feelings of pleasure and displeasure." (P. 30.)

Should we not rather say that the proposition of a purpose presupposes an expression of *will* in the subject which makes the proposition? Wherever there is will, there is also approval and disapproval, but approval is not always pleasurable and disapproval is not always attended with displeasure. Does it not often happen that we cannot help disapproving of things which please us?

Professor Höffding's present explanation of the subject does not satisfy me. The main point of my criticism, it seems to me, has not been answered, and the difficulty is not overcome. Professor Höffding declares that the strong desire for activity, development, and progress does not exist at all stages. It is itself a consequence of development and progress (p. 537). This, it may be granted, explains why a civilised society cannot help developing workers that plod and toil, finding no satisfaction unless they plod and toil; but it does not explain why (if after all the criterion of our ethical judgment remains happiness or the continuous state of pleasurable feelings) their state is preferable to that of indolent and happy savages.

Professor Höffding says:

> "*If* it could be proved that increasing pain followed necessarily on all advancement of civilisation . . . . in that case it would be impossible to combine civilisation and welfare" (i. e. a continuous state of pleasurable feelings).

Well, *if* that be so,—as Professor Höffding himself in the comparison of man to a pig and of Socrates to a fool has actually conceded to be true,—if we stand between the dilemma of civilisation and welfare, or in other words if we have the choice only between a higher stage of life and a happier state of existence, which is preferable? That which Professor Höffding considers as preferable is his true criterion of what he calls good. The other one holds only so long as it agrees with his true and final criterion, so long as it does not come in conflict with it.

Suppose we select as the final criterion of ethics not the growth and development of the life-totality, but that of procuring to the greatest number of men, as much as possible, a continuous state of pleasurable feelings,—what will be the outcome of it? Can we suppose that, if these two principles collide, we shall be able to stop growth? Can we expect to overcome nature and to curtail natural evolution so as to bring about a more favorable balance between our pleasures and pains? If we do, we shall soon find out that we have reckoned without our host.

A conflict between civilisation and welfare, (i. e. between natural evolution and our pleasurable feelings,) would not discontinue civilisation as Professor Höffding supposes, it would rather produce a change in what we have to consider as welfare. We *have to* be pleased with the development of our race according to the laws of nature, and those who are displeased might just as well commit suicide at once, for they will go to the wall, they will disappear from the stage of life. Those alone will survive who are pleased with that which the laws of nature demand.

Our pleasurable feelings are subjective, nature and the laws of evolution are objective. The criterion of ethics is not subjective but objective. The question is not what produces pleasurable feelings, but what is the unalterable order of the world with which we have to be pleased.

The question of ethics, in my mind, is not what we wish to do or what we think we ought to do, but *what we must do.* Nature prescribes a definite course. If we choose another one, we shall not reach our aim, and if we reach it, it will be for a short time only.

The aim of nature is not the happiness of living beings, the aim of nature, in the realm of organised life, is growth, development, evolution. Pleasures and pains are phases in the household of life, they are not life's aim. Experience shows that in reaching a higher stage we acquire an additional sensibility for both, for new pleasures and new pains. The pleasures of human existence in comparison with those of animals have been as much intensified and increased as the pains. The ratio has on the average remained about the same and it has rarely risen in favor of pleasures. Rather the reverse takes place: the higher man loses the taste of enjoying himself without losing the sensitiveness of pain.

Ethics, as a science and from the standpoint of positivism, has to inquire what according to the nature of things we must do. It has to study facts and from facts it has to derive rules (the moral prescripts) which will assist us in doing at once what we shall after all *have to* do. The criterion of ethics is not some standard which we put up ourselves, the criterion of ethics is agreement with facts.

II. THE AUTHORITY OF MORAL COMMANDS.

Professor Höffding emphasises "the fact that there is not merely one single ethical problem but many"—a fact which cannot be denied, for there are, indeed, innumerable problems of an ethical nature. However, we must bear in mind that all the ethical problems are closely interconnected. The better we understand them, the more shall we recognise that all together form one great system of problems, and that one problem lies at the bottom of all. This one basic problem I have called *the* ethical problem.

The solution of the basic problem of ethics will not involve the ready solution of all the rest, but we can be sure that it will throw light upon any question that is of an ethical nature.

Professor Höffding recognises the importance of system in ethics. He says:

"The systematism of ethical science is still so little advanced that it is necessary to draw out a general outline before we pass on to any single feature. The value of systematism is namely this, that we are immediately enabled to see the connection of the single questions with one another as well as their distinctive peculiarity."

It appears almost unfair toward the present state of ethical science when Professor Höffding adds:

"In ethics we are not yet so far advanced."

If we were not, we should do our best to advance so as to recognise the unity of all ethical problems. We must first recognise *the* ethical problem, before we can with any hope of success approach the many, which are dependent upon the one.

Which is the one basic problem of ethics?

We read in Matthew, xxi. 23:

"And when Jesus was come into the temple, the chief priests and the elders of the people came unto him as he was teaching and said, By what authority doest thou these things? and who gave thee this authority?"

This question is legitimate and all our ethical conceptions must necessarily depend upon the answer which we accept as satisfactory. The basic problem of ethics is the foundation of ethics, it is the justification of the ethical prescripts, it is the discovery of the authority upon which ethical rules are based. If there were no power that enforces a certain line of conduct, ethics in my opinion would have no right of existence; and if any one preaches certain commands, he is bound to give satisfactory reasons why we must obey his commands.

Professor Höffding says that ethics "starts from its own assumptions" (p. 111). Ethics should not start from any assumptions.

If we are to come to a mutual understanding we must drop all subjectivism, we must not study ethics from special points of view, from the principles or standards of any individual or group of individuals. There is not the slightest use of a person making himself any "highest and only aim" which, it may be true, "from his point of view can never be refuted." So long as ethics starts from assumptions or principles, it will be no science; for truly, as Professor Höffding says in excuse of the inability to prove principles, "The difficulty always occurs in the enunciation of a principle that a direct demonstration of its validity cannot be given."

The requirement of ethics is to arrive at statements of fact. Let us build upon facts and we shall stand upon solid ground.

Ethics in order to be scientific must be based upon the objective and unalterable order of things, upon the ascertainable data of experience, upon the laws of nature.

Professor Höffding says:

> "Religious ethics is founded on authority. Its *contents* are the revealed commands of authority; the *feeling* which impels us *to pass ethical judgments* is the fear or reverence or love with which men are filled in the presence of divine authority."

Scientific ethics can in this respect not be different from religious ethics, for it is also based upon authority. A scientific ethicist has to proceed like any other naturalist; he must observe the course of events and attempt to discover the laws in accordance with which the events take place. These laws are no less unalterable than any other natural laws, and we may appropriately call them the natural laws of ethics. The moral commands of ethical teachers have been derived, either instinctively or with a clear scientific insight, from the natural laws of ethics. The authority of the natural laws of ethics has been decked out by different religious teachers with more or less mythological tinsel or wrapped in mystic darkness; for practical purposes it remained to some limited extent the same and will to some extent always remain the same, for we shall have to obey the moral law, be it from fear, or reverence, or love.

The unity of all the ethical problems will be preserved, however much they may be differentiated. Indeed Professor Höffding in his enumeration sufficiently indicates their interconnection. He speaks of (1) the motive principle of judgment, (2) the test-principle of judgment, and (3) of the motive to action. Whatever difference he makes between these three terms, it is obvious that whether and how far judgments, tests, or motives are sound will depend upon their agreement with the authority of the natural law of ethics. The pedagogic problem is also connected with the ethical problem because upon our solution of the latter will directly depend the aim and indirectly also the method of education. Such complex motives as "ambition or the instinct of acquisition" will become "the means of attaining to true ethical self-assertion" in the degree proportional to the elements they contain which will strengthen our efforts of setting us at one with the natural law of ethics.

To sum up: The natural law of ethics has to be derived from facts like all other natural laws. The natural law of ethics is the authority upon which all moral commands are based, and agreement with the natural law of ethics is the final criterion of ethics.

III. ETHICS AND WELFARE.

I have no objection to an ethics of welfare; on the contrary, I consider every ethics as an ethics of welfare. My objection to Professor Höffding's ethics is solely directed against his definition of welfare as "a continuous state of pleasurable feelings." Welfare is according to my terminology that state of things which is in accord with the natural law of ethics, and it so happens that welfare must as a rule not only be bought, but also constantly maintained with many pains, troubles, anxieties, and sacrifices. It is true that upon the whole there may be a surplus of happiness and of satisfaction, if not of pleasures; but the surplus of happiness (important though it is) does not constitute that which is morally good in welfare. Morally good (the characteristic feature of the ethical idea of welfare) is that which is in accord with the natural law of ethics.

If the term "utility" were defined by utilitarians in the sense in which I define welfare, I should also have no objection to utilitarianism. The utilitarians, however, define their theory as "the Greatest Happiness Principle," and if "useful" is taken in its ordinary sense as that which is profitable or advantageous, it makes of utilitarianism an ethics of expediency.

IV. FEELINGS AND JUDGMENTS.

The fundamental difference between Professor Höffding and myself, and as it seems to me his *πρῶτον ψεῦδος*, lies in his definition of ethical judgments. He says:

"Ethical judgments, judgments concerning good and bad, in their simplest form are expressions of feeling, and never lose that character however much influence clear and reasoned knowledge may acquire with respect to them."

I am very well aware of the fact that all thinking beings are first feeling beings. Thought cannot develop in the absence of feeling. Without feeling there is no thought; but thought is not feeling, and feeling is not thought.* By thought I understand the operations that take place among representative feelings, and the essential feature of these feelings is not whether they are pleasurable or painful, but that they are correct representations. Judgments are perhaps the most important mental operations. There are logical judgments, legal judgments, ethical judgments, etc. In none of them is the feeling element of mental activity of any account. That which makes of them judgments is the reasoning or the thought-activity. Whether a judgment is correct or not does not depend upon the feeling that may be associated with it, but it depends upon the truth of its several ideas and the propriety of their connection.

A judgment, be it logical, juridical, ethical, or any other, is the more liable to be wrong, the more we allow the feeling element to play a part in it. Judgments swayed by strong feelings become biassed; they can attain to the ideal of truth only by an entire elimination of feeling.†

Ethics in which the feeling element is the main spring of action, is called sentimentalism. Sentimen-

* See the chapter "The Nature of Thought" in *The Soul of Man*, p. 354.

† Professor Höffding says: "The feeling of pleasure is the only psychological criterion of health and power of life." Every physician knows the insufficiency of this criterion. Many consumptives declare that they feel perfectly well even a few hours before their death.

tal ethics have no more right to exist than a sentimental logic or a sentimental jurisprudence.

The philosophy of Clärchen in "Egmont" appears to be very strong sentimentalism, and I do not believe that her demeanor can be set up as an example for imitation. Her love happiness is an intoxication. She vacillates between two extremes, now *himmelhoch jauchzend* and now *zum Tode betrübt*, and her life ends in insanity.

To consider ethical or any other judgments as feelings, and to explain their nature accordingly, seems to me no better than to speak of concepts as consisting of vowels and consonants, and to explain the nature of conceptual thought from the sounds of the letters. We cannot speak without uttering sounds, but the laws of speech or of grammar have nothing to do with sound and cannot be explained in terms of sound. When we think and judge, we are most assuredly feeling, but the feeling is of no account, and whether the feeling is pleasurable, or painful, or indifferent, has nothing to do whatever with the correctness or the ethical value of judgments.

V. PLEASURE AND PAIN.

It is very strange that, so far as I am aware, no ethicist who bases ethics upon the Happiness Principle has ever investigated the nature of pleasure and pain. It is generally assumed that pleasure is an indication of growth and pain of decay, but it has never been proved, and after a careful consideration of this theory I have come to the conclusion that it is based upon an error. Growth is rarely accompanied with pleasure and decay is mostly painless.

Optimistic philosophers look upon pleasure as positive and pain as negative, while the great pessimist Schopenhauer turns the tables and says pleasure is negative and pain positive.

An impartial consideration of the subject will show that both pleasure and pain are positive. Pain is felt whenever disturbances take place, pleasure is felt whenever wants are satisfied, and unsatisfied wants are perhaps the most prominent among the disturbances that produce pain.*

Professor Höffding says:

> "I agree with Dr. Carus that "this world of ours is not a world suited to the taste of a pleasure-seeker," if we understand by pleasure passive sensual enjoyment, an enjoyment which is not united with the rest and nourishment with which not only an immediate pleasurable feeling is connected, but whereby power is also gathered for continued endeavor."

When I say that this world of ours is not a world suited to the taste of the pleasure-seeker, I do not restrict the meaning of pleasure to "passive sensual enjoyment," but to all kinds of pleasure. There are also intellectual and artistic voluptuaries who sacrifice anything, even the performance of duty, to their pleasure, which I grant is far superior to any kind of passive sensual enjoyment. The pursuit of pleasure is not wrong in itself; but it is not ethical either. Ethics in my opinion has nothing to do either with my own pleasures or with the pleasures of anybody else. The object of ethics is the performance of duty; and the main duty of man is the performance of that which he needs must do according to the laws of nature, to let his soul grow and expand, and to develop to ever higher and nobler aims.

* See the chapter "Pleasure and Pain" in *The Soul of Man*, p. 338.

VI. PLEASURABLE FEELINGS AS AN ETHICAL CRITERION.

I know of a French teacher who has an excellent French pronunciation and speaks with perfect accuracy, but whenever he is asked to give a rule which may serve as a guide and a help to correct grammar and elocution, he says: "The chief rule in French is euphony."—"Exactly! But the same rule holds good in a certain sense for all languages."—"O no," he says, "the German is harsh and the English is tongue-breaking; only in French is the supreme law euphony."—"Now for instance," we venture to object, "you say *la harpe* and not *l'arpe;* you pronounce the *ai* different in different words you say *j'ai*, but you say *il fait* and you have again a different pronunciation of the *ai* in *nous faisons.*" He replies, "To pronounce *j'ai*, or as the Germans say *chaî* would be barbarous. To say *l'arpe*, instead of *la harpe* is simply ridiculous."—"The question is," we continued in our attempts to understand him, "what is euphonious to the ear of an educated Frenchman?"—"Well," he says, "the ear will tell you. That which jars on the ear is wrong. To say *quat'* instead of *quatre*, or *vot'* instead of *votre*, is wrong, it is vulgar. Why? it jars on the ear."

This method of teaching French appears to me a good illustration of our objection to the happiness principle of ethics. It is perfectly true that instances of immorality jar on the feelings of ethically trained minds. Why? They have become accustomed to them and look upon them as barbarous. Ungrammatical expressions and such pronunciations as do not agree with the spirit of a language are suppressed by those who recognise them as incongruous elements. Mistakes jar on their ears because they are incorrect, but they are not incorrect because they jar.

Oatmeal is a favorite dish among the Scotch. If you ask them why they eat it, they will most likely tell you, because it has an agreeable taste. But why do they like it? Because they have through generations grown accustomed to a dish which is conducive to health. Most of the dishes that are wholesome have an agreeable taste to a non-corrupted tongue. But agreeable taste for that reason cannot be considered as the supreme rule in selecting our menu. Agreeable taste is in cases of sickness a very unreliable guide and it is no criterion for a wholesome dinner. Surely the ethics of eating could not be based on agreeable taste.

The pleasurable feeling that is perceived in the satisfaction of hunger through appropriate food or in the satisfaction of any want, is not the bedrock of fact to which we can dig down; it is in itself a product of custom, of inherited habits, and other circumstances; and it can the less be used as a criterion because it varies greatly with the slightest change of its conditions.

Liberty is generally and rightly considered as a good, even though the slave may have and very often actually has enjoyed more happiness than the freed man. Stupidity is considered as an evil, although it inflicts no direct pains and may be the source of innumerable pleasures insipid in the view of others, but delightful to the jolly fool. Professor Höffding quotes from Waitz that the Indian does not progress because he "lives a happy life." Unhappiness is the cause of progress. We look down upon the Fuegians and upon the indolent South American tribe described by Humboldt. But have they not reached the aim of ethics, if happiness be that aim? Professor Höffding says in explanation of their condition:

> "That which would make such a life unendurable for us, *the strong desire for activity, development, and progress*, this desire does not exist at such stages."

If that is so, our strong desire for activity should be denounced as the source of evil. It would be ethical in that case, as some labor unions and trusts actually propose, to stop, or at least, to impede further progress. The attempt of the Jesuits in Paraguay, which to some extent was an unequivocal success, to rule the people through a spiritual dependence satisfying all their wants and keeping them in perfect contentment, cannot be condemned from that principle of welfare which defines welfare as a continuous state of pleasurable feelings.

I can see how a man can be induced to submit to a moment of pain in order to escape more pain in the future, but I cannot see on what ground one man can be requested to sacrifice himself to suffer pain or to forego his pleasures in order that a dozen or a hundred men may have a jolly time. It appears to me that a greater error has never been pronounced than that of making "the greatest happiness of the greatest number" the maxim of ethics.

For the same reason that prevents us from regarding the principle of happiness as the aim of ethics or as its test and criterion, we cannot consider self-humiliation, contrition, misery, and the abandonment of gayety and merriness as moral or meritorious. Joy and grief are in themselves as little wrong as they are virtuous. Any ethics the end of which is a morose austerity, simply because it makes life dreary, is at least as much mistaken as a philosophy which finds the purpose of life in mere pleasure, be it ever so vain, simply because it is pleasure. To pursue happiness or renounce it, either may sometimes be moral and sometimes immoral. Again, to undergo pain and to inflict pain on others, or to avoid pain, either may also be moral or immoral. The criterion of ethics will not be found in the sphere of feelings. Morality cannot be measured by and it cannot be expressed in pleasures and pains.

VII. THE SUPERINDIVIDUAL AND SOCIETY.

Professor Höffding criticises my view of "that superindividual soul-life which we call society," as based upon a mystical personification of society.

The superindividual motives of the human soul as I use the term, are actual realities, they are no less actual and concrete than are the image and the concept of a tree in my brain. I have sufficiently explained their origin and natural growth ("Ethical Problem," pp. 34–44), and feel that Professor Höffding's charge rests upon a misunderstanding. It appears to me that his term "sympathy," which he regards as the main element of ethical feelings leading to the adoption of the principle of general welfare, is much more liable to be interpreted in a mystical way. At least Schopenhauer's idea of sympathy (which he calls *Mitleid*) is undoubtedly a very mysterious thing, and its existence is supposed to be a direct manifestation of the metaphysical. I do not say that Professor Höffding uses the word sympathy in the sense of Schopenhauer's idea of *Mitleid*, but I am sure that if he attempts to explain its natural origin, he will (in order to remain positive and scientific) have to go over the same ground and arrive at the same conclusion as I did, although he may express himself in different words.

The truth is that man's ideas consist in representations of things and of relations without him, and these ideas are not the product of his individual exertions alone, they are the product of social work and of the common activity and intercourse of human society. This is true of language as a whole and of every single word which we use. This is true of all conceptual thought and most so of all ethical impulses. In spite of all individualism and in spite of the truth that lies in certain claims of individualism as to personal liberty and freedom of self-determination, I maintain that there is no individual in the sense of a separate ego-existence. That which makes of us human beings is the product of social life. I call the ideas and the impulses naturally developing in this way, superindividual, and if we could take them out of the soul of a man, he would cease to be a man. What is man but an incarnation of mankind! Social intercourse and common work produce the superindividual ideas and impulses in man, and these superindividual ideas and impulses in their action constitute the life of society.

This view is not "a mystical personification of society" under the simile of an organism, but it is a description of certain facts in the development of the human soul.

Society is not an aggregation of individuals, it is constituted by the superindividual element in the souls of individual men. The number of people in a society is for ethical purposes unessential. Professor Höffding accordingly makes an unimportant feature prominent, when he says:

"The idea of society, if it is to be scientifically employed, must always be so applied that at every point the definite group of individuals which it represents may be established."

If the greatest happiness of the greatest number among a definite group of individuals constitutes the morality of an act, would not the man who falls among thieves be under the moral obligation to renounce his property because the robbers constitute the majority?

If we leave the superindividual element out of sight, we shall naturally fall into the error of counting the individuals and deciding right and wrong by majority votes. The pleasure of a majority however does not constitute justice, and the greatest happiness of the greatest number is no criterion of that which is to be considered as morally good.

Society in the sense of a mere number of individuals will by and by create but does not constitute morality; nor can the majority of a society propose a criterion. The nature of moral goodness is not a matter of number nor of size nor of quantity. It must be sought in the quality of our ideas and motives. Moral are those ideas which tend to build up the life-totality of our souls so as to engender more and more of mankind in man, or still broader expressed, so as to keep man in harmony with the whole cosmos—with God.

VIII. THE POLICY OF THE ETHICAL SOCIETIES.

Professor Höffding considers it perfectly justified that the leaders of the ethical societies "keep these institutions as independent as possible not only of all dogmatic tendency of thought but also of all unnecessary philosophical hypotheses and speculations." So do we, for we object to dogmas, to hypotheses, and mere speculations. We consider the era of dogmatic religion as past, and trust in the rise of a religion based on truth, i. e. a natural and cosmical religion which stands on facts verifiable by science. Every religion, be it ever so adulterated by superstitions which as a rule, the less tenable they appear, are the more tenaciously defended as infallible dogmas—contains in its world-conception at least the germ of becoming a cosmical religion. The development of all religions aims at one and the same goal, namely the recognition of the truth and the aspiration to live accordingly. Those religions which remain faithful to this spirit of the religious sentiment will survive; they will drop the errors of dogmatic belief, they will free themselves of the narrowness of sectarianism and develop the cosmic religion of truth—of that one and sole truth which need not shun the light of criticism and which is at one with science.

We do not object to the ethical societies that they have no dogmas and that they do not identify themselves with a special philosophy; we object solely to their proposition to preach ethics without having a religion, or without basing ethics upon a conception of the world. And why do we object? Simply because it is impossible to preach ethics without basing it upon a definite view of the world, for ethics is nothing more or less than the endeavor to act according to a certain conception, to realise it in deeds. Can you realise in deeds a conception without having any? Can you live the truth without knowing the truth? You must at least have an instinctive inkling of what the truth is.

Mr. Salter separates the domains of ethics and science. He does not believe that ethics can be established on science, for he declares that science deals with facts, i. e. that which is, while ethics deals with ideals, i. e. that which ought to be. "We have to believe in ethics if we believe in them at all," Mr. Salter says, "not because they have the facts on their side but because of their own intrinsic attractiveness and authority."* This reminds me of one of Goethe and Schiller's Xenions in which the German poets criticise the one-sided positions of enthusiasts (*Schwärmer*) and philistines:

> Had you the power, enthusiasts, to grasp your ideals completely,
> Certainly you would revere Nature. For that is her due.
> Had you the power philistines, to grasp the total of Nature,
> Surely your path would lead up to th' idea's domain.

Ideals have no value unless they agree with the objective world-order which is ascertained through inquiry into the facts of nature. Ideals whose ultimate justification is intrinsic attractiveness and whose authority is professedly not founded on reality but on rapt visions of transcendental beauty, must be characterised as pure subjectivism. They are not ideals but dreams.

The ethical societies have as yet—so far as I am aware of—not given a clear and definite definition of good. Professor Adler treats this question with a certain slight. Concerning the facts of moral obligation he believes in "a general agreement *among good men and women* everywhere." (The italics are ours.) *The Open Court* (in No. 140) has challenged *the Ethical Societies*, saying that "we should be very much obliged to the *Ethical Record*, if it would give us a simple, plain, and unmistakable definition of what the leaders of the ethical movement understand by good, i. e. morally good." But this challenge remained unanswered.

It will appear that as soon as good is defined not in

* *What Can Ethics Do For Us*, p. 5. By W. M. Salter. C. H. Kerr, Chicago, 1891.

tautologies,* but in definite and unmistakable terms, the conception of good will be the expression of a world-conception. Is it possible to do an act which is not expressive of an opinion? And if an act is not expressive of a clear opinion, it is based upon an instinctive, an unclear, and undefined opinion. When the ethical societies declare that they do not intend to commit themselves to religious or philosophical views, they establish an anarchy of ethical conviction. Religion, as we have defined it, is man's inmost and holiest conviction, in accord with which he regulates his conduct. The ethical societies implicitly declare that we can regulate our conduct without having any conviction.

Is not an ethical society without any definite convictions upon which to base its ethics like a ship without a compass in foggy weather?

The attitude of the ethical societies in not committing themselves to any religious or philosophical view is after all—and how can it be otherwise?—a palpable self-delusion, for their whole policy bears unmistakably a definite and characteristic stamp. The leaders of the ethical societies will most likely repudiate my interpretation of their position, because it appears to me that they are not clear themselves concerning the philosophical basis upon which they stand and thus (as I am fully aware) many contradictory features appear by the side of those which I should consider as most significant.

IX. PROFESSOR ADLER'S POSITION.

Professor Adler is the founder of the Ethical Societies, he is their leader, and however much Mr. Sal-

* It is obvious that such definitions as "good is that which produces welfare" are meaningless, so long as we are not told what it is that makes a certain state *well* faring or *well* being.

ter, Dr. Coit, Mr. Sheldon, and Mr. Weston may disagree from him in minor matters, his views are decisive in the management, and the policy of the whole movement depends on him. Through his indefatigable zeal in the holy cause of ethics, his unflinching courage in the defense of what he regards as right, his energetic devotion to his ideals, and through the influence of his powerful oratory he has made the ethical societies what they now are. He determines their character and he is the soul of the whole movement. Now it is true that Professor Adler has never presented us with a systematic philosophy, but all his activity, his speeches, his poems, and the plans of his enterprises represent a very definite philosophical conception, which, to give it a name, may briefly be called Kantian Agnosticism.

Professor Adler is an agnostic, although not after the pattern of Spencer or Huxley. His agnosticism has been impressed upon his mind by Kant.

I expect that Mr. Adler will repudiate the name of agnostic, and it is quite indifferent with what name he may characterise his views. His position remains the same, whatever name he may choose to call it, if he chooses any; and he will choose none for he is too consistent an agnostic to define his position by a name.

It devolves upon me to prove my assertion and I hope to be able to do so.

Professor Adler looks upon ethics as something which lies outside the pale of human knowledge. He says in one of his lectures:

"And now one point more of utmost importance. If there be an existence corresponding to our highest idea, as we have said there is, yet we know not what kind of existence that may be. . . . . why then should we speak of it at all, why should we try to mention in words an existence which we cannot know? I will answer why. Because it is necessary to remind mankind constantly that *there is an existence which they do not know*. . . . Because otherwise the sense of mystery will fade out of human lives. . . . ."

Is "the sense of mystery" really a necessary element in human lives to make men aware of the grandeur of the universe. Is there no holiness in clearness of thought, and is ethics only sacred if it is surrounded with the hazy halo of an unknowable transcendentalism?

If our moral ideal does not come by the special revelation of God, as the dogmatic religions maintain, and if we cannot find it in nature, if it is beyond the ken of human cognition, if it is unascertainable by science, whence does it come? Professor Adler says:

"We must, indeed, be always on our guard, lest we confuse the idea of the Perfect with notions of the good derived from human experience. This has been the mistake of theology in the past, the point wherein every theodicy has invariably broken down. When we think of the Perfect we think of a transcendental state of existence, when we think of the moral law in its completeness we think of a transcendental law, a law which can only be wholly fulfilled in the regions of the Infinite, but which can never be fully realised within the conditions of space and time. The formula of that law when applied to human relations, yields the specific moral commandments, but these commandments can never express the full content, can never convey the far off spiritual meanings of the supreme law itself. The specific commandments do, indeed, partake of the nature of the transcendental law, they are its effects. The light that shines through them comes from beyond, but its beams are broken as they pass our terrestrial medium, and the full light in all its glory we can never see."

In this passage I believe to recognise the influence of Kant's transcendentalism. I differ from Professor Adler's conception of Kantian transcendentalism, but that is of no account here. One point only is of consequence. Professor Adler uses the word transcendental in the sense of transcendent and thus he changes the ethics of pure reason into mysticism. Professor Adler says:

> "Though I can never be scientifically certain, I can be *morally* sure that the mystery of the universe is to be read in terms of moral perfection."

I do not deny that moral instinct ripens quicker than scientific comprehension. Why? Because in a time when science is not as yet so far advanced as to understand the operations of the moral law, those people who instinctively obey the rules that can be derived from the moral law, will survive and all the rest will go to the wall. But the fact that we can have a reliable moral guide in an instinctive certainty which is generally called conscience, even before we attain to scientific clearness, does not prove that science will be forever excluded from the world of moral ideals.

Professor Adler's agnosticism found a very strong expression in a poem which resembles in its tone and ideas the church hymns of the New Jerusalem. The poem is very unequivocal on the point that moral action is comparable to building an ideal city, the plan of which is unknown to the builders. Professor Adler says:

> "Have you heard the Golden City
> Mentioned in the legends old?
> Everlasting light shines o'er it,
> Wondrous tales of it are told.
>
> Only righteous men and women
> Dwell within its gleaming wall;
> Wrong is banished from its borders,
> Justice reigns supreme o'er all.
>
> Do you ask, Where is that City,
> Where the perfect Right doth reign?
> I must answer, I must tell you,
> That you seek its site in vain.

You may roam o'er hill and valley,
You may pass o'er land and sea,
You may search the wide earth over,—
'T is a City yet to be!

We are builders of that City,—
All our joys and all our groans
Help to rear its shining ramparts;
All our lives are building-stones.

. . . . .

*What that plan may be we know not.**
How the seat of Justice high,
How the City of our vision
Will appear to mortal eye,—

That no mortal eye can picture,
That no mortal tongue can tell.
We can barely dream the glories
Of the Future's citadel."

How great an importance is attributed to this song by the leaders of the ethical movement may be learned from Mr. Salter's opinion of it. Mr. Salter says in criticising Unitarianism:

"Not from Unitarianism, not from Christianity, has come the song that best utters and almost chants this thought [of an ideal fellowship]. It is from Felix Adler, upon whom, I sometimes think, more than upon any other man of our day, the mantle and prophetic spirit of Channing have fallen, and whose words, I almost believe, are those which Jesus himself would utter, should he come and put his solemn thought and passion into the language of to-day."

Agnosticism is in our opinion no sound basis upon which to erect ethics. The unknowable is like quicksand, it gives way under our feet. The ethics of agnosticism must necessarily become mysticism. The ethereal dreams of mysticists need no solid basis, they hover in the air. Mr. Spencer who for some reason or other tried to escape the consequences of his agnosti-

*The italics are ours.

cism in the ethical field, adopted Utilitarianism, basing his moral maxims not upon the unknowable, as consistency would require, but upon the principle of the greatest happiness for the greatest number.

Professor Adler is not a Spencerian agnostic and here lies the strength of his ethics. Although he does not attain to a clear and scientific conception of the origin and natural growth of morality, he sounds no uncertain voice with regard to the Happiness Principle. He has on several occasions, like his great master Kant, uncompromisingly rejected any Hedonism or Eudæmonism. Among all societies aspiring to foster moral ideals, the societies for ethical culture are distinguished for their seriousness and ardor; and there can be no doubt about the cause: it is the spirit of Professor Adler's zeal not to give way to a hedonistic conception of ethics.

X. THE UNITY OF THE ETHICAL PROBLEM.

We conclude. Although the ethical problem can and must be split up in innumerable different problems, we should never lose sight of its unity.

Our age is a period of specialisation, of a division of labor and of detail work. This is true. But the more will it be necessary to survey the whole field and keep in mind the unity of which all piecemeal efforts are but parts. As soon as we lose sight of the unity in a certain system of problems, we are most liable to drop into inconsistencies. This is true of all things, of every science in particular, and of philosophy, the science of the sciences, also. It is no less true of ethics. We cannot engage, with any hope of success, in any of the diverse ethical questions unless we have first solved *the* ethical problem.

FIRST PRINCIPLES IN ETHICS.

BY WILLIAM M. SALTER.

It is the prerogative of man to ask for reasons for what he is enjoined to do or believe. An animal does not ask a reason why; a child may not—but a developed human being has a dignity with which mere blind obedience and unreasoning assent are felt to be incompatible.

It is as legitimate to question and inquire in the ethical field as in any other. There is nothing sacred about duty, right, good—in the sense of their making a region which we should not explore, or look upon with critical eyes. If we are told we *ought* to do any special thing, we have a right to ask, why?—just as we have a right to ask for the evidence of any theological creed or any scientific or philosophical proposition. Yes, more than "having a right," I may say that we should ask for reasons in the realm of morals: For, in the first place, some things which we may be told to do may be questionable and we should not wish to be imposed upon; in the second place, there are different notions of right and wrong abroad in the world, conflicting notions, and we are obliged to have some standard by which to judge between them; thirdly, the very sacredness of what is really right should make us jealous of anything that falsely goes by that name; and fourthly, even what is absolutely right should not be accepted as such by a rational being on authority, because this or that person says so, or this or that book so teaches—but only because he sees it to be so with his own eyes, because it is the deliverance, the discovery of his own reason. It may not be possible for every one to be rationalised at once; and in the meantime those for whom suffice the poets "few strong instincts" and "few are fortunate; none the less is it the ideal for every one who has the capacities of reason in him to develop those capacities, to "look before and after" and know the why and wherefore of everything he does, to bring his whole life, moral and intellectual, out into the light.

And now perhaps the first thing we need to do is to get a clear idea of what the ethical field is, which we are to explore. It is, firstly, the field of human action—and not only of actions in the outward sense, but of all that we do, whether by body or mind, so we do it voluntarily. Whatever happens in us apart from our will is outside the realm we are considering, just as much as what happens without us: the digestion of our food, for example, the circulation of the blood—though to the extent that we can affect these by our will they may come inside; if, for instance, they are feeble and imperfect and by anything we can do we can make them stronger, healthier, it may be our duty to do so. It is our life so far as it is regulated by our thought that we have to do with as ethical inquirers; so far as it goes on of itself and is ruled by laws which we are powerless to affect, it is beyond the province of ethics. Yet, more particularly, all voluntary actions may be of one sort or another, according as our thought determines. We may, for example, in taking a walk, go along this street or that as we choose. In talking with a friend, we may give or we may withhold certain information in our possession. In recollecting a promise or a vow, we may keep it or break it as one or the other thought is predominant in us at the time. Now wherever there are two possible thoughts and it occurs to us to say that one is better than the other, that one should be followed rather than the other, we enter the field of ethics proper. This by no means always happens in the case of voluntary actions; when we are off for a holiday it may not matter, within limits, what we do—whether we ride or walk or row or "lie in the sun" and do nothing; the only duty in the matter, may be, may be to do as we please. But sometimes we say, This is good and that is bad; this deserves to be done and that ought not to be done. Such judgments are ethical judgments; they are not of course descriptive of the actions, but of what the actions should be; in other words, they assert an ideal, and when they are repeated and generalised, they become formulations of a rule. Ethics is really a study of the rules of human action; if we call it a science, it is an ideal science —for it is not a study of the actual conduct of men (and so differs entirely from sociology or history), but of what that conduct would be if it conformed to certain rules; and these rules themselves are not simply the matter-of-fact rules which an individual or a people reverences, but the true rules, the rules which are intrinsically worthy of reverence.

Here then is the field for our inquiry—not nature, not man in general, not his actions, but the rules according to which he conceives he should act; and our inquiry now is not so much, what these rules are in detail but what is their reason for being, not so much how and when they arose and what is their history, but what is their justification and validity. To trace the rule, "Thou shalt not steal," for example, back to the one who first conceived it, to fix its authorship and date in the dim distant past, and follow its history since, is not the same as justifying it; customs and rules may have existed for ages and yet be without a rational basis. Ethics proper, on its intellectual side, is a reasoning about rules of conduct, it is a testing, criticising, accepting or rejecting the rules commonly proposed; and in searching for first principles in ethics, we are really asking for the ultimate reasons why we should follow (or refuse to follow) this, that or the other special injunction, for the final justification of whatever we call right.

Where shall we turn for light as to this problem? There seem to be those who think that science can settle it for us; they say that the basis of ethics is to be found in a clear knowledge of the world in which we live. And there is a measure of truth in this. If we do not understand our own being and natural laws about us we are to this extent in the dark, in our actions. Ignorance of the teachings of physiology and hygiene may cause us aches and pains that knowledge might have prevented. Ignorance of sanitary science is doubtless responsible in part for the large mortality of great cities. It is only by a knowledge of nature's forces—gravity, heat, steam, electricity,—that we can turn them to account and make them serve and benefit man. If we study the facts of sociology and history, we learn what conditions are favorable and what unfavorable to the growth and prosperity of communities. Such knowledge is of incalculable value; it is a help and guide to action—and yet there is some confusion in regarding it as the basis of ethics or as giving us an ultimate standard of right action. For who does not see that everything depends upon the use to which we mean to put our knowledge? It seems to be taken for granted that everybody desires happiness or long life for himself and for others; that the only wish of a person can be to use nature's forces for the general benefit; that all we care for is to make communities grow and prosper—in which case it would of course only be necessary to learn how these ends can be attained. But the fact is that we may desire other things; we may wish to know how to cut short our lives and how to end the lives of our people—time and again this has happened and is happening to-day, a great part of the activity of men consisting in killing one another or making preparations to; we may use nature's forces to injure as well as to benefit—a man of violence has the same motive for getting a complete scientific understanding of dynamite that any other sort of man would have; we may desire to degrade and humiliate a people as well as uplift it and make it prosperous—as England seems to have acted toward Ireland. Such scientific knowledge as I have referred to cannot be the basis or ultimate standard of ethics (however useful and necessary it may be in a subsidiary way), for one may act in complete accordance with it and yet aim at opposite things; one may have the clearest view of the world in which we live and yet play either (what we are accustomed to call) a good part or a bad part in it. The real question of ethics is, what are the true things to aim at, what is the meaning of playing a good or a bad part in the world—and, so far as scientific knowledge is concerned, for what ends shall we use that knowledge? Our very intentness on those ends (when we have discovered them) must make us resolute on finding out every possible means and observing every condition necessary for attaining them.

But if science fails us at the critical point (a certain mental confusion being involved in the very notion of its being more than a subsidiary guide for us), what else have we to do than to face the problem with our own discursive minds and by thinking of this end of our action and that, by weighing and balancing between them, try to find out that which seems worthiest, completest, most final and self-sufficient? For this, let it now be distinctly said, is what we are in search of—something, some state or condition which seems good in itself, which does not need to be regarded as a means to another end but which of itself satisfies the mind. If we ask for a reason for any action or rule, it must be because the action or rule requires a reason, being incomplete, objectless, irrational without it—as when a person going down town is asked Why? by a friend and in replying he tells his errand, while if he should say, For nothing, the friend would not know what to make of him. There are plenty of human actions, and sustained courses of conduct that have no meaning save in relation to some purpose beyond themselves. Yet on the other hand there may be things that seem so good that we do not look beyond them, things that it is superfluous to ask a reason for; they are complete in themselves and do not require any justification. It is such things that we have no reason of, things in virtue of which, or by their relation to which, all other things are good, things that it would be as absurd to ask for a reason for aiming at, as for conceding the truth of any self-luminous fact of nature. If such things can be found, if a supreme rule (or rules) can thus be formulated and if, on the other hand, all minor, special rules can be traced back to the supreme one and an explanation and justification thus be furnished for each single duty, then our problem would be virtually solved. To give a reason for everything that requires a reason, and to find those things for which no reason can be given only because they are self-evident—is all that the ethical student can ask. It is as when (to take a minor and imperfect illustration) having been in distant parts, we begin to travel homewards; at every step of the journey, at every change from sea to land, or from train to train, there is a reason for the action beyond itself; but when at last we reach the loved spot, and are safe within the dear old walls with father and mother or with wife and child, we do not ask a reason for being there—it is where we belong.

Let us, then, without attempting systematic completeness, take up a few of the duties and see if good reasons can be given for them and gradually work our way, if it is possible, toward the discovery of ends that are good in themselves. Temperance is one of man's duties; it is almost universally admitted. Yet I think it is legitimate to ask, why we should be temperate—for though familiarity with the idea may make it appear almost self-evident, it is not from the standpoint of reason really so. We take in as much air as we can with our lungs, we can hardly have too much light and sunshine—why may we not drink as much water or wine as we can and eat as much food? The answer obviously is that eating or drinking beyond a certain amount or measure is injurious to our health;

if we have gone beyond certain limits, we strain our bodily organism and weaken it. Hence, to the end of health, we must be temperate; but for this, temperance would be no virtue and intemperance no vice. Or consider the virtues of chastity and modesty; respect for them is almost instinctive in men and women who have been normally born and educated—and yet we may ask why these should be virtues and may come to see that if the race were not perpetuated as it is, if certain peculiar consequences did not flow from certain acts, if the institution of the family were not such an all-important factor in the evolution of man, there would be no more occasion for chastity and modesty than there is for refusing to shake hands with more than one person or for covering one's face so it shall not be seen. A duty is no less binding because we see the reason for it; rather it is only he who does see the reason who feels the full extent of the obligation, as knowing all the duty rests upon. This, it appears to me, equally applies to truth and falsehood. We should tell the truth to others because they need it, because without knowledge every one is more or less in darkness; and if there are ever times when we should withhold the truth it is in those rare circumstances when it may injure rather than help. Falsehood is base because it is a sort of treachery—a disowning of the bond by which we are united to our fellow men. For the same reason we have a right to the truth from others; and, moreover, we ought to give it to ourselves, or search for it, if it is not at hand; we can only grow, we can only step surefootedly in life, as we know. In brief, truth is obligatory, because it is a means of benefit; if it were in and of itself a virtue, irrespective of the needs or circumstances of those to whom the knowledge is implanted, then we should have to speak the truth though it killed people and should have to refuse to deceive a raging animal though at the risk of being killed ourselves.

But now let us take a step further. We have found that there is a reason for some of the commonly-recognised duties of life, that they are duties, because in doing them we contribute to certain desirable ends. In the one case, it is health; in another, the perpetuation of the race; in another, the benefit or welfare of men. The question then forces itself upon us, are these ends desirable for themselves alone, or have in turn we to give a reason for choosing them, just as we had to for temperance, purity and speaking the truth? Have we at this stage arrived where we can rest, have we the ultimate ends, the final goods, the first principles of which we are in search? It does not altogether seem so. What is for the good of our health should indeed at once have respect from us; and yet I think it is tolerably evident on a little reflection that health is desirable, because with it we can best do our work in life, because with it we are put in possession of all our faculties—and without it we are in a measure useless, a burden to others and a burden to ourselves. If we could do our work as well, if we could be as cheerful, if we could think and attain all our higher spiritual development as well without health as with it, health would be a matter of indifference. And if we ever allow an injury to our health, if we ever take risks with it (with the sanction of conscience, I mean), it is in aiming at some good beyond it—as mothers may in child-bearing, as explorers and pioneers may in opening up new countries to the world, as students and philosophic thinkers may in endeavoring to unravel the mysteries of existence, as reformers may in contending with old wrongs and abuses, as patriots may who risk their very life in the defense of their firesides and homes. We should keep our health for a purpose; it is not an end in itself. I am obliged to think in the same way of the perpetuation of the race. I think we may ask, *why* should we follow these deep-seated instincts of our nature? Natural as it may be to obey them, self-evident as it may seem to many that there ought to be more and more people in the world, I think that on sober reflection we are bound to ask, why? My answer would be that whether more people in the world are desirable depends upon what sort of people they are to be, how circumstanced (whether favorably or no to a really human development)—for we can easily conceive of conditions (and there are likely to be such in the later history of the globe) in which life would be a pitiful, useless struggle; and there may be inborn tendencies, physical and mental, that may make it better for some men and women not to have children now. The perpetuation of the race is a good, so far as it means the possibility of the race rising ever to higher and higher levels, so far as it means that there may be new human beings who may do better than their fathers and mothers did (or, at least as well), so far as it means the continuity and perpetuation and advancement of that spiritual something we call human civilisation and culture. No, the family, is not an end; it is a means to an end—a necessary means, indeed, and thereby a sacred institution, but still looking beyond itself; and these fathers and mothers are truly hallowed in their domestic lives who wish to bring up their children to carry still further the conquests of light, of love, and of justice in the world.

Yet when we think of the third end of which discovery was made—namely, the benefit or welfare of men, must we not say that this is a self-evident good, that no reason outside it is required for seeking it, since it appeals so immediately to us? In a sense it must be admitted that this is so. The reasons that have been given for the other ends, just discussed, are more or less closely connected with this end. And yet it is necessary that we have a clear idea of what the benefit or welfare of men means. There may be different standards by which to judge it, there may be limited notions of it; and we must not content ourselves with a phrase or a vague idea. Some may understand by welfare simply being well-situated in life, secure against enemies and accidents; but such welfare is as one-sided and incomplete a notion as health—we may ask, Why should we be thus favorably situated? what is the good of it, if we do not make more of ourselves thereby? Others may understand by welfare happiness; and surely happiness has the marks of being a good in itself. When we are happy, we do not ask why, to what end are we happy? For all labor, for all effort, for all self-denial there must be a reason; but there needs be no reason for happiness. And yet happiness, while a good (in itself), is not necessarily the good, the whole good; and such is its singular nature that it may be connected with not only what is otherwise good, but with what is unworthy and bad. Are there not those who find happiness in ruling other people and bringing them under their thumb, are there not those who find happiness in living in the eyes of the world and being continually noticed and applauded, are there not those who find happiness in giving themselves up to selfish pursuits and are never so pleased as when they have driven a successful bargain at somebody else's loss? Happiness in and of itself is innocent and is one of the first ends of our being, but when it is made into the only end, when other goods are made secondary or ignored, it may be the accompaniment of ignoble as well as noble action; moreover, in the existing state of human nature, happiness is so variable a quantity, that it can scarcely be said to furnish a standard at all (even a low or poor one), and so an ancient writer said well, "Pleasure is the companion, not the guide of virtue." We may live for happiness, if we only make it consistent with other ends of our being; we may work for other's happiness, so it be a worthy happiness, a happiness which is a harmonious part of a total good.

Physical security and comfort, happiness—these are not enough as measures of man's welfare; the one is too low, the other too variable. And how is it possible to judge of welfare save by saying that it must take in the whole of man, not only the life of the body or the satisfaction of existing desires, but the life of the mind and spirit, the possibilities of willing and achieving, the capacities of love—so that to work for human welfare means to work for the cultivation, the enrichment, the indefinite enlargement and expansion of the entire life of men, physical and spiritual? If we mean by human welfare, human perfection, if we set before ourselves the ideal of a perfected humanity —then we have an end in which we can rest, a goal that has every appearance of being a final goal, because we can imagine nothing greater beyond it, because there is no outside purpose a perfected humanity could serve which could be as great as itself. We may not be able to say beforehand all that a perfected humanity would attain, all it would be; we may not be able to present a definite picture of it—yet we know the tendencies, the capacities that await a full and complete development, we know the lines of advance in the past, we see how they stretch out before us now; we know our direction, our bearing—and what will be (or should be) in the future is only an extension, an unfolding, a blossoming and ripening of what we have now. Humanity's powers, (all it has consciously, all that may be revealed to it) passed into realisation—the mind, the heart, the will of universal man in full play and triumphant activity; that is the ideal that seems to sum up what is valid in all other ideals, that is the good which serves to measure all other goods; everything is right which tends to its accomplishment and everything is wrong which tends to defeat it and make it impossible; all our duties (which are real duties) have their ultimate sanction here—they are explained by, derived from the one supreme duty of laboring for such a consummation; every valid rule of action is only an application of the sovereign rule to work for the perfection of society, for the total development of the capacities of man.

It is only another way of stating this to say that we have now reached the point where we cease to ask for reasons. It is as with any scientific investigation; when we reach an ultimate law of nature or an ultimate fact, we are satisfied. We do not wish to go beyond it, because there is no going beyond it; and all the demands and efforts of our reason might be said to be to the end of finding something about which we have to reason no more. Such a recognition as this when made in the realm of morals is sometimes misunderstood. When we propose an ultimate rule of right action and say that no reason can be given for it, this is misinterpreted as meaning that we give up reliance or reason and abandon ourselves to mysticism; while it is reason and reason only that has brought us to the discovery of the ultimate rule, and the rule might be called (if so long a word can be pardoned) the objectification of reason—that is, reason written out into an objective law. Mysticism is, if I understand the word, a love of vague, shadowy, nebulous thoughts, a preference of twilight or the dark rather than the clear light of day; but nothing is clearer, more distinct, (to one who thinks along the lines I have just followed) than this ultimate law of right which I have stated; no reason could be given for it that is as clear as the law itself. A sense of all this is the motive for the assertion sometimes made that it is absurd for a man to ask, Why should I do right? For when one finds the real, ultimate right, the question is absurd; but this does not mean that it is absurd to ask why one should be temperate, or truthful, or chaste, or obedient to authority, all of which are right only in relation to circumstances that may change. When we find out what is right, when we discover any special minor duty that is really duty, there is nothing under heaven for us but to do it; and the question, Why? as it is sometimes raised does not mean a demand for intellectual clarification, but rather, What am I going to get by doing right? and springs from a base motive rather than a noble one. There are not a few of these specious questioners to-day—weak, timid children of fashion and conventional religion—who ask why should they rule their passions and live sober righteous lives, unless it is that they are going to be rewarded for it hereafter; so little does popular Christianity really educate the moral nature of its followers. For there is this implication in the idea of an ultimate rule of action—namely, that man has a capacity of acting in accordance with it, that there is (what we may call for lack of a better term) an instinct for the right in him, a love for the right as such, just as there is a love for the truth as such, irrespective of any personal gain save the consciousness of knowing it; this disinterested love of truth is the basic motive of science and the love of right is the basic motive of really moral conduct.

From the standpoint of the supreme rule it ought now to be possible to survey the whole field of duty and to give an explanation and justification for each minor rule. This would be necessary to complete our investigation and to give it a thoroughly scientific character. But I fear I have already taken more space than should be accorded to a single article.

THE "IS" AND THE "OUGHT."

The distinction between explicative and normative sciences is for certain purposes very commendable. Such sciences as psychology, physiology, botany, grammar, etc., explain the "is," they describe facts as they are, while such sciences as logic, horticulture, hygiene, ethics, etc., set forth an "ought"; they prescribe the methods by which a certain ideal is to be attained. Normative sciences in so far as they are practically applied are also called disciplines.

Yet the distinction between explicative and normative sciences is artificial; it serves a certain purely scientific purpose, viz. to discriminate between natural laws and rules; but it is not founded in the nature of things. The realities which form the objects of these sciences are undivided and indivisible. Hygiene is possible only on the basis of physiology; logic only on the basis of a knowledge of the actual modes of thought; horticulture only on the basis of botany, and ethics only on the basis of psychology and sociology.

It is true that as a rule a skilled gardener will raise better fruit than a scientific botanist, but the best fruit will be raised in the botanical gardens where skill is guided by scientific insight.

The ethics of mankind has up to date been almost exclusively in the hands of the clergy, who in so far as they are imbued with the spirit of dogmatism, claim to be in possession of a nostrum which was by a divine revelation entrusted solely to their care, and maintain that nothing can be learned from science. The present age, however, no longer believes in nostrums and science penetrates everywhere. Humanity has found out that ethics forms no exception among the normative disciplines and that it can be based upon science as much as hygiene and horticulture.

The greatest demand of the time is not as the iconoclast says the abolition of religion, it is not as the dogmatist says, a revival of the blind faith of ages gone by, the greatest demand of the time is a conciliation between religion and science, is the imbuement of the clergy with the holy spirit of research, not in their symbolic books only, not in the Bible only, but in the wider and more reliable revelation of God, in nature; the greatest demand of the time is the maturing of dogmatic religion into a religion of science which will finally turn the cathedrals, temples, and synagogues of mankind into churches of science.

The Christian catechisms distinguish between the visible churches and the Invisible Church, the latter being the ideal of the former. There is a great truth in this distinction. The Invisible Church is that church whose faith is the religion of science, who preaches the ethics based upon facts and stands upon the ground of demonstrable truth. The Invisible Church is an ideal; but it is not an air castle. The Invisible Church is the aim toward which the development of all the visible churches tends. So long as the visible churches grow to be more and more like the Invisible Church, they will be and remain the moral leaders of mankind.

If the churches refuse to progress with the spirit of the time, they will lose their influence upon society, and the kingdom will be taken from them and given to others. That which we want, that which we must have, and that which mankind will have after all, if not to-day or to-morrow, yet in some not too distant future is a church which preaches the religion of humanity, which has no creed, no dogmas, but avowing a faith in truth and in the provableness of truth, teaches an ethics based upon the facts of nature.

When the Ethical Societies were founded many people hoped that a movement was started which would supply the demand of a religion of science and of scientific ethics applied to practical life. This hope was not fulfilled. The founder of the ethical societies is swayed by principles which are little short of an actual hostility toward science, and Mr. Salter is not as yet free from the belief that the ultimate basis of science rests upon some transcendental principle. Science in his opinion fails at the critical point.

The Societies of Ethical Culture can be called progressive in so far only as they discard rituals and ceremonies; but they are actually a reactionary movement on the main point in question. And there are frequent instances of clergymen and rabbis who proclaim freely and boldly the advanced ideas of a scientific conception of religion. Such views are not only not heard from the platforms of the Societies for Ethical Culture, but they are stigmatised by their leader.

It seems to me that in the present article Mr. Salter has considerably approached our position. He objects to mysticism, which Professor Adler formerly regarded as an indispensable element of ethics and ethical culture, and we may hope that the barrier of his transcendentalism that separates us still may be broken down too.

Mr. Salter says:

"Here then is the field for our inquiry—not nature, not man in general, not his actions, but the rules according to which he conceives he should act."

But he exclaims with a tinge of hopeless despair, as if there were no answer to the question:

"Where shall we turn for light as to this problem?"

He answers the question by a counter-question; he asks:

"Who does not see that everything depends upon the use to which we mean to put our knowledge?"

"It seems to be taken for granted that everybody desires happiness or long life for himself and others."

"But the fact is that *we may desire** other things."

Is Mr. Salter's question unanswerable? We hope not; for if it were unanswerable, ethics could not exist as a science.

The ultimate question of ethics is not *what WE desire*, but on the contrary *what IS desired of us*. We, i. e. our personal likes and dislikes, our intentions to make or to mar, have nothing to do with the subject. Ethics does not in the least depend upon the use to which *we* mean to put our knowledge. The mere introduction of the *we* and what *we* intend to use facts for, will produce confusion. This "we" of our personal desires is the veil of Maya which deceives us and leads us so easily astray.

The "is" that forms the basis of the "ought" in ethics consists in the nature of mankind and of the universe in which mankind exists. The laws of nature, especially of human nature and of the evolution

* Italics are ours.

of humanity, are the very same thing which the dogmatic religions call "the will of God." The will of God remains and will remain, for ever and aye, the basis of ethics.

Facts are such as they are, and the laws of nature will prevail. This is the basic truth of ethics and any question whether *we* shall recognise the will of God, whether *we* shall acknowledge the truth of nature's laws, whether *we* shall adopt the rules that are derived from the "is" into our will as the supreme rule of action, is another question of a personal nature, but it does neither invalidate the basis of ethics, nor does it stand in any connection with it.

We might be dissatisfied with the laws of nature and might imagine that we, if we had created the world, should have arranged them better than they are. We might decline to respect the precepts of the moral ought. That would doom our souls to perdition, for O Man! who art thou that repliest against God? (Rom. ix, 20.) It is hard for thee to kick against the pricks. (Acts ix, 5.)

The ought of ethics remains the same whether I, or you, or anybody else, deigns to follow, or refuses to follow, its behests; for the ultimate basis of ethics is not founded upon any so-called immovable rock of our conscience, not upon our subjective likes or dislikes, not upon what we choose to do or to leave alone. The ultimate basis of ethics is of an objective nature. The criterion of ethics is one of fact and not of opinion. That which has to be the standard of moral action can be inquired into, and can be searched for by scientific methods; it can be stated with as much exactness as the mathematical or logical rules or as any other precepts of the normative sciences.

Ethics is a normative science. It is as truly a science in every respect as are all the normative sciences. The ultimate principles of the normative sciences are not of a transcendental nature, they are founded upon the actual facts of life; the "ought" derives its rules from the "is," the ideal is rooted and must be rooted in the real.

AN ANALYSIS OF THE MORAL OUGHT.

COMMENTS UPON PROF. H. SIDGWICK'S VIEW.

THE question has been raised by ethical students, How is it that man has the idea of "ought" at all?*

The ideas "right," "moral goodness," "duty," the "ought," etc., are fundamental notions of ethics. As such they should be carefully defined; yet they are frequently used by moralists without an analysis of their meaning. Professor Sidgwick says in his article "Some Fundamental Ethical Controversies," *Mind*, No. 56, p. 480:

"Different systems give different answers to the fundamental question, 'What is right,' but not, therefore, a different meaning to the question."

Professor Sidgwick adds:

"According to me, this fundamental notion is ultimate and unanalysable: in saying which I do not mean to affirm that it belongs to the 'original constitution of the mind,' and is not the result of a process of development; that is a question of psychol-

*I owe the suggestion of writing this article to Mr. Salter. He takes the view that the "ought" is an obligation of absolute authority residing beyond facts and beyond the realm of science. Thus my attention was called to the importance of an analysis of the ought-idea itself. Whether or not the ought-idea is conceived as absolute, ultimate, and unanalysable is not a merely theoretical problem, it is of practical importance; for if we suppose that the ought is absolute, ultimate, and unanalysable, we are prevented from inquiring into its nature and come under the spell of a mysticism that debars progress and further philosophical research.

ogy—or rather psychogony with which I am not concerned: I merely mean that as I now find it in my thought, I cannot resolve it into, or explain it by, any more elementary notions. I regard it as co-ordinate with the notion expressed by the word 'is' or 'exists.' Possibly these and other fundamental notions may, in the progress of philosophy, prove capable of being arranged in some system of rational evolution; but I hold that no such system has as yet been constructed and that, therefore, the notions are now and for us ultimate."

The "ought" is most certainly a fact, or to use Professor Sidgwick's words, it is "a co-ordinate with the notion expressed by the word 'is' or 'exists.'" But he who attempts to describe the meaning of the "ought" will find that it is neither unanalysable nor ultimate; on the contrary it is a complex fact of a very special kind. The expression "ought" represents a certain relation among the ideas of a living, thinking, and acting creature.

By "analysing an idea," I understand, as Professor Sidgwick expresses it, "a resolving it into more elementary notions." All our notions are descriptions of facts. Those notions which represent a complex state of things accordingly are analysable, they can be described as certain relations or certain configurations of more elementary and more simple facts. Analysing is at the same time classifying. The most elementary and most simple facts would be those qualities of phenomena which are a universal feature of reality. And it is a matter of course that something that is universal can in its turn be no further subsumed under more general views. Analysis as well as classification ends with the universal and simplest qualities of existence.

The mind of a living being consists of many impulses the origin of which is a problem that belongs (as Professor Sidgwick declares of the "ought"), to psychogony. Yet the subject is too important to be left out in ethics and if Professor Sidgwick knows of no system that can analyse such facts as the ethical impulse of "the ought," it is highly desirable to do the work.

* * *

Impulses are tendencies to pass into action. To pass into action is an incipient motion. What is motion?

Motion is change of place. Hydrogen and oxygen when brought into contact show a tendency to combine; they exhibit an incipient motion. A ball placed on a slanting surface will roll down; it is going to change its place and this state is an incipient motion. The process of chemical combination and the rolling ball are motions, but no actions; they are not deeds of rational beings.

The word "action" is used in two senses, (1) to designate the purposive deeds of rational beings; and (2) to denote a certain view of motion, which should include every kind of efficiency, not only real motions, i. e. changes of place, but also pressures where the effect of the action is to counteract another action of equal force: thus the result of $+1$ and -1 is a zero of motion, or rest. In this wider sense of the word we speak of the action of oxygen upon other elements and the action of a resting stone that exercises a pressure. Action in the narrow sense of the word, designating the deeds of rational beings, is a very complex kind of motion. There is some additional feature in action. What is that additional feature?

Action is purposive motion. What is purpose?

Purpose is the aim of the actor.

Has the rolling ball no aim? Yes it has an aim. Motion cannot be thought without possessing a definite direction. Every gravitating body has an aim. It does not always reach its aim, but that is of no account. Every chemical atom that combines with another atom has an aim. Every piece of reality is acting somehow in a definite way. The end of the direction of its action is called the aim of its action. If there are obstacles preventing a motion reaching its aim, the motion comes to a rest. That is the end of the motion, yet not the end of the activity of the moving body. The action of the moving body (i. e. in the wider sense of the term "action") continues in the shape of pressure in the direction of the aim.

These processes are described by the physicist who uses the terms kinetic and potential energy to represent the two forms of the activity of acting things. All acting things are real. Their activity is that feature which makes them real. Activity in this sense of the term is called in German *Wirklichkeit*, and *Wirklichkeit* at the same time means "reality."

Every motion having an aim, purpose must be something more than "aim"; and indeed it is. Purpose is the conscious representation of an aim. The falling stone has an aim. If the stone were conscious of its aim, we should say, that the falling stone has a purpose.

This then is the main difference between motion and action, between aim and purpose. Action (in the narrow sense of the term) is conscious motion, and purpose is a conscious aim.

Action and motion are different, but on the other hand they possess something in common. The similarity between action and motion is their spontaneity.

The gravity of a stone acts in a certain way according to the stone's position. This gravity is a quality of the stone, it is part of its existence, it is its intrinsic and inalienable nature. There is not a force outside the stone that pushes it, there is no external so-called "cause"* that makes it fall, but the stone itself falls. The stone falls because that is its nature, and when lying on the ground it exercises a certain pressure, because that is its nature. In certain positions this same nature, called "gravity," acts as motion, in others as pressure; but throughout it is spontaneous activity—spontaneous, because rising out of its own being, and characterising its real nature.

This same spontaneity is found throughout reality, in organic nature, and also in the conscious actions of living organisms. The spontaneity of living organisms is so immediate that men have always believed that their actions (in the absence of compulsion) are their own doing and that they are responsible for their actions. This state of things has been called freedom of will. And certainly this conception is not based upon error, it is true. Yet men noticing that actions performed without the compulsion of others are spontaneous expressions of the actor's character, forgot that

*This wrong usage of the term "cause" has discredited the idea of cause, so that philosophers rose to say, there are no causes whatever. Their intentions were right; there are no causes acting as agents upon things. But this wrong usage of the term cause is no reason to discard a useful idea. Causation is transformation and the term "cause" should mean only the relatively first motion in a series of motions representing in a certain process the start of the transformation which can be arbitrarily selected, and "effect" the final state of things with which the process ends. (See *Fund. Prob.* pp. 96—104.)

this is true of all activity in nature. The light burns because it is its nature to burn. The burning is spontaneous. The oxygen combines with the fatty substances of the oil in the wick not because there is a so-called "cause" operating upon it, but because the oxygen is a reality of a definite nature and to enter under this condition into a combination with certain atoms of combustible materials is this nature of the oxygen. Its action is spontaneous just as much as a man's action is spontaneous.

There is no reality but it is possessed of spontaneity, nay reality is spontaneity itself; and the constancy of this spontaneity makes it that natŭral processes, the actions of men included, can be foreseen and predetermined; or as the scientist expresses it that all nature is governed by law—not that there were a law from the outside imposed upon the world, but that the nature of everything that exists is constant in all its changes, that accordingly it exhibits regularities which can be described in formulas called natural laws.

Natural law is no oppression of nature. Natural law is only a description of its being; and nature is free throughout. Everything in nature acts not as it must, but (to speak anthropomorphically) as it wills, i. e. according to its own being.

* * *

Man's actions are distinguished from the motions of so-called inanimate nature in so far as he is conscious of his aim. The aims of so-called inanimate nature are not conscious, they cannot be called purposes. Conscious beings alone can have purposes. The problem of the origin of consciousness accordingly will also solve the problem of the origin of purpose and purposive action. We have treated the problem of the origin of consciousness at length on other occasions, which briefly recapitulated is as follows: *

Consciousness is a certain feature of our existence which is best characterised as awareness. Consciousness is not objective existence, it is not matter and not motion: it is subjective existence. Consciousness is a complex state of simpler elements and these simpler elements are called feelings. The simplest feelings a man knows of are perceived as awarenesses of certain states. Feelings as they are perceived and known have a meaning, and this meaning originates by comparison with other feelings and memories of feelings. Feelings represent something, and that which they represent is called the object. A feeling organism feels itself as a body, as an objective thing among things. This body affects and is affected by other bodies and it feels differently as it is differently affected. Although other bodies like our own body belong to and are a part of objective existence, we communicate with them and cannot deal with them otherwise than by treating them as possessing subjectivity. We regard them as conscious beings like ourselves. Their feelings, their consciousness cannot be seen, but their whole attitude indicates that their feelings are analogous to ours. It is natural that feelings cannot be seen, or observed, for they are not objective states but subjective states. They are felt by the subject that is feeling. Our own feelings would appear to others who looked into our pulsating brain as motions, so it is natural that the feelings of others can appear to us likewise as motions only. Motion and feeling accordingly are the subjective and objective aspects of reality.

* See *The Soul of Man*, pp. 23–45

Every feeling is objectively considered a motion, but not *vice versa*. Not every motion is a feeling. Feelings are in their objective aspect very complex motions. Yet while we do not say that every motion is a feeling, we say that every objective existence, is at the same time a subjective existence, and this subjective existence which seems of no account in inorganic nature, is no mere blank, it is, not feeling, but potentiality of feeling; it contains the germs of psychical existence, and this leads to the inevitable conclusion that the world is throughout spiritual in its innermost nature. That which appears to a subject as objectivity is in itself subjectivity, that which appears as matter is in itself spiritual: either actual spirit or potential spirit.

We can form no idea of the subjective existence of inorganic nature, but its objective existence is grand enough to satisfy us. The subjectivity of the sun for instance may be as grand as the enormous amount of energy that carries his light through cosmic space, an extremely small part of which is intercepted by the earth where it is the main source of light and life and joy. Yet whatever be the subjectivity of inorganic nature, apparently it does not consist in representations. Representations originate only with the rise of feelings when feelings acquire certain meanings, and when subjectivity becomes representative we call it mind.

Living organisms are active beings, and with the rise of consciousness the aims of their actions become purposes.

Suppose a conscious being were possessed of one purpose only, his action would be determined by that one purpose. Yet living beings are very complex and the memory-structures of their minds will under certain circumstances naturally suggest in a rapid succession several propositions of which one only can be selected as a purpose. The conflict among these several propositions, which are called motives of action, will cause a delay, this conflict is called deliberation, which lasts until the strongest motive has overcome the resistance of the other motives.

The strongest motive at any one moment is by no means the strongest motive at other moments. Thus actions are done which afterwards would not have been done. If a man considers a former action performed through a motive that has lost its strength, he pronounces the verdict "I ought not have done it."

This "ought" is not as yet the moral ought. The moral ought is still more complex.

If a man has a certain purpose and performs an action in compliance with that purpose but fails in realising his purpose, he says, I ought to have acted otherwise in order to attain my purpose. His means to the end were inadequate. If on another occasion he follows the same motive, he says to himself, I have more carefully to consider the means to the end I have in view.

This idea of "I have to" is again an ought, but it is not as yet the moral ought.

The choice among several motives to do a thing, or among several ways of doing a thing is the condition of any ought. The idea that this or that will have to be regretted or will fail, that another thing will not have to be regretted and will succeed, leads to the formulation of rules. These rules appear to him who has the intention to obey them, as an ought.

It is natural that those motives which promise pleasure are stronger than others. Almost all the rules of ought are to protect a man against the temptation of his pleasure-promising motives.

The idea of ought in general is a very complex idea, yet the moral ought is still more complex. What is the moral ought?

Man is a social animal. Society is not merely a collection of individuals, but the individual is a product of society. An individual that is prompted by egotistic motives alone will always fail in the end; and suppose that a certain man's fate were an exception, that he succeeded by a favorable combination of circumstances, death will defeat him after all.

A man in whom the idea of his being a member of a family, of a nation, of humanity, is a live presence, will feel bound to stand up for the common welfare with equal or even more energy than for his private interests. He is impressed with the importance that everyone in his place has to attend to the work allotted him, and he himself will be serious in the performance of what he is wont to call duty.

Duty is formulated as a norm or a prescript which is to be the highest motive for action and the intent of the moral man is to make it unbendingly strong so as to overrule all other considerations.

* * *

To sum up:

We have seen that the moral ought is not unanalysable, it is not an ultimate notion. It is a very complex mental fact which admits of analysis and a description of both its origin and its nature. The moral ought is a special kind of any ought or of any rule of action devised for the guidance of conduct. Conduct is a special case of natural processes; it is a motion plus purpose, purpose being an aim pursued with conscious intention. And aim, again, is one constituent feature of motion. There is no motion without aim. The ought grows from the realm of inorganic existence together with the unfolding of mind in animal organisms and it reaches its grandest development in the moral ideals of man.

Professor Sidgwick has sufficiently guarded his statement, saying that he merely means he cannot now resolve it into or explain it by any more elementary elements. Nevertheless it is not advisable to deal with a fundamental idea as if it were unexplainable or unanalysable and thus cast the glamor of mysticism over the whole realm of the most important and practical of sciences. There are ethical students who follow blindly the authority of such a great teacher as is Professor Sidgwick and they are too apt to forget the cautious limitation of his words preaching the mystery of the ought in its transcendent incomprehensibility.

There are always minds who love to live in the twilight of thought, who think that the unintelligible is grander than that which can be understood; and these minds seize eagerly upon every expression that throws a shadow on science, that dwarfs philosophy, and makes human knowledge appear dull and useless.

NATURE AND MORALITY.

AN EXAMINATION OF THE ETHICAL VIEWS OF JOHN STUART MILL.

I. THE MEANING OF BASING ETHICS UPON NATURE.

JOHN STUART MILL has written an essay on Nature in which he "inquires into the truth of the doctrines which make Nature a test of right and wrong." He sums up the results of his inquiry in the following conclusions:

"The word *Nature* has two principal meanings: it either denotes the entire system of things, with the aggregate of all their properties, or it denotes things as they would be, apart from human intervention.

"In the first of these senses, the doctrine that man ought to follow nature is unmeaning; since man has no power to do anything else than follow nature; all his actions are done through, and in obedience to, some one or many of nature's physical or mental laws.

"In the other sense of the term, the doctrine that man ought to follow nature, or in other words, ought to make the spontaneous course of things the model of his voluntary actions, is equally irrational and immoral.

"Irrational, because all human action whatever, consists in altering, and all useful action in improving, the spontaneous course of nature:

"Immoral, because the course of natural phenomena being replete with everything which when committed by human beings is most worthy of abhorrence, any one who endeavoured in his actions to imitate the natural course of things would be universally seen and acknowledged to be the wickedest of men."

If the word Nature is used in the second meaning, it is obvious that an imitation of nature would signify the suppression of the human in man, of that which is properly called ethical; it would deprive man of his most characteristic and noblest feature,—rationality—and degrade him into an animal blindly obeying its instincts.

Yet what is instinct but inherited habit? How have habits been acquired but by repeated action? Instinct is by no means bare of the rational element. Instinct is not totally blind. Although it may not prove rational intelligence in the individual, yet it does prove rational intelligence in the race. Instinct can be explained only as having been acquired through race-experience. The human has grown out of the race-experience of man's ancestors, and the rationality of certain instincts are a prophecy of the human. If the blindness of instinct has to be called "natural," and that element of rationality, however small it may be, which represents judgment and may be considered as the germ of humanity is to be counted as "non-natural," the whole animal kingdom from man down to the moner must be classed as part of the non-natural domain of the world. Nature in that case would have to be limited to the province of unorganised things, to stones or minerals, and the world of plants might be a disputed ground.

This conception of nature is not admissible, and it contradicts its etymological meaning, which is not as yet forgotten. The word "Nature" is derived from *nascere*, to grow, and denotes especially the evolution of organised life.

If we take "nature" in its first meaning, denoting "the entire system of things with the aggregate of all the properties," Mr. Mill declares that the doctrine that "man ought to follow nature" has no meaning. He says:

> "The scheme of Nature regarded in its whole extent, cannot have had, for its sole or even principal object, the good of human or other sentient beings. What good it brings to them, is mostly the result of their own exertions."

Certainly, that good which nature brings to sentient beings, is mostly the result of their own exertions. But if nature comprises the entire system of things, it also includes the exertions of sentient beings. That sentient beings can make efforts, is one of the most important, nay, for us it is the all-important part of nature. In other words, ethics is not something artificial in contrast to that which is natural, it is not something non-natural or unnatural; ethics is the most characteristic feature of human *nature*.

Mr. Mill has much to say about art and the artificial. He treats art as something radically different from nature. He ought to have remembered Shakespeare's lines:

> "Yet nature is made better by no mean,
> But nature makes that mean; so, over that art,
> Which, you say, adds to nature, is an art
> That nature makes. . , . . .
> . . . . , .
> . . . , . . This is an art
> Which does mend nature—change, rather; but
> The art itself is nature!"—*Winter's Tale*.

Mr. Mill tries to dispel some ambiguities that lurk in the old proposition *naturam sequi*, yet he confines his investigation to one interpretation of this rule only, and indeed to that which is the crudest and the most obviously absurd conception we can form of it, so crude that nobody has ever maintained it and, so far as I know, even thought of it before Mr. Mill refuted its proposition.

* * *

In the introductory remarks to his essay on Nature, Mr. Mill complains about the "many meanings, different from the primary one, yet sufficiently allied to it to admit of confusion." The article was apparently suggested by the reading of certain propositions of theological authors, who maintain that nature must be considered as a divine revelation; nature's doings are acts of God; the scheme of nature indicates a plan wisely premeditated and designed to serve the good of human or of other sentient beings; and that "all things are for wise and good ends. Such a view has been presented to "exalt instinct at the expense of reason."

Mr. Mill deals with these notions with great adroitness. He refutes the idea that natural processes are an indication of the Creator's designs. Natural laws act blindly; the storm rages without taking into consideration that it may do harm to sentient beings.

Now, if we consider nature as a personal being who acts not in uniformities of law, but with conscious knowledge of the consequences of his doings, and adjusting them to special ends, it would truly be ridiculous to say that we must act as indeliberately, ruthlessly, and blindly, as nature acts. Mr. Mill has succeeded completely in the refutation of this view, although it almost appears to me that a serious refutation is scarcely necessary.

The following passage might be suspected of humor, but Mr. Mill is in deep earnest.

He says:

"In sober truth, nearly all the things which men are hanged or imprisoned for doing to one another, are nature's every day performances. Killing, the most criminal act recognised by human laws, Nature does once to every being that lives; and in a large proportion of cases, after protracted tortures such as only the greatest monsters whom we read of ever purposely inflicted on their living fellow-creatures.

"Nature impales men, breaks them as if on the wheel, casts them to be devoured by wild beasts, burns them to death, crushes them with stones like the first christian martyr, starves them with hunger, freezes them with cold, poisons them by the quick or slow venom of her exhalations, and has hundreds of other hideous deaths in reserve, such as the ingenious cruelty of a Nabis or a Domitian never surpassed. All this, Nature does with the most supercilious disregard both of mercy and of justice, emptying her shafts upon the best and noblest indifferently with the meanest and worst; upon those who are engaged in the highest and worthiest enterprises, and often as the direct consequence of the noblest acts; and it might almost be imagined as a punishment for them. She mows down those on whose existence hangs the well-being of a whole people, perhaps the prospects of the human race for generations to come, with as little compunction as those whose death is a relief to themselves, or a blessing to those under their noxious influence. Such are Nature's dealings with life. Next to taking life (equal to it according to a high authority) is taking the means by which we live; and Nature does this too on the largest scale and with the most callous indifference. A single hurricane destroys the hopes of a season; a flight of locusts, or an inundation, desolates a district; a trifling chemical change in an edible root, starves a million of people. The waves of the sea, like banditti seize and appropriate the wealth of the rich and the little all of the poor with the same accompaniments of stripping, wounding, and killing as their human antitypes. Everything in short, which the worst men commit either against life or property is perpetrated on a larger scale by natural agents.

"Nature has Noyades more fatal than those of Carrier; her explosions of fire damp are as destructive as human artillery; her plague and cholera far surpass the poison cups of the Borgias. Even the love of 'order' which is thought to be a following of the ways of Nature, is in fact a contradiction of them. All which people are accustomed to deprecate as 'disorder' and its consequences, is precisely a counterpart of Nature's ways. Anarchy and the Reign of Terror are overmatched in injustice, ruin, and death, by a hurricane and a pestilence."

The passage quoted appears to me of special interest because the anthropomorphic view of nature is pushed to its utmost extreme. Mr. Mill combats here the conception of a personification of nature which is unequalled in mythology. Mr. Mill concludes from his considerations:

"Nature cannot be a proper model for us to imitate. Either it is right that we should kill because nature kills; torture because nature tortures; ruin and devastate because nature does the like; or we ought not to consider at all what nature does, but what it is good to do. If there is such a thing as a *reductio ad absurdum*, this surely amounts to one. If it is a sufficient reason for doing one thing, that nature does it, why not another thing? If not all things, why anything? The physical government of the world being full of the things which when done by men are deemed the greatest enormities, it cannot be religious or moral in us to guide our actions by the analogy of the course of nature."

Mr. Mill apparently takes the words *naturam sequi* in the sense of *naturam imitari.* To follow nature is in his conception not a conforming to the entire system of things and its laws, but the regarding the facts of nature as the actions of a person, and acting accordingly.

If "nature" is taken in the sense of the whole system of things, the precept to follow nature, Mr. Mill says, is, with reference to the irrefragable necessity of natural laws, meaningless. For every atom—so to say—obeys the law of gravitation, and every motive sufficiently strong to incite a man to action, if not counteracted by other and equally strong motives, will pass into an act; it will—so to say—obey the laws of psychical dynamics. Any advice to obey the laws of nature in this sense is not quite as ridiculous as the injunction to imitate nature, but it is meaningless. It makes no sense.

But there is another sense still—and Mr. Mill has not overlooked it—in which the doctrine of basing ethics upon nature can be conceived. Mr. Mill, it appears, has devoted little space to an explanation of it, because to his mind it seemed so very obvious and unquestionably correct. Indeed it is as unquestionably correct as the other views which he combats are unquestionably erroneous and meaningless.

The original definition of nature is formulated by Mill as follows:

> "As the nature of any given thing is the aggregate of its powers and properties, so Nature in the abstract is the aggregate of the powers and properties of all things.
>
> "Nature means the sum of all phenomena, together with the causes which produce them; including not only all that happens, but all that is capable of happening; the unused capabilities of causes being as much a part of the idea of Nature, as those which take effect."

Mr. Mill concludes:

> "Since all phenomena which have been sufficiently examined are found to take place with regularity, each having certain fixed conditions . . . . on the occurrence of which it invariably happens; mankind have been able to ascertain, either by direct observation or by reasoning processes grounded on it, the conditions of the occurrence of many phenomena; and the progress of science mainly consists in ascertaining those conditions."

Ir. Mill proposes to express the doctrine not by *naturam sequi* but by *naturam observare*. He says:

> 'To acquire knowledge of the properties of things, and make use of the knowledge for guidance, is a rule of prudence, for the adaptation of means to ends; for giving effect to our wishes and intentions whatever they may be.
>
> "If, therefore, the useless precept to follow nature were changed into a precept to study nature; to know and take heed of

the properties of the things we have to deal with, so far as these properties are capable of forwarding or obstructing any given purpose; we should have arrived at the first principle of all intelligent action, or rather at the definition of intelligent action itself."

The ancients, Mr. Mill says, were very unequivocal in basing their ethics upon nature. "The Roman jurists, when attempting to systematise jurisprudence place in the front of their exposition a certain *Jus naturale*, 'quod natura' as Justinian declares in the Institutes, 'omnia animalia docuit.'" Mr. Mill after alluding to Christianity, continues:

"The people of this generation do not commonly apply principles with any such studious exactness [as the ancients], nor own such binding allegiance to any standard, but live in a kind of confusion of many standards; a condition not propitious to the formation of steady moral convictions, but convenient enough to those whose moral opinions sit lightly on them, since it gives them a much wider range of arguments for defending the doctrine of the moment."

This is very true. But how can we improve the present state of ethics, otherwise than by being exact and trying to find out the leading principle of ethics. A leading principle of ethics, which may serve us as a standard for the rules of action and a test for right or wrong, cannot be artificially constructed. The facts upon which moral aspirations have to be based, are just as much facts of nature as the formation of crystals or the growth of plants. The conditions under which those facts are formed can be ascertained; and we can by observation and forethought predefine their consequences. They can be described in laws that are just as immutable as the laws which concern the growth of plants or the health of the body. Morality in all its phases and possibilities is deeply founded in the nature of things, and unless morality be an unexplainable fact in contradiction to all other facts of nature—there is but one way of comprehending morality and discovering its principle. This way is to study the facts of social life, the consequences of what is called immorality and the consequences of moral aspiration, to analyse them, to observe them in their origin and further development, to understand their importance, and to formulate their operation as exact natural laws.

The principle of morality cannot be contrived; it must be discovered. It cannot be devised like a work of art, but has to be found out not otherwise than any other natural law. Principles of art might be fashioned so as to suit our imagination—not so principles of morality. Artistic taste, yet even that in a certain sense only, is arbitrary, but the principles of morality are not arbitrary; they are not a product of our fancy, to suit special inherited or acquired inclinations, be they ever so lofty, charitable, altruistic, generous, or self-sacrificing. The principles of morality are to be based upon rigid truths which must be ascertained by experience and demonstrated by the usual scientific methods.

There is no choice left; but we have to base ethics upon nature.

II. THE ETHICS TAUGHT BY NATURE.

What can be the meaning of Mr. Mill's objection to basing morality upon nature, i. e. upon the entire system of things, of the universe, of which we are a part? I see only three possibilities: either it means (1) that there is no ethics at all, or (2) that ethics is imported somehow into the world from the outside, or

(3) that ethics is a purely subjective invention, that it is an artificial product of man's fancy.

If nature were a chaos, if there were no constancy of law in the universe, no regularity but only the sportive arbitrariness of an irregular play of chance, no world-order but a *tohuvabhohu* of general confusion, intelligent as well as moral action would be impossible, for no calculation of consequences would be reliable. Yet if there is a world-order, conformity to it will be possible. Upon the presence of law depends the intelligibility of the world; the regularity of law is the basis of rational action, of foresight, of responsibility, and of moral action.

The view that ethics are imported into the world from the outside is the theological theory of revelation. It is based upon the dualistic world-conception that the world and God are two distinct entities. The world by itself is supposed to be a chaos, but God brings order into it by penetrating the chaos. According to this view the regularity of law is not of the world but of God; it is not an intrinsic feature of existence, but it is imposed upon it by an extra-mundane Deity.

The view that ethics is a purely subjective invention, that it is human to the exclusion of the not human in nature, we may fairly assume, is Mr. Mill's view. Mr. Mill would have objected to the idea of considering his view as a special case of the revelation theory in ethics, but such it is none the less. What is the human but a product of nature. Those forces and laws which shaped man are the very same agencies which shaped the rest of the things in the universe. If the human be something so radically different from and in essence so extraordinarily superior to the whole of nature as to justify the idea that the human can create a new world-order instead of using the world-order that exists by accommodating itself to it, it must contain, at least in germ, a certain something that is not of this world. Man's existence in that case must be the revelation of an extra-mundane power which thus enables him to rise above nature so as to be her superior.

Mr. Mill does not accept this view. There is no doubt about it that he regards man as the product of nature. His philosophical standpoint excludes the possibility of revelation. Accordingly, he can only mean that ethics is an artificial product of man's imagination. Man shapes his moral ideals as the musician composes a sonata or as the poet conceives a beautiful dream.

There are men who believe that ethics cannot be based upon facts, i. e. upon nature, but that it must be based upon some principle. But what is the value of a principle if it is not derived from facts? Ideals are mere dreams unless they are realisable, and to be realisable they must be shaped out of the facts of experience. Principles are rules to attain ideals. If ideals are in conflict with nature and nature's laws, what is their use? If they are not based upon a solid knowledge of facts, they are nothing but worthless vagaries of the human mind and it will be a positive waste of time to ponder over them or to give them a minute's serious thought.

There is only one kind of ideal that is useful and worthy of man's attention. It is that ideal which aims at creating a better state of things upon the ground of the eternal order of things. Ideals must be based upon the terra firma of natural law, otherwise they are mere fancies.

This world of ours in which we live is a world of law, and the irrefragibility of natural law renders intelligent action possible. Intelligent action is such as foresees and predetermines the course of events. Intelligent action consists in fixing an aim and in adapting means to this aim as an end. Intelligent action is the condition of moral action. Intelligent action becomes moral through rationalising the aim of action. Mankind in the child phase of its development obeys almost blindly its natural impulses, the general intent of which has been characterised as self-preservation. Self-preservation remains the ultimate aim of moral action. Yet with a modification, with an amplification and an increase of man's knowledge of the nature of himself, the ultimate aim of his actions must be modified.

The question arises, Can man at all preserve his self? Is not every individual doomed to die and is not self-preservation for any length of time absolutely impossible? Yes, it is impossible, if by "self" we understand this particular body consisting of a definite quantity of living matter in a special form. This particular self cannot be preserved for it is constantly changing; through slight modifications it becomes another with every minute, with every second of its life.

Yet man's self contains a something that is preserved, that is transmitted to others. What is this part of his self? Every man has received it, or at least the greatest part of it, through heredity and education, from his ancestors. It is his organisation including the rationality of his speech, thoughts, and actions—in one word it is his soul. His fellowman, too, has inherited it and in so far as two or several men recognise the sameness of their souls, they call each other brothers. In preserving his fellowmen's souls a man preserves his own soul.

An advanced knowledge of self necessarily changes the original impulse of self-preservation into a preservation of the soul.

Man, as a particular individual being mortal, can preserve his soul only in and through others. The nature of man's being is social and his life is ephemeral. Thus self-knowledge will teach him that he is a part of a greater whole; the most important elements of his soul originate out of his intercourse with his fellow-beings; the essence of his life, of his speech, his thoughts, his aspirations and ideals, lies in his connections with them. At the same time he must learn that his particular life is only a phase in the fuller life of the soul which has come to him out of the past animating him now and sweeping onward into the dim future. Man's real self is not the materiality of which his body consists at a given moment, but his soul. The former cannot be preserved, the latter can. Any attempt at preserving the former is thwarted by nature. If we attempt to preserve anything of ourselves, we can preserve only our soul. No other choice is left.

There is one strange fact about self-preservation. This world of ours is never at rest, there is no standstill. Any attempt at preserving life exactly as it is leads to dissolution. Preservation is only possible in growth; the preservation of life must be for its further development, it must include progress.

Such is in broad outlines the injunction that nature teaches. Such is an ethics based upon the facts of life, it is the derivation of an ultimate aim of action from nature, i. e. from the nature of the being that acts and also from the nature of the world in which this being lives. When we thus base our ethics upon the facts of experience and the natural laws that have been derived therefrom; in one word, when we base our ethics upon nature, we define those actions as moral which tend to preserve and further develop the human soul.

III. INTELLIGENT ACTION AND MORAL ACTION.

Mr. Mill says, "to make use of knowledge for guidance is a rule of prudence." But it is more; it is also a rule of ethics.

What is the difference between a prudent action and an ethical action? A prudent action may have been performed from a selfish motive merely; an ethical action is performed from a motive broader than self-interest, from a desire to be somehow of service to the development of humanity. Prudence is not morality; but prudence will lead to morality, for all immorality will defeat itself in the end. Thus prudence teaches us to avoid immorality.

Not every intelligent action is moral; but every moral action is intelligent; and it is an indispensable principle of morality to render all actions intelligent. Yet while all moral actions are intelligent, the intelligence or rationality of an action does not as yet make it moral.

A man may act in the right way against his inclinations from mere prudence. He may act in a certain way not because he wants to do the act, but because he knows that it is after all the best way; he thus acts against his will; he acts under a certain compulsion. His act in such a case may be called mere prudence. However as soon as the desire to act in the best way or to act as he knows that he should act, becomes part of his character, as soon as he performs the act done in the right way, because he wills it, his action is truly ethical.

All our actions—even those performed for our private interest, which are perfectly legitimate—should be guided by higher motives than by the impulse of a selfish self-preservation; all our proceedings, our omissions and our undertakings should be regulated by superindividual considerations; they should be in strict harmony with what may fitly be called the moral law.

The moral law has been taught us by our parents and teachers. We may accept their instruction simply on the ground of their authority, but we have a perfect right to ask, Why must we obey moral commands? And the answer would be: Because the natural course of events demands it. Nature defeats all egoistic intentions; and it sanctions the superindividual aspirations only—those which are commonly called moral principles.

There is no right in this world but it is the counterpart of duty. We have a right to ask why egotism should be overruled by higher principles. What is the duty that corresponds to this right? This duty is our obligation to inquire into the conditions of human life, so as to ascertain the principles by which our actions must be regulated. We must not rest satisfied with our moral sentiments; we must understand our sentiments, that we may be assured not by mystic intuition but by clear comprehension, that they are truly moral. We must be on our guard against ethical enthusiasm which is not based upon a clear comprehension of facts; for there are many noble sentiments which, as can be demonstrated by scientific investigation, are anything but morality. For instance, eleemosynary philanthropy, has been highly praised as the acme of morality; and yet, scientific investigation has stated with irrefutable conclusiveness that it is a wrong practice. All enthusiasm that has been wasted in this direction, can be called moral only if motives alone be considered. Objectively, they are as immoral as any criminal act committed under the influence of an erring conscience.

IV. THE ANTHROPOMORPHIC STANDPOINT OF MR. MILL.

Mr. Mill in opposing the conclusions drawn from an anthropomorphic conception of nature, imperceptibly slips into the same erroneous position. He treats nature as if it were a person and arraigns nature for immorality. He looks upon every progress as a further aberration from nature and speaks of the lower stages of savage life as "the times when mankind were nearer to their natural state." Thus he easily proves that nature is chaos and that civilisation is a conquest of man over nature. As if man were not a part of nature! "To dig, to plough, to build, to wear clothes," Mr. Mill declares, "are direct infringements of the injunctions to follow nature."

If we accepted Mr. Mill's usage of the word nature, which deliberately excludes man's exertions from the sphere of the natural, we should have to declare that man's entire being is "supernatural." The adversaries of Mr. Mill may very well thank him for his method of attack, for he furnishes evidence in support of the very conception he so eagerly attempts to overthrow. It is, of course, allowable to use the concept nature in this restricted sense, as Mr. Mill does. We may define our words as we please; but if we were to limit the word nature always to the lower stages of natural evolution, we should recognise the truth that the "supernatural" naturally grows from the natural. The supernatural has been regarded as having come into nature from spheres beyond by some extra-mundane intercession; and we discard the idea of supernaturalism simply and solely in order to avoid this misconception. If by "supernatural" is understood that higher kind of nature which evolves from the lower stages of nature, we shall entertain no objection to the word.

Nature is not a person and natural laws are not the decrees of a personal being. The order of nature is not a scheme designed for an end. Nevertheless nature has an aim. Every process of nature has an aim, every motion has a certain direction and if all the natural processes are viewed as a whole, they possess in their entirety also an aim. Our scientists have formulated the general aim of nature and call it evolution. If we look upon nature as a person, we are led to absurdities, but if we look upon nature not only as purposeless but also as aimless, we sink into a bottomless pit of errors and confusion.

Nature being no person, we cannot speak of nature as being moral or immoral. Nature is non-moral. Persons alone, individual beings, can be moral or immoral; and morality is nothing but the intentional conformity to nature and to the order of nature.

It has been said that God is moral. There is no sense in speaking of God as moral—unless it be in popular language where the usage of the phrase is to be regarded as an excusable and allowable poetic license (within certain limits even quite legitimate). God can only be called the standard of morality. God is non-moral; man only, if he conforms to the will of God, can be said to be moral.

Mr. Mill in arraigning nature for being beset with all kinds of vices, disorder, uncleanliness, and cowardice, is very emphatic in denouncing her injustice. He says:

> "It is one of Nature's general rules, and part of her habitual injustice, that 'to him that hath shall be given, but from him that hath not, shall be taken even that which he hath.' The ordinary and predominant tendency of good is towards more good. Health, strength, wealth, knowledge, virtue, are not only good in themselves but facilitate and promote the acquisition of good, both of the same and of other kinds. The person who can learn easily, is he who already knows much: it is the strong and not the sickly person who can do everything which most conduces to health; those who find it easy to gain money are not the poor but the rich; while health, strength, knowledge, talents, are all means of acquiring riches, and riches are often an indispensable means of acquiring these. Again, *e converso*, whatever may be said of evil turning into good, the general tendency of evil is towards further evil. Bodily illness renders the body more susceptible of disease; it produces incapacity of exertion, sometimes debility of mind, and often the loss of means of subsistence. All severe pain, either bodily or mental, tends to increase the susceptibilities of pain for ever after. Poverty is the parent of a thousand mental and moral evils. What is still worse, to be injured or oppressed, when habitual, lowers the whole tone of the character. One bad action leads to others, both in the agent himself, in the bystanders, and in the sufferers. All bad qualities are strengthened by habit, and all vices and follies tend to spread. Intellectual defects generate moral, and moral, intellectual; and every intellectual or moral defect generates others and so on without end."

It is certainly true that "to him that hath shall be given, but from him that hath not, shall be taken even that which he hath;" but it is perfectly useless to complain about it. It is neither justice nor injustice, but it is a law of nature or if you prefer the expression, it is the will of God; and *we* have to mind it.

To speak of the injustice of nature is just as anthropomorphic as to speak of the morality of God.

Mill's mistake is that he argues from an antiquated theological standpoint which is, even among theologians, not at all the universally accepted view.

Morality may be described as our attempts to improve the given state of nature, but it certainly can never improve the order of nature. All the improvements we can make upon the given state of nature, have to be based upon the unalterable order of nature, and he who attempts to formulate any rules of action, be it in the department of industrial enterprises, in social and political reform, or in the realm of moral aspirations, will have to do it after a careful study of facts. The irrefragable laws of nature form the immovable basis upon which we have to take our stand. Whatever action we undertake, before we plan or devise, we must take heed of the laws to which we have to conform. The laws of nature and among them the moral laws, are not flexible, they are stern and immutable. If we cannot understand the nature of things in scientific abstractness, and if (in order to understand the earnest necessity that the moral law must be obeyed) we represent the order of nature as a personal being, it will be well to remember the parable of Christ in which he compares God to a hard man, reaping where he has not sown and gathering where he has not strewed. If we have received one talent only, there is but one way to keep that one talent; we must go and trade with the same and make with it another talent. But if the very knowledge that we have to deal with a hard man, induces us to be afraid, so as to go and hide that one talent in the earth, then, that one talent will be taken from us.

The parable of the talents is very instructive. Its doctrine seems severe on the poor, especially those who are poor in spirit; but it is just as much severe on the rich. Christ spoke to the poor and his application was made so as to impress their minds, that he who has received little is no less responsible for that little, than he who has received much for the much he has received. "For unto whomsoever much is given, of him shall be much required, and to whom men have committed much, of him they will ask the more." If Christ had spoken to the rich, the learned, and the great, he might have made a different application of the parable and might have told them of the servant who having received five talents had not only buried but wasted the rich gift. There are perhaps more men ruined through having received too much than by having received too little. The temptations are greater in the former case, and the dire necessity of the latter case often exercises a wholesome and educating influence.

If justice means that every servant, whether he increases the talents he has received or buries them in the earth, should in the end receive an equal share, Mr. Mill would be justified in denouncing the course of nature as unjust. But it appears to me advisable that any one who thus indicts the very order of nature for injustice, imagining that the whole universe is wrong and he alone and perhaps also a few fellow beings of his with him are right, should first revise the logic of his conception of justice; for it is in such a case most probable that on close scrutiny he will somewhere discover a flaw in his idea of justice.

*
* *

Mr. Mill's objection to basing ethics upon nature was made to oppose a theological conception of ethics. Our traditional religions, we must know, are in their intentions monistic, they are dualistic only if the allegory of their symbols is taken as literal truth. In opposing the theology of traditional religions Mr. Mill attacked erroneously their very heart, the monistic meaning of their doctrines instead of striking at the dualistic interpretation of their mythology. Thus if Mr. Mill were right in his objection to basing ethics upon nature—i. e. upon the unalterable, the eternal in nature, upon the law of nature or to use the religious and most pregnant term, upon God—if Mr. Mill were right, there would be two alternatives left: Either there is no ethics at all, which view Mr. Mill would not accept, or the dualistic interpretation of theology is correct, that ethics is an extramundane factor.

When ethics and the conditions of ethical ideals are found and can be proved to be an immanent part of nature, the dualistic interpretation of the old religions will have to be surrendered while their monistic meaning which is after all the core and living spirit of all religious aspirations will appear in a stronger light than ever.

AN AMERICAN MORALIST.*

BY PROF. L. M. BILLIA.

DR. PAUL CARUS, one of the editors of *The Monist* and *The Open Court*—periodicals which rank among the most important of the socio-philosophical reviews of the United States of America—proposes, in three lectures upon the "Ethical Problem," the adoption of a course which might be considered as a compromise between the utilitarian and the objective-moral, or, as he terms it, the "intuitionalist" school. He meets the utilitarian principle at the outset by the following declaration:

"We may say that the pursuit of happiness is a natural right of man, but we cannot derive the moral "ought" from the pursuit of happiness. And the mere pursuit of happiness is not sufficient to make a complete and worthy human life. On the contrary, the mere pursuit of happiness wherever it prevails unchecked in the soul of man is a most dangerous tendency, which unfits man for business as well as for family life, and above all for ideal aspirations. What is the reason that trustworthy persons, competent workers, dutiful men and women are so rare? It is simply because most people are too eager in their pursuit of happiness.

"The pursuit of happiness is not wrong. Enjoyment is not a sin, and recreation is not improper. Yet it is wrong to make happiness the sole aim of existence. We cannot live without enjoy-

* Translated from the Italian. The article appeared first in *Il Nuovo Risorgimento Rivista di Filosofia, Scienze, Lettere, Educazione e Studi Sociali* (Milan), a Roman Catholic magazine, and was republished in pamphlet form.

ment; enjoyment keeps our minds healthy and buoyant; yet enjoyment is not the purpose of life. Recreation is the rest we take after our work is done. We do not work in order to have recreation; but we seek recreation in order to do more work.

"If the pursuit of happiness is not sufficient to make man's life complete and worthy, what then is needed to make it so? We all know what is needed: it is ethics. Then let us have ethics—not mere theories about pleasurable sensations, but true ethics—ethics that are nobler than the mere pursuit of pleasure."

If these lofty conceptions do not suffice to gain our sympathies for him, the author acquires a new claim on us by virtue of the following declaration:

"I shall be glad to learn from my critics; and wherever any one will convince me of an error, he will find me ready to change my opinion and to accept the truth whatever it be."

Both from a scientific and a practical point of view, I find his disagreement with those who would promote the elevation of moral life without regard to philosophical or religious opinions, or without fundamental principles, a very serious matter.

Dr. Carus's book had its origin in a controversy between the author and the "Society of Ethical Culture," represented by *The Ethical Record*, of Philadelphia. Although we cannot agree with him in his position that supernatural revelation is an impossibility, we, nevertheless, approve of his conception of the necessity of a philosophico-scientific basis of ethics—a necessity which, in our opinion, is a logical objective exigency of speculative thought, and, socially, a subjective exigency of our time and of modern education. This view is, in our opinion, fully in accord with Antonio Rosmini's "Philosophy of Ethics" and "Philosophy of Right (*Diritto*)."

The author, possessed of a happier memory than

ours, very well recollects the time when man was an animal, living in herds with others of his kind; and he knows also, that at that early day higher ethics had received but little development. But, as little by little a higher ethics grew, society emerged from barbarism into the light of civilisation. And here criticism grows somewhat laborious; for, notwithstanding his earnest profession of scientific research, the author's method of procedure is that of the statement of aphorisms and definitions, each of which we should be justified in calling in doubt. In fact, it is these very aphorisms and definitions from which he proceeds, that should, first of all, have been submittted to critical examination—even from a historical standpoint—if the author really wished to give ethics a scientific basis. In agreement with Comte's conceptions of the three natural stages of development, he declares that the question, whether ethics is a science and can be founded upon a scientific basis, is the same as that of the reconciliation of religion and science, or of the development of religion from infancy to its state of maturity, from dualism to monism, from the mysticism of a vague supernaturalistic speculation to the light of positive certainty, from an authoritative and credulous faith to the faith of scientific knowledge.

However correct and honest the intentions of the author may be, we consider as truly deplorable his arbitrary conception of religion, which, in his presupposition undiscussed, and, for him, admitting of no discussion, is nothing but a human fact, while to us the elevation of man to the Absolute is itself a work of God. If the author's supposition were true, his course would have to be approved of, although the difficulty would remain, whether a scientific religion could be understood by the multitude, who might know it generally, but not scientifically.

Nor are we less surprised at the author's confounding the ideas "vague," "supernatural," and "fantastic"; the fantastic, the ideal, and the supernatural being three orders much at variance with facts. Altogether, Dr. Carus's point of departure differs in nothing from that of Comte.

And thus, when he comes to establish the "basis" of ethics—always in aphoristic form—he states the hypothesis, that knowledge is a representation of facts—a definition of which our readers know, beyond doubt, is disputable.

It is true, the author attempts to found ethics upon reason, upon the immutable and necessary order of things, and he deserves praise for thus having elevated himself above the level of the utilitarian; but, in default of tradition and through excessive fear of the supernatural and mystical, he falls into the error of a material monism and fails, at the same time, to give his doctrine a foundation.

However, the author is worthy and capable of something better, as may be seen in his beautiful observation in censure of the ferocious and pharisaical theory, which pretends to derive all moral sentiment from egotism. Here he is entirely in accord with the Italian school, and I doubt if the remarks he makes could be improved upon.

Only it is deplorable that, owing to his disregarding a great part of ancient and modern philosophic speculation, he should not be able, while face to face with the utilitarians, to perceive others than the ranks of those whom he terms intuitionalists, wrongfully accusing them of ignoring and of refusing to demonstrate, by natural and scientific methods, the reasons or motives underlying morality, of making duty a mystery, etc., etc. All this we naturally read with something akin to ill-will here, in the home of the philosophy of right (*diritto*); in fact, in Europe generally, where for so many centuries the supreme motives of the good have been scientifically investigated.

He likewise touches upon the problem of freewill and believes to have found its solution, but does not seem to be well aware of the main difficulty, which consists in this, that, on the one hand, the fact of freewill is attested by the consciousness; on the other hand, that will without motive is an absurdity. Certainly. But, with the usual defect of Anglo-Americans—the tendency to vaporings, as in the McKinley bill, so in philosophical speculation,—the work of centuries,—he falls into a twofold error: historical and philosophical. His classification of those who have entered into an investigation of this problem into theologians, who hold freewill a will without motive and an inscrutable mystery, and freethinkers, so called, who place it among illusions, is much too superficial. Assuredly, these two views are both false; but, if our author had kept accurate account of philosophical tradition, and above all, if he had paid closer attention to Italian philosophy, and to that of Rosmini in particular, he would have observed that the difficulty has been by many not only recognised, but also surmounted.

In fact, the doctrine of practical judgment, in our opinion, while, on the one hand, it justifies the existence of freedom of choice, is not satisfied with merely affirming it, but demonstrates the operation by a keen analysis; and, on the other hand, confutes in the best possible manner determinism, physiological, as well as psychological and rationalistic. And what is this "best possible manner"? That of conceding, or rather, of comprehending whatever truth there may be in those views, in order the better to avoid the fallacies they may contain. An act not determined by a reason is an absurdity. Decidedly. But a free will consists precisely in the ability to determine, in the ability to make real a given reason, a given impulse, a given sentiment. How is freewill reconcilable with the evident subjection of our acts to the status of the nervous system, the status of health or disease, adventitious or constitutional, individual or hereditary? Free choice is an act of reflection, or rather, one of the higher acts of reflection. Now, reflection requires a certain status of order and calmness in our functions, which, for instance, does not exist, at least not without great expenditure of force, in fever, hysterics, excessive pain, extraordinary somnolence, or any ardent superexcitation. But it is none the less true that these same conditions, favorable or unfavorable as they may be to reflection, and to the exercise of free choice, have for the most part their origin in liberty of choice itself, as in disease which has been neglected or aggravated, or criminally transmitted to descendants, or in cases of exaltation not restrained at the outset, or to assume a less ignoble case, in any excessive lassitude or strain, whether of muscle or brain, consequent upon hard labor.

At times Dr. Carus recognises the difficulty, but then again, following the imperfect theory of some German moralists, he confounds liberty of will with freedom from passion, and ends by admitting liberty solely in connection with the Good. Now, it is very true that liberty makes for the Good. It is very true that he who does good is freer than he who works evil; that the practice of virtue not only educates and refines sentiment, but also strengthens freedom of will, just as, on the other hand, yielding to certain vices weakens, and, in the end, almost entirely nullifies it. But it is none the less true that liberty presents itself in connection with the Evil as well as in connection with the Good. So true is this that, before entering on the examination of certain crimes, men often sustain fierce struggles with themselves in the endeavor to silence the voice of nature, of conscience, of blood; as may especially be noticed in criminal cases of a political nature, and in all those which are executed with open predetermination and which are designed to some end of vast importance. Nor is it the case that those who have preceded Dr. Carus have not well distinguished between necessity and compulsion—a very old and well-known distinction. On the contrary, he himself does not well distinguish *libertas a coactione* from *libertas a necessitate*, in which freedom of choice precisely consists. *Libertas a necessitate*, we repeat, does not in itself denote absence of reason, but determines to itself the preponderant reason.

We must say, however, by way of *causerie*, as the French would put it, that we have been better entertained than we at first expected to be, by this work of the author of "Meliorism."* We find two good reasons for not being displeased with it.

The first is the author's innate goodness and loftiness of spirit, which constantly reveals itself in his combating egotism, in his lifting up his readers out

* This is the title of another of the author's works, and, in fact, the one which he applies to his system.

of the slough of "Spencerianism," and in the fact that he reposes the supreme ethical law in *truth*. Although rejecting his doctrine of representation,* we cannot but congratulate Dr. Carus on his happy declaration: that ethics should recognise as its principal basis the search for truth and adaptation thereto; that an honest inquiry into truth is the condition of all ethics, and that faithfulness and obedience to truth includes all the laws that a system of ethics could contain.

* For the convenience of our readers, especially the young and strangers, we may repeat the reasons upon which we reject the theory of representation: That which is known is the truth; that which is known is the idea. Idea and truth are entirely wholly one, and are wholly one also with the object thought of. If, instead of saying that the idea is the object thought of, we say that the idea is, through sense-reminiscence, a representation of the object, it would come to pass that we could never think of any object, but always of its representation; therefore, I could not think: one, two, three—the thought itself would be impossible. Moreover, the representation could not be thought, if not by means of a certain resemblance or similitude with the object thought of; this similitude is what is actually thought: it is a common element; it is the unity of the representation and that which is represented. Idea in this sense is the representation of many things similar to each other, but this is not its definition. (See Rosmini, Psychology, vol. II, p. 1339.)

ROSMINI'S PHILOSOPHY.

BY DR. PAUL CARUS.

PROF. L. M. BILLIA is a Roman Catholic and a disciple of Antonio Rosmini-Serbati. There is a deep-seated and radical difference between our view and that of our critic, and yet there is also in some points of great consequence a striking agreement. As there is no hope of a conversion on either side, we may forbear arguing the case and be satisfied with a simple statement, which will contrast the two world-conceptions. But before entering into a discussion of the present subject, it seems advisable to sketch the philosophy of Professor Billia's great master, who may fairly be regarded as the most representative Roman Catholic thinker of modern times.

Rosmini was born in March, 1797, in Roveredo, Tyrol, the eldest son of a wealthy and noble family. He attended the Lyceum at Trient and the University of Padua, and selected in 1821 the ecclesiastical calling with the avowed purpose of giving to theology a sound philosophical basis. In his love of the church and eagerness for reform, he became the founder of a new religious order, the Society of the Brothers and Sisters of Charity, popularly called in Italy "The Rosminians." He joined Piedmont in 1830 and Pope Pius IX. in 1848, under whose reform-ministry he became the papal minister of education. At the outbreak of the Roman revolution, he retired from public life and died July 1st, 1855 at Stresa.

In spite of all his devotion not only to the church but also to the Pope personally, whom he followed into his exile at Gaëta, one of his writings "On the Five Wounds of the Church" has been placed upon the Index.

Rosmini's numerous, and partly very ponderous, writings are little accessible to the English speaking world. His works were collected (according to Meyer's Konversations-Lexikon) in seventeen volumes (Milan, 1842–44), and he wrote, according to Davidson, not fewer than ninety-nine various publications, books, and among them very voluminous books, articles and pamphlets, on philosophical, theological, ethical, legal, and miscellaneous subjects. Among them are claimed to be the most important ones, "Nuovo saggio sull' origine delle idee," 3 vol.; and "Philosophia del diritto." The best known Italian works on his life are by Thomaseo (Turin, 1855) and Bernardi (Pinerolo, 1860).

There is a translation extant of Rosmini's "Nouvo saggio sull' origine delle idee," entitled "New Essay on the Origin of Ideas" (London, 1883–84), published by the English branch of the Rosminians which is attached to the ancient church of St. Etheldreda, Ely Place, Holborn. The most convenient work for English readers will be Davidson's book "Rosmini's Philosophical System" (London, 1882).

In order to overcome doubt and unbelief Rosmini attempted to establish a rational basis of the Christian faith, thus to work out a conciliation of reason and religion. He opposed the sensualism and empiricism as represented in Italy by Gioja and Ramagnosi, and propounded a philosophical system which in accord with Descartes's idealism was expected to be in agreement with the doctrines of the church.

The Encyclopædia Britannica characterises Rosmini's philosophy as follows:

"Rosmini, contemplating the position of recent philosophy from Locke to Hegel, and having his eye directed to the ancient and fundamental problem of the origin, truth, and certainty of our ideas, wrote :—'If philosophy is to be restored to love and respect, I think it will be necessary, in part, to return to the teachings of the ancients, and in part to give those teachings the benefit of modern methods' ('Theodicy,' n. 148). Pursuing, therefore, the now generally approved method of the observation of facts, he most carefully examined and analysed the fact of human knowledge, and obtained the following results:

"1) That the notion or idea of being or existence in general enters into, and is presupposed by, all our acquired cognitions, so that, without it, they would be impossible.

"2) That this idea is essentially objective, inasmuch as what is seen in it is as distinct from and opposed to the mind that sees it as the light is from the eye that looks at it.

"3) That it is essentially true, because 'being' and 'truth' are convertible terms, and because in the vision of it the mind cannot err, since error could only be committed by a judgment, and here there is no judgment, but a pure intuition affirming nothing and denying nothing.

"4) That by the application of this essentially objective and true idea the human being intellectually perceives, first, the animal body individually conjoined with him, and then, on occasion of the sensations produced in him *not by himself*, the causes of those sensations, that is, from the action felt he perceives and affirms an agent, a being, and therefore a true thing, that acts on him, and he thus gets at the external world,—these are the true primitive judgments, containing (*a*) the subsistence of the particular being (subject), and (*b*) its essence or species as determined by the quality of the action felt from it (predicate).

"5) That reflexion, by separating the essence or species from the subsistence, obtains the full specific idea (universalisation), and then from this, by leaving aside some of its elements, the abstract specific idea (abstraction).

"6) That the mind, having reached this stage of development, can proceed to further and further abstracts, including the first principles of reasoning, the principles of the several sciences, complex ideas, groups of ideas, and so on without end.

"7) Finally, that the same most universal idea of being, this generator and formal element of all acquired cognitions, cannot itself be acquired, but must be innate in us, implanted by God in our nature. Being, as naturally shining to our mind, must therefore be what men call the light of reason. Hence the name Rosmini gives it of ideal being; and this he laid down as the one true fundamental principle of all philosophy, and the supreme criterion of truth and certainty."

We are in sympathy with the aspiration represented by Rosmini, of rationalising the Christian faith. We do not believe that Rosmini was successful in his efforts; indeed, we think that he could not be, because he took a wrong start and was blinded by the firm and fore-determined conviction that the Christianity of the church was undeniable and indubitable truth. Nevertheless, we regard the effort of any man of conciliating his religion with science and rational thought as praiseworthy, and we go so far as to say that the gist of Christianity, i. e. the main tenets of Christian ethics, admit indeed of a perfectly rational foundation. We deny, however, the possibility of rationalising the dogmas of the church. We see in them only the crystallised mythology of past ages, which, when regarded as a mythology, is profound, venerable, full of oddly and mysteriously expressed truths, but when regarded as truth itself, are utterly absurd.

We agree with Professor Billia in substance while we disagree in form. We agree in rejecting hedonism, or the pleasure theory in ethics, and we agree in accepting the ethics of a stern search for truth. Neither of us can think of speaking of ethics as independent of a definite world-conception. Both of us regard morality simply as the practical application of our deepest religious convictions concerning that which we have found to be the truth. Yet we disagree as to the form in which we cast our convictions. Rosmini and his school favor mystical expressions and extol the tradition of the church in comparison to the results of modern science. We, on the contrary, do not rest satisfied until the mysteries disappear like fog before the sun; and while we place little reliance upon ecclesiastical traditions, we rely mainly upon that which God's revelation in nature teaches us through science.

Thus my Roman Catholic critic who enjoys the advantage of living in the cradle of an ancient civilisation and the very home of the "Filosophia del diritto" jokes at my ingenuousness of accepting the theory of evolution. He does not attempt to overthrow the theory of evolution, and does not seem to expect me to take the trouble of proving it to him. I hope, he will not be offended when I openly confess that the smile was fully reciprocated on my part. It is not ignorance of the philosophical and ecclesiastical traditions, nor a horror of the supernatural that prevent me from accepting an ecclesiastical philosophy as is that of Rosmini's. Yet Professor Billia, it appears to me, does not appreciate the full weight of overwhelming proofs which give evidence to the truth of the theory of evolution.

Professor Billia, so it seems to us, still regards religious truths (i. e., the moral tenets which confessedly contain the gist of religion) as incompatible with the results of modern science. This may be excusable in the face of the fact that almost all modern ethicists who accept the theory of evolution, Spencer, Höffding, Gizycki, etc., are hedonists. We trust that the theory of evolution, far from overthrowing the moral truths of religion will give them a scientific and reliable basis. If evolution is true, we must live in obedience to the law of evolution. In that case, we cannot fashion our lives according to our pleasure, for the facts of nature sternly demand, by penalty of degeneration and perdition, a constant progress and higher development of our souls. Here we are in accord with the old Hebrew and Christian tradition. Ethics is not subjective; our rules of conduct are not self-made; there is an objective authority which must be obeyed, whose will is plainly recognised in the laws of nature and in the course of evolution.

We have no "fear of the supernatural"; we simply regard its conception as an error. To Professor Billia religious truths are acquired by a supernatural revelation, and scientific truths by a natural revelation. The former only are regarded as holy and infallible, not the latter, which are rather dubitable and unreliable. To us all truth is holy. In so far as truth is a statement of fact, a description of some feature or part of the objective reality in which and of which we are, truth is always divine. Thus religion, or our attempt of living the truth, no less than science, or our search for the truth, are in one respect "human facts" and in another respect "a work of God."

The main difference between our Catholic critic and ourselves consists in this: that he regards the traditional authority of the Church as ultimate, while we replace it by the authority of objective truth, provable according to the usual methods of science.

We do not intend to enter into a discussion of minor points; so we abstain here from repeating our doctrine of freewill, simply stating that we do not feel guilty, as Professor Billia maintains, of having confounded "liberty of will with freedom from passion"; on the other hand, we do not see how the Italian school can boast of having solved the problem, while claiming to have confuted "in the best possible manner determinism, physiological, psychological, and rationalistic." We further abstain from discussing whether or not and how far there is an agreement of our position with Auguste Comte's positivism. We concur with Comte in the recognition of the scientific method; we depart from his agnosticism and many details of his philosophical views; and, finally, we only hint here that when the author of "The Ethical Problem" spoke of the "intuitionalists," he did not have reference to the "Objective school" of Rosmini. Intuitionalism is a peculiarly English phenomenon, which can only in one point, indeed, in the main point, be compared to Rosmini's view, viz.: in its strange tenet of the intuitive apprehension of truth. This latter point, however, is of sufficient consequence to deserve a few additional remarks.

Professor Billia regards it as a matter of course that "the doctrine of representation" is wrong. By doctrine of representation he understands our proposition that knowledge is a representation of facts and that truth is a correct representation of facts. According to his view "idea and truth are wholly one, and are wholly one with the object thought of." This sentence, if I understand this rather mystifying explanation correctly, means, that ideas are directly perceived in the same way as sensations—the *Anschauungen* of our senses. Our sensations (i. e., in Kant's terminology our *Anschauungen*, often translated by "intuitions") are not subject to doubt; they are immediately perceived as real; and a similar immediateness has been attributed by many philosophers to certain very general or universal truths.

Rosmini regards "being" and truth as identical. We make a distinction between reality and truth. Sensations are "real"; we cannot say that sensations as such are either true or untrue. For instance, I feel a slight pang of hunger in the stomach: Is there any truth or untruth in this feeling? Or a certain color sensation takes place in the eye: Is there any truth or untruth in this sensation? Sensations are simply real; they are the data of our experience, out of which we construct our ideas. But these ideas if they properly represent the objects sensed, are true; if not, they are untrue. Truth and untruth always presuppose mental activity. If I, having a color-sensation which is a subjective hallucination, judge that there is an object before me, I am mistaken; the sensation in that case is not wrong, but my judgment of it is wrong. The sensation is right enough; it is caused somehow according to the laws of nature; but I have allowed myself to be misguided by its appearance.

Thus truth is never a thing of immediate perception, but always the product of mental activity. The very laws of mind would have to be reversed, should truth be directly perceived as are sensations.

Professor Billia assumes that if an idea, "through sense-reminiscence," were "a representation of the object,"

"It would come to pass that we could never think of any object, but always of its representation; therefore,

he adds,

"I could not think one, two, three—the thought itself would be impossible."

Why? Is this not self-mystification? Let us not stultify ourselves. By having and thinking a representation, we think of the object represented. A certain feeling, being caused somehow, say by a certain sense-impression, comes to represent an object, and thus it stands for it; it symbolises it. This is the nature of thought. Whenever the symbol is felt, the object represented in it is thought of.

There is a long distance between Alessandria in Northern Italy and Chicago in the prairies of Illinois, but it almost seems to us that the distance between the spiritual roads of Professor Billia and ourselves is greater still. Centuries seem to lie between us. But in spite of all our divergencies we observe with pleasure a certain concurrence in some most important points. We have in this sketch attempted to represent the case with faithful impartiality, not attenuating and not extending either the differences or agreements.

FAITH AND REASON.

A REVIEW OF FECHNER'S METHOD OF CONCILIATING RELIGION WITH SCIENCE.

GUSTAV THEODOR FECHNER is the founder of psycho-physics, i. e., the science which determines the relation between sense-stimuli and sensations, thus explaining the interdependence between bodily functions and psychical phenomena. Prof. E. H. Weber had set up the law that the increase of a stimulus to be appreciable must always bear some fixed and definite proportion to the intensity of the stimulus with which it is compared. For instance if we can just distinguish between 16 ounces and 17 ounces, we shall be able to distinguish between 32 and 34 ounces, not between 33 and 34. The fraction $\frac{1}{16}$ must be the same. This fraction, the smallest noticeable difference, which is to be found out by experiment, is called the "difference threshold" of muscular sense.

Fechner took up Weber's investigations and stated Weber's law with greater precision in a mathematical form thus: "The sensation increases as the logarithm of the stimulus." He made this law of the relation that obtains between body and soul the basis of a new branch of science which he called "psycho-physics."

We must add that the law is approximately true in the case of sight, hearing, pressure, and the muscular sense, it is most exactly true of sound, but it is uncertain for the chemical senses of smell and taste. It is most exact in the middle regions of the sensory scale but becomes unreliable when we approach either the lower or upper limit of sensibility.

Fechner called attention to the duality of sensation and motion; yet he proposed to conceive this duality as two aspects only of one and the same thing. Fechner's philosophical ideal was monism, yet we must add that, in our opinion, he has not fully realised his monistic ideal. His imaginative powers were those of a poet and we find that his views of God and soul and immortality are sometimes bordering on or even entering into that kind of fanciful spiritualism which is generally called supernaturalism.

* * *

This is a short description of Fechner's position and importance as a psychologist. At present we do not intend to give any further explanation of his metaphysical, or psychological, or philosophical views, but to describe his attitude toward religion. No one perhaps could feel more deeply and earnestly the demand of the soul to have science and religion conciliated. He was a man of science; his life was devoted to most intricate investigations and experiments, but he never lost sight on the one hand of the religious importance of scientific work and on the other hand of the indispensability of religion to science.

Fechner argues:

Knowledge and faith are intimately interconnected. Science cannot live without faith. I know that I have a sensation of red or green or yellow, I also know that the sum of the angles in a plane triangle are equal to 180 degrees. But I do not know in the strictest sense of knowledge that another man has the same color-sensation when he looks at the same objects. I do not even know that space is tri-dimensional, I may have (and we cannot say that we do not have) good reasons for believing the one and the other, but this belief, certain though it may be, rests upon our faith in the regularity and cosmic order of the universe, which is the result of an inference but not an object of direct knowledge. Fechner starting from such considerations, says, it is the duty of the man of science not to abolish faith but to replace it so far as possible by exact knowledge.

Faith originates because we need it, we are in want of it, it is a necessity of life. We cannot extend our knowledge without faith, we cannot act without it, and that faith an essential feature of which is the aspiration to extend knowledge is superior to the self-sufficient faith of the Moslem who burns the books and spurns science.

The basis of religion lies deeply buried in the nature of man and human society, so deeply that many cannot detect it. Many propose the principles of humanity or pure ethics as a surrogate in the place of religion. But they forget that these principles of humanity are a product of religion and would not exist without it. Humanity and religiosity rise and sink together. We may imagine the stones in the foundation of the building useless, because they are hidden from sight, but if we should take them away the house must fall.

Religion holds and keeps human society, and human society is such an immediate presence as the air we breathe. To discard religion and keep humanity or ethics is about the same as to propose that we can dispense with the air so long as and because we have breath.

Fechner maintains that there are three essential elements in religion and no religion is perfect unless it proposes a belief in all three. These three elements are the belief in (1) God, (2) an immortal soul, and (3) spirits. God is to him not only the ground of all existence but also the soul-tie of all spirits among whom Christ is our ideal as the foremost revealer of God.

* * *

We do not intend to give further explanations of Fechner's views and are satisfied in having outlined his religious standpoint. We shall now attempt to construe his views satisfactorily to our world-conception.

Fechner's conceptions of God, the soul, and the spirit-world are not without fantastic notions, and we cannot accept the arguments he proposes, especially for the last and most favorite of his three religious ideas. We do not deny the spirituality of the world, for we ourselves are spirits, not pure spirits but spirits after all, and our innermost nature is spiritual. But we deny Fechner's peculiar conception of a spirit-world above the spirituality of nature.

Let us see whether we can give to Fechner's views an interpretation that will stand the test of scientific critique.

The idea of a spirit-world is strange, but if interpreted allegorically it has a deep significance. Among Christians it finds its expression in the mythology of angels, saints, and devils. Yet this idea of a spirit-world, although it is mythology, contains (as all mythology does) a great and important truth. If we decipher the mythological meaning of the belief in saints and translate it into a statement of facts, we should say that the soul-life of all humanity is one great stream; all sentient creatures that lived on earth since organised life began form one great empire, one large republic of interdependent citizens. A man's life does not begin with birth, nor does it end with death. There are no individuals in the strict sense of the word. The soul-life of past generations flows through the present generation into future generations. Our ancestors' souls are not lost; our dead are not dissolved into nothing; they continue; so long as we speak their language, think their ideas, and act according to their maxims; they are with us all the time and will be with us even unto the end of the world. In so far as their presence is effective of evil, they are demons, in so far as it is effective of good, as their influence leads the race onward and upward, they correspond to the saints of the church.

Is there also a truth in the belief in angels? Certainly there is! If those features of nature's all-being which produce and uphold the spiritual world of man's soul-life, are called in their harmonious totality God, we should say that the single powers of nature tending to advance God's work in the world, are, mythologically expressed, his messengers and servants. If we conceive the sun merely in his physical effects, we are overwhelmed with his grandeur, his awfulness and beneficence. Through him we receive directly and indirectly most of the boons that produce and sustain life. The sun is not a mind, yet we stand in a relation to the sun that is, on our part, of a personal nature. We can and often do regard him with gratitude, and to represent him as an archangel of God is by no means an inappropriate allegory. It is mythology, but the mythology has a meaning.

Our consciousness is the effect of the subconscious spirituality of our organisation. This subconscious spirituality is, as it were, our attending angel, our familiar, the spirit that nourishes and bears our mentality, it is the pedestal upon which our conscious life rests.

It is a wrong conception of nature to think of nature as a dead machine regulated by the law of inertia. Nature is life, nature is spontaneity, nature is spirituality.

If we weigh the materialistic conception, (which considers solely and exclusively what we define as the objectivity of nature i. e. matter in motion, dropping that source of psychical life which we call the subjectivity of nature), if we compare materialism with the mythology of ancient and modern religions, we should say that the former is radically wrong and the latter, the modern and even the ancient religions, are right in the face of the former. The latter are wrong only in so far as the truth is symbolically expressed and not in exact scientific formulas. But the truth is there nevertheless.

*
* *

Fechner concludes a little volume which he has written on the subject, with a peculiar confession. He says in his "Drei Motive und Gründe des Glaubens":

"As free as the position is which I advocate in this work and have advocated in former writings, yet the orthodox position where I have met it elsewhere, has on the whole, though not in every case, pleased me better than the free. . . .

"To this firmness of faith is attached a wonderful blessing. When I observe that many enjoy this blessing even now and apply it in their principles and actions, in as far as it is possible in this time of imperfection, relying partly on the need of such blessing and partly upon the truth and goodness of the principal tenets of the Christian religion, I am thereby filled with a secret admiration and joy. I see in this on the one hand an expression and on the other hand an acceptation of the meaning and fact of a perfect religion, an acceptation, which can only take place in so far as the respective religion is looked upon as that which according to its idea it intends to be in completion, and in so far as its historic sources are considered entirely reliable. . . .

"Religion should furnish to reason the highest, safest, and surest points of view; and now it is left to the function of the individual reason to govern, to improve, to judge and to sift these views; that is to reverse the whole subject, and in the place of the unity settling all things which we must expect from religion, we now get in addition to the other causes of dissent we already have, also the confusion and contention about religion itself, so that we easily lose all religion."

Let us pause here for a moment and ask, What is "the individual reason"? Reason is reason in so far only as it agrees with that feature of reality which makes of the world a cosmos. Objectivity accordingly is the nature of reason; and "individual reason," denoting a subjective kind of reason is a contradictory term.

The individual reason (supposing that the term means subjective rationality, a rational taste or fancy) is not and cannot be an absolute criterion of truth. That is not true which pleases the taste of a rational being best, but that which agrees with reality; not that which satisfies one's conception of rationality, but that which is in conformity with actual facts. There are some people who believe that that is right which their conscience tells them to be right, and that that is true which pleases their peculiar sense of rationality best. But their position is false. The standards of truth and error, and of right and wrong, are objective not subjective; and the very instrument of reasoning, man's organ of arranging the facts of experience in proper relations, his mechanism of formal thought is but a copy of the world-order, an imitation of the ways of nature, and a systematised recognition of the forms of existence. Through reason the scientist can formulate the regularities of the universe in laws and through reason alone living beings are enabled to set themselves purposes for their actions.

Religion is the recognition of authority. It stands on the recognition of something that is independent of our wishes and tastes; of something that is as it is whatever we think of it; it stands on the recognition of reality. But religion is not based alone on the recognition of reality, it implies also the demand of finding out the nature of reality. Religion demands cognition, and so the proper employment of reason is an essential part of religion.

*
* *

Fechner proposes three principles which lead to faith, (1) the historical principle, (2) the practical principle, and (3) the theoretical principle. The first and second are the main stays of orthodox religion for they lead to religion whatever it may be, the third principle, however, which includes critique and science, is that which purifies religion and leads on to that ideal religion of which the mythological conceptions are dim prophecies. Fechner continues:

"And why then do I not place myself upon the ground of unconditional faith in what has become historical? I cannot, and hundreds and thousands cannot. The theoretical principle asserts itself, too, and must assert itself. And if implicit faith in what has generally been accepted, for those who have such faith, has its advantages which nothing could replace, yet with the impossibility that all have it and that reason be sacrificed to faith under all circumstances, another task of history comes into play, that is the task to make the advantages, which those believers alone can have almost exceptionally and yet not in a perfect degree, because they look upon the yet imperfect religion as already perfect, the common property of all, by really advancing religion to its perfection and thus making it possible for it to reach its culminating point.

"It must finally arrive where reason will be fully satisfied and will be a pillar of the faith it now constantly shakes, instead of demanding impossible sacrifices of reason in behalf of faith. And for this end indeed the introduction of new positions in history is needed; the efforts of a reason no longer tied to rigid dogmas and its attempts to overthrow what is destined to fall at some time, require the greatest diversity of aspirations, a ceaseless fight from all sides and the failure of most of these efforts, so that, after all the false courses are exhausted and done away with, the right course may at least surely and safely remain."

There is much truth in what Fechner says and we sympathise with the position he takes; yet we propose to go further:

Fechner's third principle is the most important one of all. Without it the other two principles cannot produce religion. Without it, religion would be dogmatism, and would cease to be religion.

Fechner concludes his book "Die drei Motive und Gründe des Glaubens" with a poem which may be regarded as his confession of faith. Some verses express the author's sentiment in the words of Christian mythology and we must know his scientific faith in God as the all-and-one in order to avoid misconstruction. We here present a translation (made by Mr. E. F. L. Gauss, of Chicago, for this special purpose) which faithfully preserves the rhythm and the character of the original even in most of its details.

"In God my soul is resting;
He lives and therefore I;
Life is in and about Him,
I cannot live without Him,
He cannot let me die.

"In God my soul is resting;
Say that it ends who lists:
I have no care, for surely
For aye rests there securely
What now in Him exists.

"In God my soul is resting;
My life with all its trim
In Him is bound and hidden,
And when He shall have bidden
My soul returns to Him.

"In God my soul is resting;
Though hid He from its sight,
The witnesses descending
Reveal Him without ending,
Foremost the Christ, the Light.

"In God my soul is resting;
The angels' host I see
In His pure heights of Heaven
In glory move, and even
One of them doth bear me.

"In God my soul is resting;
The tie of souls is He,
Faith, Love, and Hope forever
Will shun the soul's endeavor
Till this we fully see.

"In God my soul is resting;
In Him are ever rife
The truth, goodness, and beauty
That purpose be in duty
And harmony in life.

"In God my soul is resting;
What could the parcel be?
Far what I'd fain be grasping!
Fear not, soul, in thy gasping
Salvation comes to thee.

"In God my soul is resting;
He is its very source.
His will my acts commandeth,
And though my will withstandeth
He holds His steady course.

"In God my soul is resting;
Although He never sins,
Yet with His children's ailings
He also bears their failings
And them to duty wins.

"In God my soul is resting;
Comfort in grief, sublime!
He's love and must unfold it,
And never can withhold it,
I still abide my time.

"In God my soul is resting;
This be my final word.
Though storms my bark encumber
Yet peace attends my slumber:
He's my eternal port!"

We regard Fechner's method of conciliating Religion with Science as an attempt in the right direction, but we cannot say that we are fully satisfied with the conclusion at which he arrives. His expositions do not clearly show the boundary line between Faith and Reason, and thus his Faith actually interferes with his Reason.

There is one way that will hopelessly confound the issues between religion and science, which is, when faith performs the function of science. There is another way that will take out of life purpose, charity, and comfort, which is when cold and unimpressible reason performs the function of faith, i. e. when the sentiment and enthusiasm of the heart is chilled or entirely replaced by the figures of dry calculations. There is but one way that will reconcile science and religion and that is when science and faith harmoniously work together, each of the two in their coöperation performing its own function.

Faith when it performs the function of reason is called creed. Creed is injurious, but faith is wholesome. He only who is faithful will conquer.

Reason when it performs the function of faith is craftiness and guile. Craftiness is a vice but rationality is the human in man.

Faith is not knowledge, but an attitude of the soul. Faith is a moral not a mental quality. Faith is character, strength of will, loyalty to truth. There is no religion in a man unless he be faithful.

Reason is the arranging and systematising of knowledge so as to represent facts correctly, or in one word, so as to construct truth. Reason must be the torch in the hand of faith, so that faith may walk on the right path.

Reason without faith makes of man a machine without sympathy, without tenderness, without enthusiasm for his ideals. Reason in the soul without good-will, constancy and moral stamina, is a torch in the hand of a vicious man, and the mischief it works is great.

Faith without reason is superstition. It is like unto a man that is groping in the dark. He has eyes but either they are blind or he shuts them to the light. There is light and he might use the light to illumine his path, but he scorns the light. He rather relies upon what he imagines to be an inner light which is in reality luminous hallucinations that appear to him when he runs his head against the objects of his surroundings.

To sum up: Irrational faith is as much irreligious as faithless reason.

INDEX.